7/15/13
$22.95

VETERANS' JOURNEYS HOME

VETERANS' JOURNEYS HOME

Lori Holyfield

Paradigm Publishers
Boulder • London

Copyright © 2011 Paradigm Publishers

Published in the United States by Paradigm Publishers, 2845 Wilderness Place, Boulder, CO 80301 USA.

Paradigm Publishers is the trade name of Birkenkamp & Company, LLC, Dean Birkenkamp, President and Publisher.

Library of Congress Cataloging-in-Publication Data

Holyfield, Lori, 1960-
    Veterans' journeys home : life after Afghanistan and Iraq / by Lori Holyfield.
        p. cm.
    Includes bibliographical references and index.
    ISBN 978-1-61205-051-5 (hbk. : alk. paper) — ISBN 978-1-61205-052-2 (pbk. : alk. paper)
    1. Veterans—United States—Psychology.   2. Veterans—Mental health services—United States.   3. Afghan War, 2001—Veterans—United States.   4. Iraq War, 2003—Veterans—United States.   5. Post-traumatic stress disorder—United States.   6. Afghan War, 2001—Psychological aspects.   7. Iraq War, 2003—Psychological aspects.   I. Title.   II. Title: Life after Afghanistan and Iraq.
    UB369.H65 2011
    362.860973—dc23

                                                                                  2011024444

Printed and bound in the United States of America on acid-free paper that meets the standards of the American National Standard for Permanence of Paper for Printed Library Materials.

Designed and Typeset by Straight Creek Bookmakers.

15 14 13 12 11   1 2 3 4 5

This book is dedicated to all who carry the wounded hearts of war and to those who help them on their journeys home.

Vets Journey Home USA contact information:
1-800-236-4692

Contents

Acknowledgments

The seeds for this book came about through two phases of research. Phase one included the Veterans Oral History Project, affiliated with the Library of Congress "Experiencing War Series" and the University of Arkansas, Barbara and David Pryor Center for Oral and Visual History, and Special Collections, Mullins Library. For phase one, I wish to thank first and foremost those veterans who were willing to share their war experiences and participate in the oral history project. Without their willingness to be interviewed, there would be no book.

Two excellent graduate students aided in the interviewing and transcription process. Without the help of Crosby Hipes and Melodie Griffis, I would still be transcribing interviews today. Funding for their assistance was provided through a generous grant from the University of Arkansas Women's Giving Circle. Other generous funds from the Department of Sociology and Criminal Justice, Jones Family-Community Institute, and a personal contribution from colleague, Dr. Ania Zajicek, combined to assist me with the completion of phase two of the research.

For phase two, I wish to thank my graduate assistants Maggie Cobb and Ashleigh McKinzie for their valuable library research. I also am indebted to colleagues and friends—Marcella Thompson, whose keen editing skills were invaluable, and Denise Cobb, whose close reading and insightful comments as the spouse of a veteran were exceptional. For phase two, I give special thanks to all those affiliated with Vets Journey Home. Without their advocacy and dedication, this book would have ended without the hope for healing our returning veterans that I now know exists. Consequently, 50 percent of the proceeds from this book will be donated to Vets Journey Home as they continue their important work.

Finally, I consider myself extremely lucky to have a family that supports my academic endeavors, which often require travel away from home and seemingly insane periods of writing with little or no interaction. Their collective wisdom and ripe sense of humor kept me grounded when my heart was heavy with war. Last, but certainly not least, I am especially grateful to my grandsons, Klint and Kirk, for their joyful reminder that unconditional love endures life's most significant challenges. May you never know the pain that accompanies war.

Introduction

On September 11, 2001, I stood squeezed into the small office of my friend Deb along with several colleagues on campus. We huddled around her small television, watching the tragedy unfold. As we watched the Twin Towers fall, first one, then the other, we stood, as did millions of Americans, motionless and in shock. Each of us had to teach class within the hour. In whispered tones we struggled with what we would say. How could we hold our composure? I was jarred from my thoughts when I looked at the clock. I wiped the tears and rushed to the auditorium and my class of 350—first-year students. Some had already heard the news and others listened in terror. After some discussion and tearful speculation about what was to come, I needed something that would help us through the next 90 minutes, something to temporarily calm the rising tide of fear we all felt. I asked them to take a few minutes and imagine they were writing their grandchild a letter that would be locked away in a time capsule for fifty years. "How will you remember today?" "What will you tell your grandchildren about 9/11?" I collected the letters, many of which are reproduced in the epilogue, but one in particular stood out.

Dear Grandson,

Today is unreal to me. This morning four commercial airplanes were run into two major buildings. The World Trade Center and the Pentagon have collapsed and the last plane was downed in

Pennsylvania, unknown as to why. Car bombs are going off in random places. Today terrorism is real. Many people have mentioned Pearl Harbor—maybe because this is how they felt at that time. I wish I had not woken up this morning. While I was on my morning run, oblivious to all this terror, people were dying—alone and scared. Today hate is real. Why anyone can justify killing another amazes me. The world is not meant to be this way. Today was not meant to happen. History books and movies, though they make us cry, don't prepare us for this. I want to call my parents and tell them I love them. It is unknown as to how the day will end but I am telling you, I am thankful you were not here today. I hope your generation never has to deal with this. I pray you never have to cry for thousands.

All my love,
Grandmother

Sociologists have shown that fear is a powerful motivation for politicians and that fearful messages from those in political power can lead us toward devastating outcomes because political strategies can "tap the emotional churning" of the public.[1] President George W. Bush was quoted in the *Washington Post* on September 12, 2001: "Any country that harbors and protects him [Osama bin Laden] is our enemy. We must carry their war to them."[2] As the saying goes, "Hindsight is 20-20 vision." Americans today know much more about the erroneous link between 9/11 and our current wars with Iraq and Afghanistan. But as the time capsule exercise demonstrated, the collective fear that was generated from the tragedy of September 11, 2001 was so palpable (and accessible to political strategists), it would lead to the longest wars in American history.

Politicians don't fight wars—soldiers do. This book is dedicated to all those who serve in the military and especially to those who experience the trauma of war and its emotional aftermath. There are two reasons I've written this book. The first is personal. I am the daughter of a veteran who fought in the Korean War, an invisible one for much of society, or so my father thought. Everyone called him by his last name, "Kirk," and like so many of his generation, Kirk was not only a veteran of war, he was a product of his time, trapped in a working-class masculinity that confined him to a rugged exterior. He felt the full range of emotions that make us all human but was constrained by what he believed he could and could not express.

My father passed away at a relatively young age; accounts of his war experience as an Army artillery specialist would fit in the palm of my hand. Talk of his war experience was taboo in our family. It's not that I didn't ask—I did. I wasn't interested in hearing the grisly tales of combat so much as I simply wanted to better understand his emotional pain. I've seen the "thousand-mile stare" that he would mask with alcohol and work. We all knew that my father had a wounded heart, and like so many families of veterans we lived with the demons that accompanied him home from war that had no name.

Second, I have always been intrigued by the management of emotions within organizations, a sphere of our lives we seldom admit is subject to social control. But just as our behaviors are guided by societal norms, our emotional expressions are guided by prescribed rules as well. In December 2006, while driving home from the office, I heard an interview on National Public Radio.[3] It was the story of a returning soldier at Colorado's Fort Carson who had been shamed by his commanding officer and his unit after self-disclosing he was suffering from Post Traumatic Stress Disorder (PTSD). I listened as other soldiers revealed that rather than being treated, they were being discharged for "personality disorders" or "patterns of misconduct" because of missing formation or alcohol and substance abuse, known symptoms of PTSD and strategies for self-medicating the wounds of war. Receiving less than an honorable discharge meant these soldiers would not be eligible for benefits, adding insult to injury. Military life, I would come to learn, includes some of the most stringent emotion norms found in modern society, and these norms follow soldiers from basic training to war and back home again.

During the interview one soldier described telling his supervisor that he had almost killed himself and that he was going to miss formation and check himself into a psychiatric ward. Before he could get to the hospital, his sergeant sent a group of his fellow soldiers to arrest him, pounding on his door and telling him he was AWOL. The sergeant told the reporter that he proudly orchestrated the shaming of soldiers by others in his unit. "I don't like people who are weak-minded," he told the reporter, adding he would never be caught seeing a therapist. I was stunned as I realized the depth of emotional pain and humiliation these soldiers must have felt. The report ended by revealing that the sergeant later admitted to having been diagnosed with depression and "anger issues" and that he was now seeing a therapist as well. He regretted his actions and voiced this in the interview, hoping others would learn from his mistakes. I couldn't help but wonder how things might have been different for my father had he been able to talk openly about his own wounded heart. I feared for those young men, worried they would be condemned to a private war of emotional pain. How might it affect their families? From there, the project was born.[4]

I began talking with some of the early veterans returning from the wars in Iraq and Afghanistan. I began to interview soldiers and reservists but noticed they were hesitant to share their experiences with civilians. "Unless you've been to war, you can't understand," one young soldier explained to me. But I wanted to know more—if returning veterans could talk about their experiences while they were still visceral and raw, perhaps it could be cathartic in some way. In 2007, I partnered with the Library of Congress (LOC) to conduct oral histories for the "Experiencing War" series. Many of the oral histories from this project are now available at the LOC online archive.

I knew only two soldiers at the start. Army Lt. Colonel Rick Mayes, a former police officer and instructor for the campus ROTC, and Naval Petty Officer Eric Heath, a campus police officer, were both students in our sociology graduate program. I told them what I was hoping to do and they were both kind enough to serve as guinea pigs for the project. If it had not been for their generosity and willingness to be interviewed and provide further contacts, I don't know that I would be writing this book. It was their stories that prompted me to go further.

Rick has been with the Army and National Guard since he enlisted in 1977. He returned to serve in the ROTC program on campus after decades as a police officer. His jovial demeanor seems at first unexpected for someone who was in command of thousands of soldiers in his MP (military police) battalion. His main duties in Iraq were the training of Iraqi police and protecting the main supply route up from Kuwait. I have no doubt that Lt. Colonel Mayes is highly respected for his deep sense of duty and his wry humor. One of my favorite memories of Rick was his unique way of presenting material in class. During a graduate seminar for field methods, he arrived to class with his handouts and presented the bullet points in song, to the tune of "Rawhide." I suppose he could be described as a class clown at times, but for Lt. Colonel Mayes, the missions, the men and women who served under his command, are precious commodities and he is very serious when he speaks of them.

Eric, like most I would interview, joined the Army National Guard at the age of 17. In 2004, Eric transferred to the Navy reserves and served in Operation Enduring Freedom. His family has a long tradition of military service. Eric is soft spoken and his gentle demeanor seems inconsistent with the work he was assigned during Operation Enduring Freedom. As a petty officer, his assignment was that of prison guard for U.S. soldiers at Camp Arifjan. Eric reflected on the moral ambivalence he felt about guarding U.S. soldiers for their "criminal" actions during combat and remembers asking himself more than once: If he were in the same combat situations of those he now guarded as prisoners, might he not have done the same thing?

Both Rick and Eric helped me early on to understand that the best way for a civilian to honor a veteran is to provide a space for his or her story. Army National Guard First Lieutenant Points aptly describes the need for oral histories: "First person stories are the best way for people to know what's happened, what goes on. If you don't tell your story, nobody's [going to] know it and you'll have somebody looking back at numbers and stats and trying to write what happened. But when somebody has taken the time to tell their story, they could've had a first-hand account of what's happened. It helps you think about a lot of things, too—just sort through what's happened to you and think about some things. [Storytelling] puts it all in perspective."

I would come to learn that most returning veterans feel as if civilians not only *can't* understand war experience, they don't really *want* to understand war or its gruesome details. Veterans quickly learn when they return home that the specifics of combat are too murky, too disturbing for some, illustrating Americans' felt ambivalence and cultural *disease* with the current wars. I learned that well-intentioned civilians don't ask because they are not sure what to say. Others are politically opposed to the war and mistakenly dismiss the experiences of those who serve with the policies they criticize. Many succumb to compassion fatigue and shy away from asking veterans about their experiences because of their own discomfort. But our discomfort often leads veterans to retreat from social settings and, in some cases, choose not to reveal their military status at all. The result is that they hold their emotions in, talk among themselves, or isolate, sometimes to the point of self-destruction.

Burdened with economic downturn as well as environmental and natural disasters, we find ourselves surrounded by a media that focuses on celebrity and political spectacle.[5] Veterans, I would learn, are suspicious of the media and prefer to talk about war in their own words. Army Sergeant Hurt, who spent two tours in Iraq, explains: "One of the worst things about being in Iraq is knowing that [American citizens] don't have a clue. The news gets it wrong, everything wrong from what I've seen. I would say from the people I know, civilians, probably 95–98 percent, a large, large number, the rule, not the exception but the rule, is that people don't know what's going on over there.... I'm just saying I don't think a lot of people get their information from veterans, from people who've been there, who've done it. I think they get it all from the news, which is completely inaccurate. They get it from these third sources, from people who've never been there, and I think it's important [to] whatever degree they can, for veterans to explain what happened over there, how that affects them, how that affects everything, because otherwise civilians aren't going to understand. And they need to understand."

For Hurt and other veterans, telling about their experiences is also a way to honor those who have died in war. "They are owed the respect that people back home know what happened, why it happened, what was going on over there so people understand what the picture actually looks like. They don't have a picture in their mind from some third source that was never even there, you know what I mean? I think at the end of the day by making people understand to the best of your ability what happened there, you're pretty much showing respect to the people who didn't come home. That's the way I look at it."

Others argue that we are a culture that simply cannot acknowledge the abject suffering that war creates. So we engage in a *collective amnesia* of war among much of the citizenry, leaving the trauma to those who experience it along with their families and a small community of mental health professionals and clergy who serve them. Edward Tick describes the process this way in *War and the Soul* (2005): "They come home stumbling out of hell. But we don't see them as they have become. Instead, we offer them beer and turkey dinners, debriefing and an occasional parade, and a return to routine jobs and weekends in the shopping malls."[6] In the end, those who serve carry the burden of war for society as a whole. For Americans, Ilona Meagher adds, "it is our responsibility to pay close attention to what happens to our troops after the parades and medal ceremonies are over."[7] A single death in combat is a tragedy, but for many who survive combat the tragedy continues. War scars the soul.

While my research has included many returning veterans who have not experienced the trauma of war, I was inspired to write about those who do. It is true that most participated in combat at varying levels by the sheer fact that they were placed in country. However, my aim here is to introduce those who carry visceral and raw memories of their experiences to highlight the challenges that combat and military service create for veterans upon return to civilian life. The voices from this group of soldiers echo those of thousands of soldiers who experience disruptions to families, jobs, and finances associated with extended or repeated tours.

Indeed, among those veterans between the ages of 21 and 39, over half (51.7 percent) report severe impairment in transitioning to civilian life. Among female veterans, rates of depression have reached nearly 17 percent.[8] Annual suicide rates have steadily increased since 2002. Notably, over the past year there have been several months in which there were more military suicides stateside than service-related deaths, and those numbers continue to rise.[9] Finally, unemployment rates for veterans returning from Iraq and Afghanistan have risen sharply—from 6.1 percent in 2007 to 14.7 in 2010. Unemployment rates for reservists and the National Guard has quadrupled since 2007, hovering at 10.6 percent.[10]

Book Overview

This book is divided into two parts. Chapters 1–4 are based on oral histories of veterans returning from Iraq and Afghanistan. Here a trajectory of military service is provided to reveal today's changing military and the enormous challenges soldiers face upon return to civilian life. Chapter 1, "War, Those Who Fight It, and the Shifting Image of the Warrior," provides a brief introduction of today's war, the growing number of "signature injuries," and a profile of today's soldier. This chapter includes a discussion of the shifting images of warriors to highlight the complexity of the warrior archetype within the masculine institution of the military.

Chapter 2, "Socialization and the Contemporary Warrior," details current practice and socialization techniques of basic training. It follows some from this group as they go from training to become soldiers—to combat—where their military identities are both confirmed and confronted. These veterans best capture the overall experience of what transpires in the transformation from citizen to soldier (a generic term I have applied to all branches of military service). Their stories honor those who were not included, describing the necessary rituals and rites of passage that mark the creation of soldiers as individual identities are erased and reshaped for military service. As chapter 2 reveals, basic training is especially illustrative of this process.

Chapter 3, "Reluctant Edgework and Nonstandard War," incorporates the raw memories of war, as recalled by individuals after serving in combat. One veteran aptly describes it as the "nonstandard" war in which civilians, unclear missions, changing rules of engagement, and ethnic and religious divisions complicate U.S. efforts. These oral history accounts illustrate the psychological challenges and moral ambiguity that accompany combat—what it does to bodies, minds, and hearts. Good soldiers sometimes experience an unraveling of the self, damaging our "civilized natures and established identities."[11]

Chapter 4, "Sister Soldiers: Women and Military Service," is dedicated to females who serve in the military and explores some of their experienced marginalization as well as their success. Sister soldiers are faced with a unique set of challenges. These range from having to prove themselves, being scrutinized more heavily, harassment, and emotional adjustment to feeling marginalized and, in some cases, experiencing violence from within the ranks.

Chapter 5, "Military Masculinity and Combat: The Perfect Storm for PTSD," provides an in-depth discussion of trauma and the signature injuries of war (Post Traumatic Stress Disorder and Traumatic Brain Injuries). Mental health professionals, veterans' advocates, and lay readers interested in understanding the trajectory of discourse surrounding PTSD should find this chapter helpful for further study. Because combat trauma occurs in a particular context, I expand upon the emotional aspects of prolonged episodes of combat to provide a context for the growing phenomenon of psychological injuries. Throughout these chapters, the reader should become more informed of the moral and emotional wounds of war, the contemporary meaning of the warrior archetype, and the challenges faced in military and in post-combat civilian life.

Chapters 6–8 focus on hope for those who have been wounded by war. This work is the culmination of a year of ethnographic study of a program assisting veterans. Chapter 6, "A History of Vets Journey Home," follows the trajectory of Bamboo Bridge, a nonprofit program for combat veterans from Vietnam, to its current incarnation as Vets Journey Home (VJH). This little-known program, whose mission is to heal veterans of all wars, combat and noncombat, is effectively assisting those seeking to heal the trauma of war. Staffed by volunteers, mostly veterans themselves, it draws on a combination of therapeutic tools from emotional intelligence[12] and psychodrama[13] to counseling and the "mythopoetic" men's movement.[14] The program is free to veterans and active-duty service members and is funded solely by donations. Indeed, 50 percent of the proceeds from the sale of this book will go to Veterans Journey Home.[15]

Chapter 7, appropriately titled "Welcome Home," draws from one year of ethnographic observation with Vets Journey Home to describe how the program works. With the permission of participants and VJH staff, I take the reader into the deep emotional process work that occurs during any VJH weekend. I draw on verbatim excerpts to highlight the process of healing trauma. In addition to describing the work done by veterans, I have also included excerpts from a VJH weekend that was designed for veterans and their spouses. As one wife of a veteran diagnosed with PTSD observed, "Healing the veteran is only half the solution." This chapter reveals that trauma from military service affects not just veterans, but all of us as family members, friends, and communities.

As Patricia Clason, cofounder of Vets Journey Home, explains, "I think a critical piece is that a vet doesn't have to have PTSD to have emotional wounds from the experience of war. Also many vets function well when they return and don't realize some of the subtle effects of the emotional wounds of war (minimal ambition, emotional distance, etc.) until divorce, job loss, difficulty maintaining a job, or achieving goals happens to them or the pattern emerges. Even then, many of them aren't treated by therapists and live lives of mediocrity and getting by." The goal of Vets Journey Home is to change the trajectory for veterans from all wars. Remarkable in its depth, VJH assists those who are struggling to heal the emotional *and* moral wounds of combat without glorifying war. Rather, the focus is on the soldier and his/her journey forward through the telling of one's story. Tools are provided to help soldiers understand their wounds and begin the healing process, strengthening their ability to forgive themselves and others and develop deeper levels of self awareness. Moreover, Vets Journey Home provides a true "welcome home" to veterans. It can and should be taking place in every community throughout the United States.

In chapter 8, finally, "The Power of Ritual and the Importance of Story-Telling," I return to the oral history project in which veterans were asked the simple question, "Why should veterans share their stories?" Their collective wisdom reminds us all that soldiers need a safe place to share their experiences of war, one that necessarily focuses on and honors these men and women for their sacrifices.

CHAPTER ONE

War, Those Who Fight It, and Shifting Images of the Warrior

After the attack on the Twin Towers and the Pentagon, the Bush administration moved quickly to declare war against Osama bin Laden, the Taliban, and al-Qaeda operatives in Afghanistan and (soon after) Iraq. On September 14, 2001, President George W. Bush told the nation, "Our responsibility to history is already clear: to answer these attacks and rid the world of evil."[1] With this, the "crusade" against terrorism began. On October 7, 2001, U.S. and British troops launched the first airstrike against the Taliban in Afghanistan, demanding the surrender of Osama bin Laden to no avail. Soon the focus turned to Iraq. Linking Saddam Hussein to the 9/11 attacks, the Bush administration was able to convince the American public that Saddam was housing weapons of mass destruction and that a preemptive attack on Iraq was necessary.

The first U.S. forces marched into Iraq in March 2003. Today approximately 50,000 U.S. troops remain in Iraq as the Obama administration increases forces in Afghanistan. Although President Barack Obama's withdrawal of U.S. troops in August 2010 was seen by many as a step toward returning Iraq's sovereignty, troops are expected to remain in country through 2011, and some predictions are longer. Meanwhile, sectarian violence and numbers of suicide bombings have risen against the Iraq police forces in 2010, causing many Iraqi politicians and soldiers concern regarding Iraq's potential for a sovereign government.[2]

The wars are not over for U.S. troops, who are now being built up again in Afghanistan. The stated goal now is to counter terrorism and bring a degree of stability to Afghanistan and to dismantle and defeat al-Qaeda and the Taliban in both Afghanistan and Pakistan where Osama bin Laden was killed. As those who serve will attest, this objective will require a massive and sustained U.S. commitment in Afghanistan. General David Petraeus reports that U.S. troops are now in the throes of a propaganda war with the Taliban and an unstable government. Recent news reports state that the Taliban are capitalizing on Afghan citizens' distrust of President Karzai and are creating a perception of a "puppet regime" controlled by the United States.[3]

As the United States continues its efforts to fight terror in both Afghanistan and Pakistan alongside NATO troops, it will be the "ground pounders" who fight the war. Those who serve in combat occupations (e.g., combat engineers, infantry, and artillery) within the military are the ones most at risk for death or injury as well as the signature injuries of war (Post Traumatic Stress Disorder and Traumatic Brain Injury) in contrast to those who serve in support specialties (MOS) such as administration and medical fields. This does not mean, however, that support personnel are not pulled into combat in Iraq and Afghanistan, where the lines between militarized and demilitarized zones are no longer clear.

Approximately 1.64 million U.S. troops have served in Operation Iraqi Freedom (OIF) and Operation Enduring Freedom (OEF), which includes Afghanistan. Over 1 million active duty forces and over 400,000 reservists have been deployed to Iraq and Afghanistan specifically.[4] Our volunteer military is half the size of the military during the Vietnam era. As a result, active duty forces are spent. Men and women who serve have seen their tours extended (a process known as *stop-loss*), or they return home only to find they are expected to serve multiple tours. The Army has taken the brunt of the hit simply because it constitutes 75 percent of the "boots on the ground" in both Iraq and Afghanistan. Many U.S.

Army troops (67 percent) have deployed to OIF or OEF, and a recent report from the RAND corporation reveals that almost half of those deployed have served two tours, 21 percent are serving or have served three tours, and approximately 9,000 troops have been redeployed four or more times.[5] National Guard units and reservists have been called up in numbers not seen since World War II.

Signature Injuries of War

At present, almost 6,000 U.S. troops have died in OIF and OEF operations and nearly 33,000 permanent injuries have been reported along with an estimated hundreds of thousands of Iraqi and Afghanistan civilians killed.[6] As of summer 2010, the Department of Defense figures indicate that approximately 18,000 U.S. troops were wounded so seriously that they were listed as "WIA Not RTD" (Wounded in Action, Not Returned to Duty). One-third of Marines, nearly 40 percent of Army personnel, and approximately half of the National Guard report mental health problems and readjustment issues. Among those deployed, an estimated 14 percent are currently affected by Post Traumatic Stress Disorder (PTSD), while only half seek treatment.[7] These rates exceed those recorded for Vietnam, with more recent estimates expected to be even higher.[8] As many as 300,000 returning veterans are suffering from possible PTSD or severe depression. Moreover, an estimated 320,000 have experienced a probable Traumatic Brain Injury (TBI) during deployment, yet more than half reported they were never evaluated by a physician for their brain injury.[9] Both PTSD and TBI have now been dubbed the signature injuries of war in Iraq and Afghanistan.

Today's Soldiers

Who serves in today's all-volunteer U.S. Armed Forces (Army, Navy, Marine Corps, Air Force, and Coast Guard)? Compared to those who served under the draft in Vietnam, today's all-volunteer forces are more likely to have high school diplomas and to score at or above the median for the Armed Forces Qualification Test (AFQT).[10] However, these numbers are not as optimistic in recent years because the Armed Forces continue to need more new recruits. The military uses AFQT scores to determine who is trainable and most likely to complete their contracts. A high school diploma is considered the best indicator of this outcome. Performance on the AFQT and education backgrounds (high school diploma) combine to determine placement into specific "tiers" or categories. For example, those who place in tiers I (HS diploma) and II are seen as above average; those placing in tiers IIIA and IIIB are considered average; those who place in tiers IV and V are considered below average or markedly below average.

Prior to 2007, the goal of the Department of Defense was for 67 percent of recruits to score at least in the 50th percentile (levels I through IIIA). This goal has been lowered to 60 percent for the Army to meet its recruitment goals, and according to a recent report, the cap on the number of recruits scoring IV has risen from 2 percent to 4 percent, again to keep recruitment numbers up.[11] The percent of those placing in tier I has declined in recent years, reflecting the strain placed on the military.[12]

Age and racial composition have not changed significantly since Vietnam, although gender has. The average age of today's military recruit is still young at 18; nearly half of today's active duty force is between the ages of 17 and 24. By comparison, this age group makes up less than 20 percent of today's civilian cohort of prime working age. While women were barred from reaching numbers above 2 percent prior to 1967, today they constitute 14 percent of the enlisted force.[13] The Congressional Budget Office reports that African American males continue to join the military at higher rates than their white-male counterparts and other racial minorities. Today, African Americans constitute 29 percent of the Army's enlisted force, a disproportionate number, although they are less likely to serve in combat MOS than their white male counterparts when all branches are included. White males continue to have a higher representation in combat occupations—they constitute 68 percent of the military and 75 percent of the combat MOS versus African American service members at 13 percent of combat MOS (versus nineteen percent of overall force). Hispanics are underrepresented in the military at 11 percent versus 14 percent of the overall population.[14]

While today's force is more diverse than in previous wars, "grunts" are still young working and middle class kids from throughout the country. They enlist as naïve young men and women who want to serve their country, get a college education, and experience mobility. Research continues to reveal that those from lower socioeconomic backgrounds are more likely to join the military.[15] Not surprisingly, those with resources choose college over the military.[16] Once in the military, those from disadvantaged backgrounds score lower on entry exams and are more likely to find themselves in combat occupations.[17] Thus, while the average education and diversity of today's military is slightly higher than during the Vietnam draft, socioeconomic status still influences who joins.[18] It is also still the case that those from the highest and lowest socioeconomic brackets are less likely to serve.[19] Finally, the southern region of the UnitedStates still produces proportionately higher active duty forces and reservists than other regions, while the northeast has the lowest recruitment rate.

The Shifting Image of the Warrior

Throughout this book I will refer often to the term *masculinity* because as training and service reveal, gender is performed, reinforced, and reproduced in military culture. By performance, I mean that males especially are encouraged to display characteristics that match an American ideal of manhood.[20] In *Unlocking the Iron Cage* (1996), sociologist Michael Schwalbe provides a definition of *traditional masculinity* as a normative stance that men believe they must enact in order to be respected in American culture. A man must demonstrate himself to be "rational, tough, indomitable, ambitious, competitive, in control, able to get a job done, and ardently heterosexual."[21] From military slogans and recruiting advertisements to popular film, novels, and nonfiction accounts of war, the images of combat continue to be decidedly masculine.[22]

While it is important to note that images of the warrior remain masculine, some scholars have identified a shift in the warrior image, one that includes a degree of vulnerability and modified masculinity.[23] War historians tell us that public opinion has evolved to the point that war is no longer seen as honorable so much as necessary. Others argue that since Vietnam, the once "grand narrative" of "patriotic duty, masculinity, sacrifice and service"[24] that sent acknowledgment of war trauma underground for World War II veterans has given way to a postmodern turn of trauma-centered institutional typecasting.[25] Coverage of war by the media has greatly influenced this shift, and although the wounds of war remain consistent, the public images have not.

In *The Warrior Image* (2008), historian Andrew Huebner documents the shifting images of the warrior since World War II. During that conflict, the grimmest images of death and carnage were managed through propaganda films and military media. Evidence of the psychological wounds of more than 1.3 million of those who survived the war were filtered through military propaganda, Huebner argues.[26] A war that resulted in the deaths of over 405,000 Americans (battle and nonbattle deaths) portrayed returning World War II veterans as triumphant and invulnerable. It was the last war that would achieve this honor. Public optimism for the "good war" combined with military culture to present a traditional masculine image of military life. It would not be until the end of World War II that the uglier side of war would begin to surface. Cultural images in which veterans were at first portrayed as brave, invincible, optimistic, and composed began to deteriorate as the war dragged on. Between Japanese death marches and Hitler's atrocities, media depictions became more disturbing, and the shift in imagery revealed stoic and brave yet fatigued and dejected men returning from war. Moreover, after the atomic bomb, America's ability to return to innocence faded.

William Styron has written about the enduring metaphors of Auschwitz and Hiroshima and his experiences as a young soldier. He writes, "If in the First World War nationalistic ambitions largely fueled the conflict, World War II was the incubator of a poisonous and worldwide racism." He recalls images of Japanese soldiers as rats with slanted eyes and "repulsively coiled" tails. "After VJ Day," he continues, "there was a space of a year or so when it was truly possible to conceive of a world without war. Progenitors of the baby boom, most veterans were diligently amorous." Styron recalls that the "gloom descended soon after Winston Churchill's Iron Curtain speech." For Styron, the "nervous bravado" that had held sway during his service in the Pacific gave way to a sense of the "future closing down permanently" when he was called back up for active duty in the Korean War. "Back in infantry training, I had the nightmarish perception of war as a savage continuum, not a wholesome if often lethal adventure men embarked upon, as in World War II, to strike down the forces of evil, but a perpetual way of life in which small oases of peacetime provided intermittent relief."[27]

Public portrayals continued to shift through the Korean War as the misery and fatigue of war blended with stoicism. But Americans were not able to stomach a war that dragged on because it lacked the grisly images and motivation for war that Pearl Harbor had provided. "To many Americans," Huebner writes, "the Korean War seemed a colossal waste of time, money, and especially lives.... Five million Americans served on active duty during the Korean War, almost a third of the figure for World War II."[28]

Huebner reveals that by the Vietnam era, soldiers were portrayed as traumatized, emotionally wounded, and permanently scarred. Psychological and emotional wounds became visible as American culture shifted its focus to an image of American soldiers fighting wars that allowed policy makers and politicians to save face. Soldiers were no longer shown as trusting of their higher-ups in command. Rather, they were portrayed as exploited victims of U.S. foreign policy and military brass.

Evan Wright echoes this sentiment in his 2004 book, *Generation Kill: Devil Dogs, Iceman, Captain America, and the New Face of American War.*[29] An embedded journalist in the early days of Operation Iraqi Freedom, Wright characterizes many of those returning home as reluctant warriors who joined for honor and purity but left Iraq cynical and jaded. He describes many of the young Marines he interviewed as predisposed to cynicism and distrust because of lessons learned in Vietnam. Those interviewed by Wright speak of expected dishonesty and incompetence among authority figures. A recent survey of active duty forces asked the question, "How many of your NCOs/POs in your immediate unit are good leaders?" Only 14 percent reported all were good. Forty-three percent said "most" were. Twenty-three percent reported only "some" were, and 16 percent reported only a "few" were good leaders.[30]

From these shifting images we learn that the historic warrior archetype of both protector and aggressor consistent with the ideal of traditional masculinity is more difficult to sustain in today's military culture. Just as the culture at large is involved in political and social change, so too are the armed forces. Women serve in combat zones regardless of their support positions, even though many males continue to resent their presence. As of January 2011, General George W. Casey announced that the U.S. Armed Forces were in the process of reconsidering the current official policy that bans females from combat military occupational specialties.[31]

Until December 2010, gay and lesbian soldiers remained pinned to the margins of military life with the "Don't Ask, Don't Tell" policy. Many, however, continue to resent their presence. The Department of Defense is now in the process of a shift in policy, but it will take effect slowly, by most accounts. More important, there remains significant resistance among the ranks. For example, the comprehensive Department of Defense report of November 2010, revealed that 28 percent of Armed Forces personnel reported that their personal morale would be negatively or very negatively affected by the repeal of "Don't Ask, Don't Tell." The highest resistance was found among Marines (approximately 40 percent) and the Army (approximately 30 percent). Among those who reported they would consider or leave the military sooner because of the repeal, almost one fourth of Armed Forces said they would (26 percent Army, 38 percent Marines).[32] Incidents of abusive attitudes toward gays, lesbians, and racial minorities can be found throughout the ranks.

In addition to a shifting military culture, soldiers work alongside local citizens of the countries they occupy and with private contractors who earn salaries that far exceed the average soldier's pay. Social workers, psychologists, and embedded media are more actively engaged in war zones than in previous wars. Combat stress units are deployed now with official acknowledgment of trauma, although diagnosis and/or self-disclosure remain risky.

All these factors indicate a changing military culture, and this change is apparent in the attitudes expressed by many returning soldiers who share their stories of life after combat. From their experiences, we are able to see how the complexity of modern warfare, the experience of combat trauma, and the demands of return to civilian life have impacted, to varying degrees, the masculine symbol of the rugged (heterosexual) male soldier. Evidence of these changes will unfold throughout the book.

CHAPTER TWO

Socialization of the
Contemporary Soldier

S ociologist Emile Durkheim wrote of the power of rituals and rites in his seminal work, *The Elementary Forms of Religious Life* (1912). Here, Durkheim describes how ritual is the vehicle for social solidarity, the seed for collective effervescence and "felt emotions."[1] Rites, both negative and positive, "can have sacredness; indeed, there is no rite that does not have it to some degree,"[2] Durkheim argues. Initiation rites such as those found in basic training reflect a powerful transformation as civilians are brought out of the "profane" world where their commitments to a variety of communities (e.g., work, leisure, social networks) are replaced with focused and repetitive rites of passage that encourage commitment to the elite community of the military (not unlike the rebirth ceremonies of some religions).[3]

Conscious solidarity building occurs in basic training that provides symbolic weight to the words *honor, duty,* and *sacrifice* in the name of defending the nation. Although it is acknowledged that today's military culture is far more complex, these oral histories reveal that military training continues to be laden with symbols. The flag, the uniform, military parlance (e.g., "Hooah" or "HUA" and "Semper Fi"), the march cadence, the rifle, awards, badges, honors, the salute and emblems of rank, status, and commitment to sacrifice carry significant meaning for many soldiers long after their initiation and service (e.g., "Once a Marine, always a Marine!"). Durkheim explains that this is only possible because of symbols; they have the power to take "the place of the thing, and emotions aroused are transferred to the symbol."[4] Memories of basic training reveal that the military still provides for such emotional bonds, so much so that soldiers consider one another family, but this is not without consequences.

Rituals and initiation rites, both benevolent and malevolent, are socially contagious, which means that the shared understandings and emotional force spread throughout a specific group.[5] They serve to separate the sacred group life from the profane. Interestingly, however, Durkheim predicted that military life "wrongly or rightly" will lose its standing as the last bastion of "passive obedience" in modernity.[6] I imagine that Durkheim would look at the complexity of today's military culture, its rigid bureaucratic structure and technological advances, and argue that the profane has contaminated its sacred potential. He might also argue that delineating the sacred from the profane is less possible for today's soldier, who can easily access the latter via media and information technology. Soldiers in Iraq and Afghanistan can remain in touch with friends and family through Internet, blogs, live streaming video, texting, and cell phones, and many of them do readily admit that this phenomenon is a mixed bag.

I don't know if Durkheim is correct, but there is certainly evidence that the cultural landscape of military life is shifting beneath the boots of soldiers on the ground. From basic training through experienced combat trauma and return to civilian life, the growing paradox is revealed. The once monolithic standard of masculinity that held sway has cracked open, but there remains a gap between the organizational discourse and the lived experiences of soldiers. Thus, while historians have perhaps accurately depicted the changing images of soldiers and the warrior archetype in the public arena, remnants of it remain in the highly emotional, integrative, symbolic aspects of basic training that are now juxtaposed with marginalization, alienation, and social isolation. Today, the military itself is a mixed bag. What remains constant, however, is that war still wounds the heart and there is little that training does to prepare for this outcome.

Basic Training and the Proving Ground for Masculinity

After enlistment, recruits go to basic combat training or "boot camp," as it is sometimes called. Basic training includes what are often called the red, white, and blue phases. The red phase is often considered the most difficult because it begins with hazing rituals and degradation rituals by drill sergeants. Recruits are in a new environment and may or may not be prepared for the aggression and physical demands of obstacle courses, repelling exercises, sprints, and long marches accompanied by muscle spasms and fatigue. As time goes on, recruits learn how to eat military prepared meals (MREs), run long distances, and develop respect for their drill sergeants, whom they learn quickly are not their friends. They learn very early to respond to command with "Drill sergeant. Yes, drill sergeant." Basic training is structured to be difficult. Drill sergeants are tasked with weeding out those who are physically unfit or are not mentally ready for military service.

Rifle marksmanship occurs in the white phase (weeks 4 through 6), sometimes called the "gunfighter" or "rifleman" stage, with skill-building and team-building exercises and weapons training. Soldiers come to know their weapons during this phase. Weapons training during the white phase involves learning to shoot at simulated human targets with M-16 rifles. Hand-to-hand combat maneuvers are practiced and the word "Kill!" becomes commonplace. While most recruits view the use of simulated human targets as simply techniques for learning to shoot "center mass" and perfect their aim, the technique is described as a major difference in recent warfare.

In *On Killing* (2004), Lt. Col. David Grossman has written about the psychology of this process, explaining that the necessary transformation requires a full understanding of the task at hand before engaging in the heat of battle. While being interviewed for the documentary film *The Ground Truth,* Grossman explains such transformations are needed prior to the heat of battle "because somewhere inside the mid-brain in most healthy members of our species is a resistance to killing their own kind."[7] Derogatory nicknames are provided to assist in the objectification of others. Empathy for civilians is not necessarily downplayed during basic training, but recruits learn that collateral damages are to be expected. The psychological preparation often requires dehumanizing the enemy. "The hardware in enabling killing has not changed that much. The rifle, the pistol, it hasn't changed that much," Grossman explains, "but the software [pointing to his head] has changed phenomenally." Learning to shoot "center mass" and the added dehumanization serves to create combative solidarity and help soldiers resist the temptation to shoot above or to the left or right of the enemy, a common practice in all wars.[8]

The blue phase is considered the home stretch—those who have made it through the dreaded red and white phases will be tested in field tactics, skills demonstration in their respective military occupational specialty (MOS), and teamwork capabilities. Recruits will participate in field exercises and simulated combat conditions. Command may bring in Arabic speakers dressed in Middle Eastern clothing and stage scenes that might occur in country so that recruits can practice social interaction skills. At this point, soldiers are monitored for independent displays of conformity to codes of conduct, ability to work as a team, physical fitness, and expression of the values of military culture. Recruits who display these characteristics will graduate basic training and move into their next phases of specialty. Those who don't succeed will either be "recycled" (held back) or kicked out.

After basic training, soldiers then proceed to their respective specialty training for the military occupational specialty. This might include Advanced Individual Training (AIT) or (OSUT) a combination of basic and AIT. Air Force recruits go on to technical training for their Air Force specialty code (AFSC), and Navy recruits and Coast Guard go on to schools for their "A" rating. At each phase of basic and AIT, military rituals and initiation rites are embedded in the structure to create a soldier.

This is accomplished with remnants of the traditional masculinity standard. In patriarchal organizations men have historically been depicted as emotionless, but this is misleading and is starkly absent in combat, though reality runs opposite the discourse. "Men are assumed not to show fear, sadness or even joy; anger may, however, be thought to be appropriate for men at least in some organizational settings."[9] In other words, soldiers must embody mastery over weaponry, technology, and certain emotions—all things that threaten the rational. By successfully demonstrating mastery, "individuals are implicitly actualizing the gendered division between rational and irrational, between men and women."[10] Thus, while the reality is that military masculinities are complex—gays, lesbians, bisexuals, transsexuals, and heterosexual females are all part of military culture— the discourse employed in military training continues to draw on a firmly masculine model, one that capitalizes on bravado and associates manliness with brute force, rational control, and dominance.

Recruits, regardless of sexual orientation or gender, are socialized to either embrace or at the very least tolerate the demonstrated masculinity if they are to complete military training and service in an organization in which male heterosexual prowess continues to dominate despite official policy. Once in the armed services, a vocabulary laden with denigration of feminine traits is made available to male recruits along with gender slurs.[11] For example, in early 2011, Naval Aircraft Carrier Commander Captain Owen Honors was fired for producing and participating in a raunchy video that demonstrated extreme homophobia, gay bashing, and sexism.[12] His use of homophobic humor and the sexual objectification of gays and females in the film lend credibility to sociological criticism that military culture uses such humor to handle its own apprehensions and anxieties about traditional masculinity.[13] In addition, equating women and homosexuals as sexual objects "provides ready images for portraying power and hierarchical position."[14]

Indeed, the amount of ritualized masculinity in basic training, accompanied by aggression, discipline, control, physical dominance, degradation, pain, and the censorship of a host of emotions otherwise associated with the feminine, cannot be overstated. But it is equally true and important to acknowledge that positive emotional bonds are formed, a sense of duty and group loyalty is created, and empathy for one's fellow soldier is instilled, so much so that males and females often speak of their fellow soldiers as family members. This said, the changing military culture that includes females in combat zones and the soon-to-be open recognition of sexual orientation may also render problematic the older "band of brothers" concept familiar to many heterosexual males. Indeed, the resistance to the recent repeal of "Don't Ask, Don't Tell" reveals there may be bonds available, but not to all equally.

In basic training drill sergeants are seen as father-like figures that both demonstrate and accept from recruits only those emotions that are associated with a masculine ethos. This is especially true in the early stages but may shift as recruits gain more status and respect from their command. Once this occurs, drill sergeants sometimes soften their stance and allow themselves to display more concern for their soldiers, establishing emotional bonds.

In early phases of basic training, males especially are expected to reflect the organizational belief that rationality and emotional control are necessary for effective soldiering. Ironically, this is achieved via dramatized emotion management and displays from drill sergeants. New recruits are exposed to exaggerated male aggression and hostility. Life at boot camp means living betwixt and between, as the recruit transitions from civilian to potential soldier. From here it begins—a rigid structure and 16-hour days, demanding routines, physical training, exhaustion, and the creation of a new identity. Drill sergeants model what is expected, demonstrating that aggression and violence are necessary for combat readiness. The moral ambiguity of war is eliminated, or at least held in check, during basic training as individuals shed their "civilian skins for [military] uniforms."[15]

As Marine Sergeant Carpenter explains, the goal of the military is to "break you down from civilian status all the way to the point of nothing, and then build you back in the image in which they perceive." He describes how he handled his recruits during basic training: "We're not here to babysit. We're not here to hold your hand. You're man enough to make the decision, own up to it. If you didn't know what you were getting into, life lesson! Guess what? You just learned one!" Sergeant Carpenter was especially annoyed by recruits who "whined" about their training. "America didn't become what it is today because of people who sat around and cried like little babies." His comments mirror the dominant discourse of basic training that associates vulnerability with weakness and femininity, placing limits on what males [and females] can and cannot express openly.[16]

It seems that everyone remembers the red phase, the first words from their drill sergeants, and the highly animated introduction to what lies ahead. On day 1, recruits don't know that the hazing rituals will soften over time, although some say it starts again when they arrive for specialization training. Aggression from drill sergeants is sometimes referred to as "getting smoked" or as "shark attacks." The personal narratives that follow illustrate how recruits understand this highly symbolic rite of initiation of basic training.

Staff Sergeant Woodmansee was born in 1984 and served two tours in Operation Iraqi Freedom with the 42nd Infantry regiment, Baghdad (Bravo). Joining the Army National Guard just out of high school, he felt more prepared for the physical aspects of basic training at Fort Jackson but remembers, "You're getting smoked constantly. You're getting smoked all through basic training; less as you go along. At AIT [Advanced Infantry Training], they basically pick up on the exact same idea. When you first get there, they're gonna' smoke ya', they're gonna' establish 'Hey, just because you're out of basic [training] doesn't mean you're where you need to be as far as being a soldier, cause you're just a basic training soldier graduate, that's it.' So it's kind of like they again establish dominance. You do fireguard stuff again, these random [activities]. I remember painting rocks for about 10, 12 hours for two days. Flip a rock over—if it's a different color you paint it." The point of the exercise was to demonstrate willingness to follow orders.

In all phases, basic training involves learning obedience to command, respect for authority, placing the mission first, and never accepting defeat.

A deep sense of loyalty is fostered for the uniformed family. Recruits participate in drills in which they march, run, stand at attention, and endure a grueling regiment of physical training. They learn to perform random and impossible tasks when ordered, how to load and fire weapons, how to absorb verbal assaults from drill sergeants without flinching, and how to think about the possibility of killing or being killed. Most soldiers understand and accept the hazing for its stated outcome: to create composure under stress and instill a moral grammar that can endure the reality of combat.

Specialist Lewis enlisted in the Army Reserves in 2002 at the age of 21, expecting to be called up for active duty. He served in Iraq during the early phase of the war [Operation Iraqi Freedom I]. For Lewis, basic training was a new experience. He also trained at Fort Benning, Georgia. "[I] really didn't know what to expect. I think I got 15 minutes of sleep the first night I was there [be]cause the bus got us there at like four o'clock in the morning—drove us around base. They wanted us disoriented so we couldn't, if we decided to bolt, we wouldn't know where we were going. Finally got off the bus, got into there, they held us there together, and then we finally got to the barracks when we had enough time to lie down for 15 minutes before the lights came on."

Lewis's first shark attack occurred when he was standing during reception. "First thing my drill sergeant said to me that I remember was, 'I know you're not gonna' drop this bag!' because we had to [stand] there all in a line holding up our duffel bags, trying our best not to drop them 'cause if we drop [them] we've gotta' pick them up and hold [them] longer." He remembers a huge building equivalent to two football fields where most of the punishments took place. "Whenever we got in trouble, we got sent to the wall of the building. The wall is about 30 feet high so it was really distinct. If you didn't make it down and back in a certain amount of time, you had to go back again. Then they got creative and they started telling us we had artillery fire coming in. We normally would always get artillery fire right through the big patch of rocks in the field."

Specialist Harper enlisted in the Army Reserves in 2003 at the age of 19 with the hopes of paying for college and served one tour in Operation Iraqi Freedom. "Can I cuss?" he responds, when asked to recall his basic training at Fort Jackson, South Carolina. Harper describes his first shark attack as follows: "You're sitting there and they drive around post so you don't know where you're at, and you've got two rucksacks, pretty big rucksacks, and you're sitting there. You're driving up and a guy gets on the bus with a drill sergeant that yells, 'What's taking you so long? Get off my fucking bus! What's taking you so long? You've got two minutes, get off, get off, get off! Run up, get off the bus as fast as you can!' Two rucksacks—it's pretty tough." The physical training and long cold marches were difficult but left him with a good feeling for "getting it done." Being acknowledged by drill sergeants for his hard work was also important: "I remember drill sergeants actually shaking your hand, showing you some respect. That was pretty good."

First Lieutenant Iglesias joined the Army in 1995 at the age of 22 and served three years active duty with the 3rd Infantry Division. He attended basic training at Fort Benning before serving fourteen months in Korea. In 1998, he enlisted in the Army National Guard and has since served in Egypt for six months and Iraq in 2004 and again in 2008. Basic training included a lot of hazing but was "pretty much as I expected," he remembers. Nicknamed "Inges-ass" by his drill sergeant, he remembers being punished for leaving his laundry overnight and being made to do push-ups, twenty-five for each article of clothing left. "It was like six hundred push-ups. I knocked like two hundred out the first day. Then basically he strung it out all throughout my basic training and it equaled about a thousand pushups, because you knock out twenty-five, then he would say, 'I didn't hear you' or 'What's the count now?'"

Iglesias was naïve when he enlisted. "I didn't know all the system as far as recruiting goes, and the pitfalls of that. I should've been more leery because when I went in I wanted to be 11 Bravo, Airborne and Ranger, that kind of stuff, and I just signed the contract basically 11X and I fell in with the mechanized role which, looking back on it I'm sort of glad I did, cause I had some good times with 3rd ID [infantry division], but it wasn't what I wanted. I didn't know it until halfway through basic and it was too late." He remembers, "The joke was, 'We don't need to throw a Bradley out of a C-130.'"

First Sergeant Mayfield attended basic training for the Army six days after his high school graduation in 1984. After four years of active duty, Mayfield joined the Army Reserves and later the National Guard as an unassigned infantry man. In the interim he worked as a police officer until his unit was called up to serve in Iraq with the 39th Brigade in 2004–2005. Mayfield was enamored with the military as a boy. "[I] played war with my friends, built a lot of model airplanes and tanks and stuff. I was just drawn to it. I can't really, you know, there wasn't any specific patriotic reason or anything like that. It was just a calling, I guess.... I wanted the infantry field because to me that was the field to be in if you were going to be in the Army. You know, if you're going to be a soldier, you've got to pick up a rifle and fight. And that's what the infantry is all about."

Also stationed at Fort Benning, Mayfield remembers basic training as a place where the boys were separated from the men. "Well, a lot of that stuff you try to forget about. I mean, it's just frantic.... You're running on borderline exhaustion," he explains. "So you know, sometimes you've been awake so long you start hallucinating. You're not sure what they're telling you. But, you know, it's just getting the basics of how to be a soldier ingrained in you.... I mean, it's a formative time in a young man's life. I say 'young man' not to be sexist, but Fort Benning is the home of the infantry, the home of the Airborne, the home of the Rangers, so it's a pretty high testosterone environment. As a matter of fact, I've heard it called the Benning School for Boys."

Although basic training is coed today, Mayfield remembers basic training, then and now, as an opportunity to move into manhood, to "develop that toughness and that vigor that young men have and develop it into a killer type mentality, basically. We were all, you know, ate up with it. We lived it and breathed it. We were all just enamored with it.... Every boy, man [laughs], man-boy that I know of, they want to test themselves in battle. I think that's why they go out for the contact sports, the thrill seeking. They're trying to just see if they've got what it takes. That's kind of why I went in. I use the male pronoun, not to be sexist but that's just not how little girls are raised."

Sergeant Reinold was 19 years old when he joined the Army National Guard in November 2002. He remembers being "stoked" about boot camp. "I know that everybody remembers the times when it was real rough, like, the very first two weeks. It is called red phase—you get there and they're in your butt the whole time, chewing you out and you can never do anything right. They give you these tasks that seem so impossible, like tell you [to get into] a certain type of uniform, and they give you like a minute to go up there and get it on and come back down. And we lived two floors up and we had to come back down to the drill pad, so, of course you never made it [laughs]. And every time you didn't make it, you know, you'd have to do push-ups or something. And they did that to show you it's important to make your times because otherwise people get hurt! So he [drill sergeant] hurt us."

Basic training was easy for Reinold because it resonated with his emotional orientation growing up. "I was a real closed-up kind of guy when it came to emotions. The good thing about basic training is they teach you to be a soldier and a soldier doesn't show emotion. They teach you to just shut it off, completely shut it off. It's called the soldier's switch. That's why a guy can keep fighting even though his best friend just got his head blown off, keep on fighting through it and stuff. And when that switch is on, you know the whole time I was over in Iraq, I didn't care about anything. I was going to follow orders. That's all that mattered. Complete the mission—God forbid they ever leave me out of a mission, 'cause I swear that I would have lost my purpose on earth if they did something like that. [Be]cause you're all rough and tough and you're ready to fight and you would never even show an emotion." Reinold firmly believes that censored vulnerable emotions were the key to his success during combat. His earlier emotional orientation that led him to be "closed up" also mirrors traditional masculinity, in which boys are taught early to separate themselves from their felt emotions.[17]

Getting smoked was nothing new for Specialist Hooker, either. He grew up in a military family and enlisted in the Army in 2007 at the age of 22 to help pay for college. He remembers being the butt of jokes as well. "You don't walk into the military with the last name Hooker and become a Private Hooker in basic training and not receive some slack. I can't tell you how many jokes I've gotten from drill sergeants. It's all good fun, you know." He also recalls the first day of boot camp as a vivid lesson in watching his "six" [keeping alert and "having someone's back"]. "Oh yeah, first day, I'll never forget the first day [be]cause I left a space in between the seating whenever we sat down at the table to fill out some last-minute paperwork. And I got labeled a Bravo Foxtrot, the buddy fucker, because I left a space. The drill sergeant informed me, 'That's how people die because you're not paying attention!' So the first day was quite miserable. Which, you know, I was pretty used to that. I had a father as a drill sergeant. He [the drill sergeant] wasn't going to rain down any fire on me that I wasn't used to."

As memories of boot camp reveal, exaggerated aggression by drill sergeants is purposeful and outcomes hinge upon recruits' ability to absorb hostility without reaction. Displayed anger is no accident in military training. It is a dramatized behavior that complements the organizational goals of the military. Moreover, anger has been identified for its use in energizing, organizing, and regulating social and interpersonal behavior.[18] Sometimes aggression can be a true expression of anger and other times it serves the instrumental function of dominance.[19] Obedience to command and respect for authority is not only valued but is considered key to whether one lives or dies in combat. Those able to "handle" their emotions are considered better suited for combat.

While recruits are being tested for their composure, they are also being prepared to display anger and aggression as an appropriate response to threat. Fear is evident but must be controlled. Masculine composure and control of emotions were viewed by sociologist Erving Goffman as virtuous, indicative of "character," and "akin to courage and integrity," whereas sociologist Thomas Scheff likens the suppression of vulnerable emotions (e.g., fear) to a character flaw, one that can result in a "lethal addiction to the cult of masculinity."[20] Like guilt or shame, fear fits into a category of emotions that Scheff describes as "vulnerable," often associated with the feminine. Men, more so than women, are expected to suppress vulnerable emotions during basic training. However, prolonged suppression of vulnerable emotions has its costs. Accordingly, suppression may give rise to a negative response over time, meeting what are perceived as threats to self with either "silence or violence."[21] This may reveal itself in basic training, but it is more likely to reveal itself in combat, where life and death are at stake, or on return to civilian life as soldiers continue to be held to gendered stereotypes.

As recruits learn the skills of combat, they learn that loyalty to the group surpasses individual needs. Routine activities are built into basic training to instill the importance of always "having your six covered" [watching your back or watching someone else's back]. Preparation for these moments is anticipated with strong combative solidarity. But sometimes the exaggerated displays of aggression from drill sergeants can cause recruits to question this process. For example, Sergeant George was 19 when he joined the Army in October 2000. He served three tours in Afghanistan before his contract ended in 2008. Like so many, he joined the Army for both pragmatic and ideological reasons. George enlisted in 2000 with the support of his family and saw it as an opportunity to get an education and "climb the socioeconomic ladder," but he also saw enlistment as a way to "achieve some sense of manhood."

At first, George liked basic training and understood the "character-building" aspects of it, but he became disheartened by things he witnessed. "There were a lot of things that I thought were strange or inhumane," he explains, "but I just went with it because I thought I was doing something for my country and I trusted that I was being trained with my best interest in mind and the best interest of the country in mind." He looks back upon himself now as naïve. "The one thing that really stood out to me in basic training and the thing I always go back to was the racism." He was only 19 when he witnessed a racially motivated crime against a fellow soldier during boot camp. "He [an African American] wound up getting beat almost to death by a couple of white dudes.... Just seeing his face contorted and barely recognizable was very strange and I just didn't understand that level of hate and what they were trying to accomplish with that, but I found out later in the military that that level of hate and violence is kind of the vibe that everyone is grooving on while they're in."

George also remembers numerous hazing rituals. One in particular occurred when a drill sergeant came into the barracks unannounced and flipped a bunk. "He just flew in and flipped the top bunk and the kid flew off the bunk and broke his arm and he was 'recycled' [held back due to his injury] obviously—the kid, not the drill sergeant." For George, much of the aggression from drill sergeants was "completely unnecessary." "Does that turn someone into a warrior?" he asks rhetorically, adding, "What does that do to everyone else in the room because that's now acceptable behavior because your mentor is doing it?" The same drill sergeant was notorious for throwing MREs at recruits during training. "He would throw them at them and say their name just before it hit so they would turn around and it would hit them in the face." George was especially happy when basic training ended and he was able to attend Airborne school. Yet in spite of his drill sergeant's poor leadership, he left with a sense of group solidarity, "of accomplishment and just achievement across the board."

From these excerpts, we can see that although exaggerated aggression does not always have the intended outcome, especially for those who lose respect for command, many accepted the masculine rites of passage as a necessary aspect of initiation to military life. Some embraced it. Recruits learn this normative posturing within military culture from their first day at basic training. This allows young male recruits especially to leave the three-phase process of boot camp with a sense of accomplishment. Thus, while the image of a warrior may have changed in the public arena and technological savvy has supposedly replaced physical prowess, the enactment of masculinity has not changed significantly in military training. Demonstrated aggression to subordinates is pervasive and remains highly symbolic in the early socialization phase.

Males who embrace the masculine ethos can access a discourse in basic training that allows them to acknowledge their experiences as a proving ground for their masculinity. However, the experience also creates a site of strong emotional communion, a preparation for the glue that provides them with a sense of belonging, solidarity, respect, and empathy for fellow soldiers, as revealed in the next chapter. This reveals a false duality between discourse— that men are emotionless and the feminine represents non-rational and emotional—and the lived experiences of soldiers. Male recruits who do not live up to masculine stereotypes, such as not demonstrating physical prowess, hesitating to pull the trigger, or revealing some perceived insecurity, may be called a derogatory feminine or homosexual term.[22]

Masculine organizations misleadingly partition off particular emotions in favor of instrumental behavior to fulfill rational goals. The military necessarily does this to prepare soldiers, capitalizing on obedience and minimizing resistance. But the narrative of early training that frames the masculine and feminine in a hierarchical trajectory perpetuates an essentialism that does not serve soldiers well, both male and female. As the following recollections from female soldiers and the combat experiences of the next chapter reveal, the unequal power relationships and the masculine predilection to dismiss or repress vulnerable emotions can turn on males, who are left with a sense of ambivalence about their experienced emotions of combat trauma. It shapes the discourse and directs females and males to express their emotions in particular ways.

Women and Military Training

There are notable differences in the ways male and female soldiers talk about basic training. Women join the military for reasons very similar to those men have, such as getting a college education or out of sense of duty, and no doubt have similar experiences on arrival. But their discourses about their early experiences reveal the emotion work in organizations that falls along gender lines. This is explained in part by research that reveals female recruits are still more heavily scrutinized for their ability to demonstrate similar qualities to their male counterparts.[23]

In her seminal work, *The Managed Heart*, sociologist Arlie Hochschild (1983) reveals that our emotional expressions are often a reflection of the unseen weight of dominant ideologies (e.g., men are strong and women are weak) and the shadow of social structure (e.g., the military is a man's world). While ideology provides a framework or "framing rules" for cognitive understanding of a given situation, "feeling rules" or "emotion norms" guide us in how we are to feel about given situations. Gender socialization leads to a division of emotional labor between males and females, and this process is revealed in the emotion work and emotion management strategies (managing the expressed emotions of others) that occur in basic training.

Notice that male recruits seldom if ever talked about the need to adjust their emotional orientation to the situation. According to Hochschild, women are said to do more emotion work than men because of their lower status relative to males. I see evidence of this in the fact that female recruits are quick to reveal their adjustment strategies and their emotion work. Interestingly, I found that females are more likely to verbalize vulnerable emotions when looking back over their time at basic training, but this is not because women are biologically inclined to feel vulnerable emotions more than their male counterparts. Rather, the explanation hinges upon gender performance, subordination, and social deference.

Hochschild argues that women hold the task of mastering anger and aggression by being nice or assuming a submissive posture. When they don't, there are real consequences. These rules are compounded because women (and homosexuals) have weaker "status shields" and are less able to fend off the displaced feelings of others. Some argue that in masculine organizations men are more likely to experience joy in reinforcing domination over other men, whereas their domination over women is taken for granted.[24] Perhaps this helps to explain why women are more willing than men to discuss their vulnerable emotions on arrival at basic training and are more likely to describe their attempts to manage their emotions. Also, they may be allowed a broader vocabulary in talking about their experiences. For example, females express joy, sadness, anger, and fear to both males and females equally. However, men have been shown to express more joy and sadness to females but are more likely to express anger and fear to other males.[25]

Men may be even more constrained because their task is that of mastering fear and vulnerability by holding their composure and/or by exercising anger and aggression toward others in a struggle for dominance, a role that is dramatically modeled for them in the military. It is in the telling of their stories that the emotion work strategies reveal themselves.

Unlike their male counterparts, females are being trained to participate in a work culture that renders them marginal from the start. Women recruits are understandably less likely to celebrate the bravado and masculinity they encounter during basic training, though most do take it in stride and adapt by stepping in to manage their emotions. Many anticipated the challenge of being in a male-dominated organization and others struggled with it. Some revealed they felt the need to "act" more masculine in order to succeed while others attempted to keep a low profile so as not to stand out and minimize their hazing experiences. Some denied the existence of gendered differences. Others found themselves struggling to adapt to their marginalization. Each spoke about institutional rules that minimized contact with males and each described in some fashion, her emotion work strategies to survive basic training. For some, it was a reminder of the power dynamics; others saw it as a challenge to overcome.

Like their male counterparts, women are betwixt and between their citizen and soldier roles, but they are also in a work environment that restricts them because of their gender. Notably, few males expressed vulnerable emotions or the need to adjust to the emotional climate of basic training. Rather, most drew upon a masculine discourse to describe their experience, such as the ability to fend off or ignore the exhibited aggression during smoke or shark attacks. Some praised the absence of emotions altogether. Conversely, females talked about their emotional experiences in their personal narratives.

For example, Senior Air[wo]man Hook served in the Air Force during Operation Iraqi Freedom. Hook was 22 years old when she enlisted. Short of money for college, she enlisted and attended basic training at Lackland Air Force Base in San Antonio, Texas. Basic training was "scary," she explains. "We flew in, we had tons of layovers, then we finally got down there in the middle of the night and they bus you up there. You are like pulling up and you see all these TIs (drill sergeants) and you just know you're about to get it! So we didn't get any sleep that night—like zero! They yelled at us and threw our stuff around, but it was really scary. I think pretty much everybody cried." For a male recruit to openly admit that basic training was "scary" or that he "cried" on arrival would be a violation that could bring about serious sanctions. Hook learned quickly to manage her emotions and toughen up. "I just did what I was told and acted like I was mad and they left me alone." Her "sister flight" [female unit] was located on a separate floor from the "brother flight," but drills and training were coed. She remembers the strict rules of segregation between males and females. There was to be no interaction except "when nobody was watching."

Tech Sergeant Soliz joined the Air Force in 1997 at the age of 20. She served one tour in Operation Enduring Freedom and continues to serve in the university ROTC program today. Soliz's father encouraged her to join the Air Force. He felt she would "receive better treatment as a woman." A self described "Daddy's girl," Soliz recalls, "I was really dependent on my parents and leaving them—it was just really hard. Just the shock of what the, what did I get myself into? The first two weeks I cried myself to sleep every night. I think everybody did. And then after that it was the routine and so I got used to it." She remembers laughing and smiling inappropriately when being yelled at by her drill sergeant (training instructor) after her arrival at Lackland. It was surprising to her because her father had never yelled at her as a child. The subordination and aggression took her by surprise and she found her male commander intimidating. She remembers his first comment to her was, "Wipe that smile off your face." Soliz also came to a quick understanding that in order to succeed she would have to adjust to the masculine culture. In other words, she engaged in emotion work to adapt to her situations and remembers thinking, "I can't act this way, [I've] got to be tough like the guys were."

Sergeant Bonham served in Operation Iraqi Freedom. She joined the Army in 1998, her senior year of high school. She felt that military service would provide her with a way to "instantly support myself." She struggled with whether to join the Army or live at home with her mother and attend a community college but found that "the recruiters were just so willing to do all the paperwork and everything, so it was a lot easier to join the military." For Bonham, the most memorable aspect of basic training was "they just smoke the hell out of you by making you do a lot of miserable stuff." She remembers the combination of push-ups and forced water consumption that caused many in her cohort to throw up. "They called us all up into the base and they started making us do push-ups. I was in gymnastics, so I was pretty physically fit, I didn't have much problem. But then they make you stand up and drink a canteen of water and then you do more push-ups and jumping jacks, and eventually, and then you have to go get more water. . . . People are like throwing up. And I was not about to drink all my water and start throwing up! I'm like, 'Yeah, you can yell at me. I'm not [going] to do that.'" Like other females, Bonham also learned early to "go with the flow" in order to stay below the radar of her drill sergeant. "I was so afraid. I was just waiting for it to get scary and bad, but I just kind of went with the shuffle. We went through and I didn't really get called out. . . . There was a lot of getting moved around from one place to another, standing, waiting, sitting and waiting, and things like that."

It is interesting to see how quickly female recruits adjust to the masculine backdrop. Perhaps they have prior experiences with gendered stereotyping that accompanies them in to basic training and is reemphasized in the military. Emotion work appears to assist female recruits, who are not just subordinates but are, in some cases, resented for their mere presence.

Tech Sergeant Douglas has spent her career in the Air Force. Douglas has now served three tours[26] in Operation Enduring Freedom (Afghanistan) and continues working for the Air Force ROTC. She enlisted in 1991 and attended basic training in San Antonio as well. Douglas remembers arriving late at night and her first shark attack. "People are yelling at you. You are picking up your bags, you're putting them down. You have no idea who's who or what you're really supposed to be doing. . . . But I remember the next day . . . we were just laying in our bed, everybody was afraid to get out of the bed and we could hear all these people yelling, like they were having a field day.... We all wanted to see what it was, but we were afraid to get out of our beds and then finally our TI [training instructor] came in and we got out of bed pretty fast [laughs]." There is no doubt that male recruits experience similar feelings upon arrival, but to express this would be taboo for most males, revealing that males and females are vulnerable to the management of their emotions but in gender-specific ways.

Staff Sergeant Hewitt enlisted in the Army in 1985 when she was a senior in high school. She served active duty for three years, then reenlisted in the Reserves after taking a year off. She served in Operation Enduring Freedom (Afghanistan, Delta Company) in 2003 and trained at Fort McLellan, Alabama, and later at Fort Leonard Wood, Missouri, for her AIT training. Hewitt found comfort in her all-female unit: "You're all in the same boat, so you kind of cling to each other." Her first day was especially memorable. "He [drill sergeant] dropped me for push-ups. I was going upstairs, because my platoon was the first one there before the other platoons started coming in and you had to make sure all your buttons [in the older uniforms] were done. I was on the way upstairs and he, I don't know if he saw it or guessed it or what, [but] one of my buttons was undone and he dropped me on the stairway. I'll never forget that. I was traumatized because I was going to go and get back on the floor to do them and he says, 'No!' He dropped me on the stairway. It's like 'Oh, my God!'"

Acknowledgment of fear comes more freely for females, who are not so constrained by the masculine ethos. They seem more aware of their marginal status as well and thus quickly engage in the management of their feelings to adapt. Because her specialization was in a more masculine field, Hewitt struggled with males who perceived her as less capable of performing her job. Specialty training was "very scary....When I first went in, people really didn't know how to handle me because I was a female and a mechanic because the things that I worked on were way bigger than me! And this stems from basic training ... and it amazed me because it's like, 'Come on, guys, I've been through this. You all can stop handling me like a little egg. I'm not [going to] break!' When I got to my permanent party in Virginia, I wasn't very big and so people would, soldiers, my commander—they would look at me and it's like, 'Do you know what you're doing?' and it's like, 'Yes, I've been to school for this, sir.'"

Army Specialist Little joined the Army at the age of 17, just months before 9/11, and remembers hearing about it from her drill sergeant, who received the news on his cell phone. She remembers thinking to herself, "Oh, my gosh! We are going to war and we haven't even finished basic training!" Little was surprised to find she had survived basic training. "I wasn't scared," she remembers, "It was just a shock that I was there, that I had made it because everybody was like, 'Oh, you're not going to make it. You're going to want to come home.' So I was really relieved that I made it there because it was a big, like a big accomplishment." Little recalls that "most of my friends were males." She distanced herself from the females in her unit, viewing them as weak or manipulative, and adapted a paternalistic view of her cohort. "Some of them [females], I don't even know why they were there for basic training's sake! There was a lot that either got hurt on purpose or couldn't *handle* [emphasis] it. We had a girl go AWOL after the first weeks of training."

Little also remembers the strict rules about interactions between males and females but felt the males on her base were easier to talk to when the opportunity presented itself. She is both critical of and sympathetic to the ambivalence males felt over the presence of females in basic and advanced training. "Because the guys, I guess the whole girl thing—they want to treat us differently, but then they were like, 'You're in the Army, so you need to toughen up, too.'" She continues, "We had some men that thought that girls shouldn't be in the military, [that] 'it's not tough enough anymore' [or] 'I wish I'd joined the Marines because girls are girls,' and you know, they were very sexist about it." On the other hand, "If the girls were able to do what the guys did, they thought, 'Oh, wow!' You know, 'Maybe she is learning, she doesn't mind.' So they didn't really care."

Sergeant Ferretti was working three jobs in 2002 when she joined the Army Reserves at the age of 21. She served in Operation Iraqi Freedom in 2003–2004. Ferretti's experience with basic training at Fort Leonard Wood, Missouri, was very different. She was somewhat surprised because she expected more hazing than she received. "I was expecting to be yelled at, and it didn't happen really.... It was actually disappointing, because you see all these movies and you think you're going to get yelled at and treated like a private and scary and intimidating, but they basically held us for about two to three weeks waiting for our basic training to begin."

For Ferretti, basic training was essentially noneventful until she was seriously injured. She broke her hip in three places after falling during a grueling course exercise. "It's like a 25-foot tower and I was one of an unfortunate few that fell, but it didn't occur to me that I had a serious injury at all. I continued through the course and I fell a couple other times too, in not so serious positions, but then we did a 20-mile road march. I did the whole road march on a fractured hip. Finally, our last PT test, I collapsed, right after I ran my two miles, right at the end I collapsed and I couldn't get up any further. That's when I realized I had a serious injury." Ferretti was loyal to her unit and proud that she was able to return. "I came back and I was in good enough shape to start after only two weeks."

Like their male counterparts, female soldiers are equally dedicated to their units. Most are confident that they got from basic training what they needed. Some are equally nostalgic about their experiences, but they also cannot forget their place in military culture because they are constrained by a variety of conditions that will be addressed in chapter 4.

Conclusion

In *The Ritual Process: Structure and Anti-Structure* (1969), anthropologist Victor Turner describes the power of ritual in transforming both attitudes and behavior. The intensity of basic training consists of manipulation of symbols of the magnitude Turner associated with religion, which features "rites of passage" that "accompany every change of place, state, social position and age."[27] Each phase, each rite of initiation includes "storehouses of meaningful symbols" regarded by soldiers as authoritative and crucial to group survival.[28] A transformation must occur to prepare for war, and it is heavy with symbolism, imbued with sometimes dramatic and repetitive rituals of dominance, aggression, obedience, sacrifice, and reward. And as this group of soldiers reveal, there is no room for negotiation.

In *Asylums* (1961), sociologist Erving Goffman identifies the notion of a "total institution" as a rigid setting in which individual identities are broken down, reformulated, and separated almost entirely from former identities in order to serve the institutional mission.[29] Early socialization into military culture is reminiscent of the total institution, where autonomy gives way to conformity. Another way to think about this process is to view the military as an exclusive community that necessarily defines itself in opposition to civilian life.

In *Dilemmas of the American Self* (1989), sociologist John Hewitt provides an astute description of an exclusive community and its consequences for personal identity versus social identity. "Personal identity locates the individual on the larger and more abstract stage of society,"[30] Hewitt states, whereas "social identity is tied to membership in a community."[31] Military socialization exaggerates this process, demanding that its members identify exclusively with their community, creating boundaries and moral grammar to facilitate conformity and separation from soldier and citizen. Whereas in civilian life we find ourselves negotiating the poles of "exclusivity" and "autonomy," military life results in a social identity that is constructed through "an overpowering identification with a single community."[32]

Sustained identity at either pole is difficult to maintain without serious consequence to one's understanding of self. Joining any branch of the U.S. military necessarily translates into being a member of the total institution, that "exclusive" community with stringent and binding rituals that requires "extreme commitment" and "rigorous maintenance."[33] The soldier identity is achieved through sacred rites of passage that come with their own rights and obligations. As these personal narratives of basic training illustrate, males and females alike develop a deep sense of obligation to their fellow soldiers and an expressed respect for command with little exception. Drill sergeants, hazing rituals, regimented structure, discipline, and managed emotions combine to instill in recruits a military ethos/moral grammar that will serve to filter all they come to experience. They leave basic training as "just" soldiers, willing to both kill and die for the values instilled in them. Once they have shed their civilian skins, they wear their military uniforms proudly.

As the next chapter reveals, basic training experiences are sometimes worlds apart from actual combat, where trauma and its accompanying fear are prevalent and acknowledged by both males and females. Some of the stereotypes upheld and supported in basic training unravel during actual combat. Others find their way into military service and can harm soldiers in significant ways.

CHAPTER THREE

Reluctant Edgework and "Nonstandard" War

War "porn," as it has been dubbed—video accounts of soldiers at war—is now rampant on the Internet. YouTube videos reveal journalists and civilians being killed by emotionally numb soldiers who point and click their joystick as if the people scattering below are video targets, then joke about the carnage they impose. Indeed, some argue that violent videogames have contributed not only to the dehumanization of the enemy in combat, but also to the growing number of voyeurs who are addicted to watching it.[1] There are sociopaths in every war—those who delight in the killing and can't wait to pull the trigger. But these examples are the extreme. The vast majority of those who serve are averse to killing, taking extreme measures to avoid it. Most stagger home from the hell of war morally and emotionally wounded in addition to any physical injuries they have sustained.

It is through combat and service that deep bonds are formed, not so much with the institution but rather with other soldiers who have lived it and seen firsthand the carnage of war. They've witnessed the deaths of their military brothers *and* sisters and know that in war civilians *are* killed. Families and communities are destroyed. Indeed, one study reveals that among civil wars today, 90 percent of casualties are civilians as opposed to the start of the twentieth century, when 90 percent of those who died were actual soldiers.[2]

As taught in basic training, the ideal soldier is rational, in control, and able to display mastery "over the environment, other others, and over ideas."[3] As the following oral stories reveal, this is often an illusion. In today's wars, the enemy is often unknown. Training, many soldiers argue, comes undone in combat, where daily missions and objectives are often a moving target. As one veteran explains, "Insurgents don't have to play by the rules, but we do."[4] His sentiment reflects the overall mission not to kill civilians that places the preponderance of risk on U.S. troops. But the "just war theory" that soldiers adhere to is often rendered just that—a theory.

Soldiers find themselves in the middle of tribal politics, ethnic strife, and religious divisions. They may be building bridges, roads, or schools on Monday, joking with the locals or drinking tea with tribal elders. On Tuesday they find themselves jumping out of Humvees and Bradleys that are "cooking off" with improvised explosive devices (IEDs) and rocket-propelled grenades (RPGs), often placed by the same people they were assisting on Monday. To make matters worse, rules of engagement can change on a dime, causing some to resent command and perceive procedure as "Monday morning quarterbacking."

Insurgents lurk in places not typically seen as dangerous (e.g., a local bakery or restaurant) and hide behind mobs of children waiting for chocolate or bottled water. A soldier can be killed while directing traffic or escorting government contractors to and from work sites. Soldiers work side by side with private security workers who earn five times their salary and are not nearly as scrutinized for their actions.[5] Combat operations in both Iraq and Afghanistan are not at all stable, and life there moves back and forth on an "in-control" and "out-of-control" continuum. Troops cannot control the conditions under which they will face a situation in which "failure to meet the challenge at hand will result in death, or, at the very least, debilitating injury."[6] Prolonged uncertainty combines with episodes of real terror to create what I call *reluctant military occupational edgework.*

The original term *edgework* was coined by sociologist Stephen Lyng to describe the purposeful activity of risk taking that involves negotiating the boundary between order and chaos, life and death, sanity and insanity, and a "desire to control the seemingly uncontrollable."[7] Edgework is implicitly understood in a masculine framework, motivated by a need to experience independence and self-mastery while being on the "edge" of chaos. Control of emotions, such as fear, during edgework experience is of extreme importance, although many often describe feeling a temporary "rush" or sense of omnipotence afterwards.

As a sociologist, Lyng purposefully resisted psychological profiling that would label those who engage in edgework as a particular type of person (e.g., thrill seekers). Rather, he contextualized edgework as a social-psychological response to life in contemporary society. Historically, the focus has been on voluntary risk-taking pursuits that combine skill, preparation, and composure during experiences that verge on complete chaos, situations most would regard as entirely uncontrollable. In the past, the social-psychological concept of edgework has been used to explain participation in high-risk leisure pursuits, such as skydiving,[8] BASE-jumping,[9] or mountain climbing[10]—all activities that include both body and mind through mastery of skills and techniques. Few would have considered discussions of reluctant edgework in war since an important aspect of the conceptualization of edgework has been its voluntary nature.

In his more recent work, Lyng and others identify a growing body of research that examines institutionally anchored edgework.[11] Attempts to appropriate the common themes found in edgework can be seen now in a variety of cultural arenas, including occupations. Commercial and pseudo-edgework can be sold to consumers,[12] and the concept of "occupational edgework" can be found in the areas of insurance [13] and business/finance.[14] Accordingly, many institutions now demand or encourage edgework qualities in order to function in a "risk society."[15]

These more recent discussions expand beyond individual pursuits, revealing that edgework is situated in the culture at large. Mountain rescue teams engage in stages of edgework[16]; police, firefighters, ambulance drivers, and emergency workers all experience episodes of edgework that involve a "clearly observable threat to one's physical and mental well-being or one's sense of an ordered existence."[17] Military combat operations most certainly fit within the category of occupational edgework, and early socialization of military recruits capitalizes upon the edgework potential. Lyng writes: "One could argue that the skills, competencies, and symbolic resources deriving from leisure edgework" are applied now as human capital "to navigate the challenges of the risk society."[18] Contemporary institutions simultaneously "both push and pull" their members "to edgework practices."[19]

Military marketing strategies valorize and combine the images of both edgework and masculinity, exemplified by the use of such slogans as, "Accelerate your life" (Navy) and "Discover adventure" and "There's strong, and then there's Army strong" (Army). Recruitment efforts also tap into a potential edgework orientation, such as desire for risk, mastery, and technological savvy. Various military advertisements boast of having the newest cybertechnology and up-to-date equipment (such as the Air Force's "meanest, baddest bird on the planet"). These slogans combine to present an image of military engagement as elite, masculine, and risk taking, distinguishing those who are willing to sacrifice themselves (i.e., "The few. The proud. The Marines.").

Thus, while the concept of edgework seems at first glance something that would take place outside a highly regimented institution such as the military, it is in many ways the quintessential contemporary example of occupational edgework. Individuals join the military for a variety of moral and pragmatic reasons. Some may join with an orientation toward edgework, while others crave the routine structure of military life. After all, most military personnel don't experience combat or the extraordinary risk to life. Indeed, most join to serve their country and defend the nation and to receive educational benefits, no doubt with the hope of not having to use their weapons.[20] However, military training prepares all individuals for the possibility of war, endorsing an edgework orientation should they find themselves in combat. One component of this is the boot camp experience described in chapter 2. Control of fear is reinforced, along with the suppression of other vulnerable emotions. Aggression is institutionally sanctioned and taught through discipline and obedience to command. Repetitive drills, weapons training, and simulated human targets are used for the purpose of reducing hesitation to engage the enemy under specific rules of engagement. A new language of military jargon replaces "killing" with colloquial terminology and a moral grammar that inoculates soldiers and dehumanizes the enemy (e.g., people become "targets," Muslims become "towel heads" and nations become "evil doers"). Military training is in fact a staging event for "reluctant" edgeworkers who may find themselves in situations that involve ultimate risk of life and death.

While no empirical studies of military edgework exist per se, the term itself originates from Milovanovic, who places "military occupational edgework" on a continuum from in-control to out-of-control edgework.[21] Combat is located just beyond in-control "packaged edgework" because it includes "rules of conduct built into the activity."[22] Placing combat near the middle of the continuum makes sense given that precautions are taken, rules of engagement are defined, rigid codes of conduct are enforced, and risk is minimized when possible. Out-of-control edgework is at the other end of the continuum, including extreme thrill seeking and illicit risk taking, a phenomenon many soldiers find themselves attracted to after their combat experiences. More extreme examples of specific military edgework would include war atrocities and "righteous" slaughter.[23]

Military occupational edgework during combat can move on the continuum depending on one's experience, from routine missions and reconnaissance patrols to spontaneous out-of-control edgework that occurs outside the wire (e.g., ambushes). Drawing on an example of a company point man in Vietnam, Milovanovic writes: "The degree of excitement and adrenaline rush while on 'point'—M-16 on fully automatic, intensely scanning the situations in front—was at a dizzying level. Along the in-control and out-of-control dimension, oscillation between the two poles took place: in control while on point, moving to out of control while in the midst of a firefight."[24]

Military edgework during combat reflects the paradox of institutionally anchored edgework. In other words, soldiers learn to anticipate uncertain situations under "hyperreal" conditions (i.e., kill or be killed) within a hyperrational and regimented structure. But war is chaotic and messy, sometimes negating much of the preparation and codes of conduct, especially in urban warfare. The moral grammar that is intended to hold up the American myth of a "noble" warrior unravels in episodes of reluctant military edgework along with the body's ability to withstand assault after assault on the nervous system, an issue I address in chapter 5.

Not all those who engage in military edgework will experience psychological trauma, but most will experience some degree of moral and emotional trauma. For those who have support systems and can experience reintegration outside the margins of the military, the wounds may heal over time. Others remain the walking wounded, with no place to rest their heavy hearts. Army Reserve Captain DeCoster, who served with the 113th Combat Stress Unit in Baghdad (2007–2008), speaks to the wide potential for trauma: "It wasn't like in World War II, where we're going after objectives and we were fighting. These guys, during our time, they were driving around waiting to get blown up. That's kind of ironic. People will make the qualification and say, you know, 'Well, you weren't in combat,' but anyone that drove around in Baghdad was in combat, because that's what combat was."

Voices from Combat: U.S. Army National Guard, Bravo Company

Staff Sergeant Woodmansee served two tours in Iraq. He was 17 when he joined the Army National Guard and turned 19 midway through his first tour in Iraq (2003–2004) with the 39th Brigade (Bravo Company). Trained as a military intelligence analyst, he was stationed in Taji for his first tour and then at the Baghdad International Airport during his second tour, a very different experience from his first. Woodmansee believes he is one of the lucky ones who served in Iraq, insofar as he never had to fire a weapon at a "target." He feels for those who did, however. "There were guys that had it a lot worse, guys that had to pull the trigger that had to live with some of those experiences. They had a lot harder time." Rather, Woodmansee would find himself, like so many soldiers and especially those called up from the National Guard, a reluctant participant in military edgework.

"I definitely was there during attacks when we got ambushed, IEDs going off, roadside bombs going off," he explains. "I had a car bomb go off about 20 meters away from me. I know of at least no less than five instances where I personally was being shot at, as opposed to the group of soldiers I was around. Plus, however many times there was of me being in a convoy, where the convoy as a whole was being shot at, so yeah there were combat situations. I did earn my combat action badge there. And it's really odd that actually I never fired back and still fell into the criteria for the award. But there were numerous times that had I been able to positively identify a target, I would've pulled the trigger. Thankfully, I never had to pull the trigger."

Woodmansee describes the first time he was shot at, likening it to a scene from the movie *Black Hawk Down*. "I can remember the first time I got shot at—I was doing a guard detail at Taji. It was sectioned off for the ING [Iraqi National Guard]. They used to be the ICDC, the Iraqi Civil Defense Corps, then they transitioned into the Iraqi National Guard, which transitioned to the Iraqi Army now. But at that time, the ING were doing training at Taji. Since they were local nationals on the post, we had to have U.S. forces there to guard them and make sure they weren't through the wire or whatever. And I can remember the first time I got shot at; I was out there in their little barracks area looking at the perimeter because we had an Iraqi National Guard tower manned by Iraqis up there on our FOB [Forward Operating Base]. I [was] making sure we were awake, checking out our little area outside the perimeter. I turned around and was walking around doing my little patrol area. Have you ever seen that scene in *Black Hawk Down* when he talks about whenever it's close you hear a hiss, but if it's really close you hear a snap? I kind of heard something and looked over and saw some dirt kick up to my right, and thought that was kind of weird. Then I heard it and it registered what was happening, and the first thing that went through my mind completely was, 'Why are they shooting at me?

51

I'm Lee Woodmansee. I haven't done nothing to this guy. Why are you shooting at me?' And at this point I was already running to go turn the lights out because we had these big floodlights that would cast a silhouette on the tower and on us. So I ran to turn the lights out and by the time I got there, which was maybe 20 meters away—I had lights turned out, and I was pissed off at this point. I'm turning around, like I'm crawling back to the fence. I'm going to crawl up in that tower and get some retribution. So I went from 'Why are they shooting at me? I haven't done anything to them' to 'They just shot at me!' to 'I'm pissed about it, and now I'm ready to go back out there!' And that all happened in a 30-second span, but I remember it clear as day because it never registered what it was kicking up next to me. In hindsight that was a pretty odd mix of emotions. All the subsequent times after that, I can say there was a certain feeling of excitement."

Woodmansee is aware of the potential for such experiences to have lasting effect on the body. "A lot of guys will describe it as almost fun, just the amount of adrenaline you have going through you. But about 5, 10 minutes after the firefight's over, you just want to lay down and go to sleep. I mean, you're so tired because the adrenaline's now gone. It's like crashing from an energy drink. You just want to lie down. I can remember that the first time, too. After I got my breathing calmed down, I was just so tired, and that was at the very beginning of the night," adding again, "so it's an odd mix of emotions, to say the least."

The physiological conditions of edgework that Woodmansee so aptly describes become emotionally charged and embodied experiences for some. The physiological conditions are interpreted in hindsight, but prolonged conditions can lead to a hyperalert state that cannot be easily undone. Like other types of edgework, combat entails an *embodied* experience. The adrenaline rush triggers the release of dopamine (the body's pleasurable reward to the brain for having experienced danger), leaving many with a remarkable memory of the hyperaroused state.

During his first tour, Woodmansee's brigade lost forty-two soldiers. "We had forty-two KIA [killed in action], and that's not even counting the numerous other soldiers we were working with, who aren't technically part of our brigade, who died alongside or wounded or whatever." After returning from his first tour of twelve hour shifts, late nights playing videogames, and months of continuous indirect fire, he found it difficult to sleep. A typical conversation for Woodmansee and his brother, who also served in Iraq, included comments such as, "Oh, only two wounded today? That's not bad. We only had five IEDs. Anybody get killed? Well, one. Yeah, that's not too bad. That was normal conversation," he explains. "Hyperalertness there is normal. Back in the States—far from normal. So scaling that down a little, still being really alert, on guard a lot of times, is still not normal." These "typical" conversations were not welcome back home, he remembers. At one point, his father pulled both him and his brother aside and told them to tone down their conversations. "Like I said, some of it was fun getting to kick in doors and whatever, but [we] just needed to tone it down, needed to cut some of that out."

Woodmansee recalls sitting at the end of his cot during months of explosions. "I can remember numerous times always having my body armor with my weapon shoved down into the cavity where my body is, my helmet stuck on top of that. I would lean up, take my weapon out, kind of lay with my helmet on my head, and get on the floor with my body armor on top of me [and] go to sleep in the floor wearing body armor basically. And some of that, it just became normal so I didn't sleep real well. Literally, the first night I was home in my bed, we have a swing chair, a little swing hanging off of the roof on our porch. And we had a lab [Labrador retriever] at the time, and the lab jumped onto the swing and the swing hit the door or hit the wall right there by my head. I freaked out because I mean it sounded, everything rattled the way an explosion makes a rattle! And that was kind of a wake-up call [thinking], 'This is going to suck if this is the way it is.' So that was a little hard for the transition—just sleeping and getting used to not being hyperalert, not having a conversation that involves some guy getting maimed. And that was, I think, the biggest transition for me. Aside from like road rage, things like that, yeah, there were times when I'm checking windows, looking at rooftops, checking guardrails and overpasses, stuff like that."

For Sergeant Woodmansee, the second tour would be easier. Security at base was tighter and contracted out to a private security agency. Housing conditions had improved, the constant barrage of indirect fire had diminished, and the bases were closer to Baghdad proper. Units would do their patrols and return to base. Stationed at the Baghdad International Airport, he was surprised by the number of civilians now serving and the shift in security operations. "When we were in Iraq the second time, we did not do FOB security. Like the perimeter at the towers, about 90 percent of it was done by a company called EODT, and they were a contractor, private contractor we used for personal security. They contracted out to Ugandans and Kenyans who were actually in the towers and were technically civilians.[25] We had numerous software reps, numerous program managers within our battalion now. So a fourth the size of a brigade, in our battalion, we probably had upwards of 120 civilians that we worked closely with or that were like part of the battalion—I mean vast increase."

Now in college on his G.I. Bill, Woodmansee reflects on his transition from civilian to soldier and citizen soldier. He believes that not being forced to fire a weapon on a target and not sustaining any physical wounds during both tours has helped him transition after his second tour in Iraq, better than most. "I knew how the Army worked. I knew how a deployment worked. I knew how a transition went down, and I know how I handled it last time. So this time, I just jumped right back into life. No stresses, I'm sleeping fine. I can honestly say there has been no real trouble with the second deployment because I know what to expect."

For Woodmansee, the hyperalert stages subsided. He says that he is concerned, though, for the reluctant edgeworkers or "trigger pullers," who he believes are still haunted by their experiences. "I know numerous guys who, when they came home, they started doing X (ecstasy), started smoking weed, and that was the easy stuff, not to mention meth or whatever else they were running into." The trend makes sense to him, though, as the need for more excitement, and he says there is nothing comparable to war in the States. "I know that's the wrong way to do it," he explains, "but as far as a good way? I don't know if there's a good one. To be honest with you, I think all the training the Army does on reintegration and talking about stuff and putting on the table all the resources they have? I tune them out, about 90 percent of that. I think the Army is really inefficient in its ability to convey useful information when it comes to reintegration and stuff like that.... So I think the Army as a whole is just pretty weak in its ability to prepare soldiers for that."

Reintegration to civilian life and healing emotional wounds come from "not the Army but from talking with other veterans," Woodman-see explains. "I think the real strength there is the guys that were in Iraq with you. Me and my brother talk about some of the stuff we went through, different guys that I was on the second deployment with that were on Haifa Street [a stretch of road in downtown Baghdad where an intense battle took place in 2007 with heavy U.S. casualties], you know? Guys that were foreign observers that had to put rounds on a target.... Some therapist who the Army has, who served for six years, I mean, yeah, he was in the Army, but he never went anywhere. Yeah, he can help a little bit, but not much. Then you've got that combat vet who was there with them. He doesn't need a degree. He was there. He knows a lot more about what happened than that therapist ever will. So I think that's really the kicker, is being able to talk about this stuff. If it's on your mind, you can't just bottle it up."

Voices from Combat: U.S. Army National Guard, Delta Company

First Sergeant Mayfield was in the Army National Guard when his unit was called up in October 2003. He served in Iraq as well with the 39th Brigade, 1st Cavalry Division. His unit arrived in Kuwait in March 2004. Mayfield had served as a police officer for thirteen years prior to his deployment. He was proud to serve but also had the responsibility of a spouse and family back home. Like others, Mayfield also found himself engaged in numerous episodes of edgework, many more than he cares to remember.

Mayfield remembers stepping off the plane and feeling the blast of hot air and thinking to himself, "'Gosh dang, this is hot and it's March.'

It was the hottest place I'd ever been." But the hot air was the least of his concerns. Substandard equipment and armor were a common problem for those who served in the early phases. "They had what they called AOA kits, add-on armor kits. And there were armored doors and an armored windshield and an armored back plate and I guess that was the extent of the add-on armor kit. So you've got a canvas top over your head, which is a couple of millimeters thick and everything else is, is, you know, standard fiberglass and metal. People were scrambling."

Most of their steel plates came from a Hershey's [chocolate] plant in Kuwait that was being dismantled. "All our mechanics were, you know, they had their cutting torches out cutting out doors and we called it 'hillbilly armor' because we were from Arkansas. Guys were filling sandbags, putting them in the floor of their vehicles to protect from the blast. It kind of became an exercise in, in insanity, I guess." He likened his battalion's convoy to a scene from the movie *Mad Max*. His unit heard from those already serving in Iraq that IEDs and RPGs were to be expected. "We were trying to harden our vehicles as much as possible to prevent any kind of harm to ourselves. But it got kind of silly at the end. It looked like a combination between the Beverly Hillbillies and the Road Warrior." Mayfield remembers looking out at the motor pools as they were about to leave Camp New York (Kuwait). "There [were] vehicles, some parts were green, some were tan, some of them were rust-colored from the steel and I looked out there and I thought, 'My God, man, this must really be bad if the United States Army is going to let a rag-tag looking convoy of vehicles, looking like this, drive up into Baghdad.'"

Mayfield's unit was part of Delta Company so they were spread throughout the nine serials (convoy groups) to provide heavy fire. It was early April 2004, so it was near the anniversary of the start of Operation Iraqi Freedom. He remembers the drive to Baghdad. "As soon as you hit the main road and you're traveling, you switch on automatically. You're very alert to everything because everything is new. Is that camel walking over there, is he a threat? It's kind of senseless, but that's the survival mechanism. But you'd be driving down the road and on an overpass you'd see the 'renegade freq' spray painted." Each convoy was given a radio frequency command to use if they were "in the shit" and needed to call in Quick Reaction Force (QRF) to assist. Seeing the frequency on the bridge overpasses caught his attention. "It's like, 'Oh, that's what it was.' We had it written down in our vehicles, but to see it and realize that it was such an open, known thing—it was another wake-up call," he explains. "We were always scared to death of overpasses anyway, because they would always plant IEDs, roadside bombs, near or on the overpasses. Or they would stand on the overpass and drop grenades on you. So anytime we encountered an overpass, it was always, you know, you would kind of pucker up a little bit more."

Mayfield's unit didn't see much fire until they neared Baghdad. Like so many of his comrades, he found this was when hypervigilance kicked in. "You just keep going up a level each time. The closer you get to Baghdad, the more anxious you get.... You don't sleep." Still, Mayfield describes his missions as "routine" for the most part. He compares his experience to previous wars and is quick to say his unit had it easy in comparison. "It almost makes me feel personally bad, because you know, like the Battle of the Bulge—those infantrymen, those grunts, lived in foxholes for several weeks at a time in the freezing ground." His brigade was located in Camp Taji, an old helicopter field northwest of Baghdad, equipped with air-conditioned trailers, Taco Bell, Burger King, Pizza Hut, and Subway. Soldiers had access to the Internet and some even had wide-screen televisions. He chuckles as he describes his experience as an "eight to five" war.

Downtime for Mayfield was instant messaging with his wife or watching movies, but his age set him apart from the younger soldiers, who were more likely to play videogames that included more simulated violence between missions. "You would come into these guys' trailers, these 18–20 year old guys....You'd walk in and they're playing, like, Halo or some other shooting game. They're all into it. That always amazed me, like 'My God, man, you were in a real live firefight today and now you're down here playing Halo.' But that's how they relaxed. We each had our different ways."

Most missions were routine for Mayfield's unit, but they were mixed with "brief skirmishes" that were "very intense, very short duration."

IEDs were commonplace and insurgents were skilled at placing them. Mayfield explains, "They were pretty good at putting them in places where you felt relatively safe and you didn't expect it.... And they were hard to find, I mean, when they say, 'Oh, they usually hide them in garbage at the side of the road,' well, when you drive 15 miles and there's nothing but garbage beside the road, you just can't pick them out. Originally, they were using command detonated [ones], which meant there were wires coming off of it. So if your gunners were real sharp, or your driver or your, we call it TC (Truck Commander), they were usually the ones that were looking out. Sometimes you could spot the wires. But you know, if you're looking at a piece of electrical wire, you're pretty damn close to it." His unit learned quickly that training at Fort Hood did not fully prepare them for the reality of the conditions. They learned to use whatever means they had, especially when it came to IEDs.

There is always spontaneous terror that accompanies an IED. "When it first goes off, first thing, it scares the hell out of you. And then the vehicle is immediately filled with smoke, dust. And wherever you are on your breathing cycle, whether it's an inhalation or an exhalation, you immediately just stop, because you don't want to breathe that stuff, you know? It's just, there's explosive gas fumes, and no telling what.... So you'd stop breathing and hope to God. You try and drive out of it. And you're driving blind, I mean, you can't see—there's dust, smoke, and a lot of times we would drive out of the smoke and then find a vehicle stopped, you know, right in front of us, and you'd almost hit the vehicle in front of you."

He remembers the "helpless feeling" that would come over him each time his unit was hit "because there's nothing you can do to mitigate it at that point. Once it goes off, you just clinch up and you pray there's not another one. You don't want to clear the smoke and then find out they've got RPGs and machine guns set up, or yet another IED, and they would do that quite frequently, too. They would detonate one and then we would go through our procedures and get our standoff distance, and then they would detonate another one. Or they would detonate one on a convoy or patrol, creating injuries, and then when the QRF [quick response force] and the medics got there, they would detonate another one on them. So, it's just, it's a real hard thing to combat—you can try to prevent it but.... Eventually we got better at detecting the command detonated ones with the wires." Indeed, his unit learned quickly what to watch out for, but not before his vehicle and the vehicle immediately in front of him were struck four times by IEDs. "So I got my bell rang pretty hard several times, you know."

Mayfield remembers a tactical escort for a civil affairs team that ended in an ambush on May 23, 2004. His unit was accompanying several officials on their way to meet with locals about rebuilding some of the infrastructure in the area. The dirt road was just wide enough for their Humvees, with a 7-foot drop into a ditch below so there was nowhere to maneuver. Three IEDs had been daisy-chained together and went off simultaneously. One hit within six feet of Mayfield and his driver. He chuckles as he likens their escape to a scene in an Abbot and Costello movie. "I mean [it] just scrambled our eggs, you know.... I look over at Kerry and said, 'Drive man, get us out of here!' I didn't know how bad the vehicle might be—you just mash on the gas and hope you go!" Kerry had been knocked unconscious for a few moments. "He's literally just writhing and babbling and driving and I thought my back was on fire. I could just feel this intense heat from the back of my neck all the way down my spine. I'm like, 'Man, look at me, I'm on fire!' and I'm slapping, 'Look at me, I'm on fire, put me out!' and he finally starts getting his head clear, and he's like, 'You're not on fire.'"

The ambush was hard to swallow for his unit, who experienced daily briefings of "standard military operation" that then shifted into "city board meetings" with discussions of funding for a water system, a road improvement project, or the building of a school. It was a "nonstandard" war, he explains. "We were fighting amongst 8 million people and the enemy wasn't wearing a uniform! And there are different religious aspects to it, you know. If you are too friendly to the Sunni, then the Shiite will be mad at you, and vice versa. And there are just so many little pieces to the puzzle, it's overwhelming!" For Mayfield and others in his unit, there was a phrase, "Shoot, smile, shoot." "You go from—you would be defending yourself and then be glad-handing with the little kiddies and politicians and the locals and the next thing you know, you would be shooting at the same people!"

These conditions create resentment, anger, and confusion for soldiers who try to live up to their roles as community builders and civic leaders. Yet the burden of risk is on them, because they are in a country where a significant number of people resent their presence. Soldiers who are simply following the rules of command experience moral anguish as they vacillate between being protector and aggressor. It requires extraordinary composure to remain unaffected by the deep sense of distrust that builds over time. Hypervigilance is a necessity. Mistakes are made. Chaos is real and the ultimate goal is to stay alive.

For Mayfield and his unit, there would be more ambushes to come. Meanwhile, the rules of engagement, it seemed, were changing daily as soldiers were finding themselves in situations where they had to make split-second decisions. Mayfield remembers one incident in which a young soldier shot and killed several civilians. "All these minivan taxis had come up to the checkpoint where the 1-3 truck was and a guy got out of the sliding door and pointed a pistol at the truck and the gunner just lit him up … and the guy went down and of course, people in the van start freaking out screaming and trying to bail out, and so we lit up the van. Man, that was a lot of carnage right there. Luckily the van was all males, although there were two young children and one of them got wounded.... And three or four males in the van, I'd say, was split wide open."

Mayfield thought his years as a police officer would prepare him. "I have seen car wrecks and suicide and I have seen some pretty traumatic wounds. But he [the civilian] was sitting there, gray matter splattered all over the windshield and he was making this noise, almost like a death groan or death rattle. And there wasn't a thing we could do for him. If he was alive, there wasn't a damn thing we could do for him. I mean, put a bandaid on that? But that wasn't going to do anything. There were two other guys in the back of the van that had gaping head wounds also. We couldn't do anything for them, either. So basically we got up there, assessed the casualties, and set up security and called for Medi-vac and actually we were still with 27 Cav and their battalion commander. Their QRF and their personal security showed up, along with helicopters and oh my God, and I thought, 'This is really wild!' But you know, there was nothing we could do for those guys but let them sit there and bleed out."

Mayfield learned to disconnect from his emotions under the chaos of war. He continues, "Basically there was nothing we could do. And I remember sitting in my truck eating M&Ms because I was hungry, because you get kind of busy and forget to eat. I was eating some M&Ms out of a MRE bag and I looked down and there was a big, big blood clot about the size of a dime on my knee and there was several flies swarming all over it and I thought, 'Man, that is pretty sick!' And I thought, 'I am going to leave that on there because the flies are not going to be bothering me or my M&Ms.' It's just one of those things and I said, 'Okay, deal with it.'. . . Man, there was garbage piled up all around this place. There was the smell of fresh blood. I don't know if you ever smelled large amounts of fresh blood. It was spilled out on the ground and baking in the sun and we later found a huge pile, maybe eight dozen eggs broken open and rotting out there in the sun! Man, that whole smell there would gag a maggot! It was pretty intense. One of our guys crawled up in the van and he was literally just soaked and he was just red! And I said, 'Man, Jimmy, get out of there. You are not doing anyone any good. There is nothing you can do for him.' And he immediately was besieged with flies. Someone had a spare uniform out there and he got to change, but that was a pretty graphic deal."

Mayfield was concerned for the young soldier who had shot the civilian and was now trying to save the lives of those injured. He tried to set up a combat debriefing, but it was ineffective. Soldiers would answer questions when asked but would offer nothing. He had hoped they could get some of it out talking with the chaplain, but to talk about their feelings, when the next day might require the same emotional disconnect, seemed surreal. Meanwhile, there were forms and procedures to follow. Like most of those interviewed, he resented the enormous amount of paperwork required after each incident because while "rules of engagement are clear on paper," they seldom match the reality of what occurs outside the wire.

Army Major Taylor, an eighteen-year veteran, echoes Mayfield's concerns, stating the most difficult aspect of urban warfare for him is face-to-face interaction with civilians. "The hardest and the most surprising part to us, or to me, was the wanton disregard of what we know as chivalry in the United States, or the 'law of land' of warfare by the enemy, in using women and children to disguise themselves," Taylor recalls. "On more than one occasion, they would have women or children approach you in a crowd and the enemy would be shielded behind them. Or they would put them in vehicles to come, come up to see you, and the male fighters would be hidden in the back seat or in the trunk of a car. And they would use women and children, which is something that we as American soldiers have kind of always just assumed would not be what any civilized society would do with their women and children. It became very difficult in particular for the younger soldiers, because you then truly didn't know, any time any civilian approached you, if they were friendly or enemy even if they were carrying a flower or had a smile on their face." Like Mayfield, Taylor was concerned for the impact of a "nonstandard" war upon young soldiers.

"I was from that generation, I grew up, I guess, I was a teenager when *Apocalypse Now* came out," Mayfield explains. "There is that line in the movie where Martin Sheen says, 'Arresting people for murder here is like giving tickets out for the Indiana 500!' I mean, that really hit home. There is a lot of commentary in that movie that hit home." Referring to the incident that resulted in civilian deaths, he explains, "If you didn't see any of it, you are going to have someone come in and quarterback it after you have been in a life-and-death situation? Yeah, the guy in the van that pointed, it was a cigarette lighter, but you got a 20-year-old kid with a machine gun that has to make a life or death decision in an instant and you don't have time to verify a cigarette lighter or a toy gun or whatever. God, we had kids point toy guns at us and they were just a hair's breath of us pulling the trigger on them! You wonder first of all, 'Who is buying toy guns in a combat zone?' And you know, I guess that is the way they grew up. There is always some fighting or turmoil over there."

Mayfield made first sergeant midway through his tour, but by that time he had seen enough action to last a lifetime. His thirteen-year tenure as a police officer between his deployments still did not prepare him for the hypervigilance required in Iraq. By November 2004, he was having trouble sleeping. Security was up because of the elections and his unit was experiencing more indirect fire on the base, causing many to feel safer "outside the wire." In December, Mayfield returned home when his mother passed away. November had been an especially difficult month for his unit. It was then he realized he had become emotionally numb and disconnected from his feelings. "I couldn't even cry at the funeral." The emotional and moral strain of combat had finally hit home.

Although Mayfield is medically retired, he still yearns to be with his unit, a testament to the bonds created when soldiers survive war. "Well, I wouldn't trade my experience for anything. You know, it was good for me. It kind of made me man-up and understand more, probably mature a little quicker about what life's all about. And the combat, you wouldn't wish that on your worst enemy. But again, that's one of those experiences you wouldn't trade for anything because as horrible as it was, it created those bonds with your fellow soldiers that transcends family bonds. Boy, you try explaining that to your wife! [laughs] That's kind of hard.... It's just something that someone who's not been there will never understand. And it's hard to describe. I mean I sit here and describe it to you, but I guarantee you really don't understand it. I'll tell you, I was pretty gung ho at first, but now I question a lot of policies and the politics of it. And I know war's something that's going to be around forever, but I've really become, I'd say, protective of it [war]. I mean you don't just go to war for any damned reason. You'd better have a good reason to do it because it is so damaging. It scares me to death thinking about going to war with Iran right now because I know from my experience that the military is spent. I mean it's totally exhausted from being in Iraq and Afghanistan."

Today, Mayfield continues to have difficulty explaining his experiences to family and friends. "I told my wife a couple of times since I have been back that I will never be the same man you knew before I went over there. And she says, 'Why not?' I can't explain it to you, but I just won't. I mean, I have seen things that I will never be able to share with her. If

I do share it with her, she will not be able to understand it. Because you can't explain, you can't explain what fresh blood smells like. You can't explain to someone that constant 24/7 fear. I mean, I told a buddy of mine from high school who asked if I was scared and I told him, 'Yeah, I was scared 24 hours a day.' He said, 'Nah, you weren't.' 'Yeah, I was!' You develop an underlying fear level that goes with that underlying alert level and that is the survival mechanism."

Mayfield reflects upon the hypervigilance he still experiences but is perplexed by its prolonged effect. "You know, war is an abnormal environment and adapting to that—you just can't switch it off. When you get back, you expect everything to be normal. [laughing] I am still not normal.... I don't know. Maybe it has gone from being a switch I can turn off to one of those switches you have to hold down. You know, because you just can't switch it off. When I am driving, I still get really freaked out because we were on the road so much. That is when bad things happen! I don't know why, but since I have been back I have had a [widget] hit my windshield on the highway driving 60 miles per hour and it shattered my windshield. I have had someone throw a water bottle and hit my car and you talk about ratcheting up to overload. Being around overpasses, you know? Sometimes I just don't sleep and my wife goes, 'You know, you didn't go to sleep. Why didn't you go to sleep? You have something to do tomorrow.' 'I can't!' 'Well, why?' I can't. I can't just will myself to go to sleep. I can take all the medication in the world and it won't faze me. I will stay awake until I figure out what I am thinking about and focus on what I am doing or whatever. You stay awake to be on guard because you don't have your buddies around you any more to guard your family and you while you sleep." He adds once more, "And you know, it is just one of those survival mechanisms, I think."

Voices from Combat: U.S. Marines

Marine Sergeant Carpenter enlisted in 1999. He was 17 years old, but "I knew that's what I wanted to do, so I did it," he says proudly. He graduated basic training at Camp Pendleton in 2000, just days after his eighteenth birthday. By his third year Carpenter had already served two tours, Operation Iraqi Freedom and Operation Enduring Freedom, when he reenlisted to serve a third tour in Iraq. He was hoping to be reassigned as an instructor, but when his unit was called up, he joined them. "My Marines came and asked me to do a third tour of combat because they said they felt safer with me beside them," Carpenter explains. "So I went ahead and had my orders suspended and held off until after this third tour." He was still able to return and become an instructor, but his injuries from war led to a medical retirement at the age of 26. "I was planning on making it a full lifelong career."

Carpenter was in Iraq when the war began. He company's job was to protect the berm on the roads between Kuwait and Iraq so that the "ground pounders" could get their vehicles across. After that, Carpenter's job was with Charlie Company doing reconnaissance. He remembers seeing a lot of combat during his first tour in Iraq, more so than his return tour in OIF-3 with the weapons company. "Anything that had a weapon, that shot, moved, and communicated, was designated a target." They made it from the Kuwait/Iraq border to Baghdad in less than a month, but they experienced a lot of engagement. "We engaged several soft targets, several hard targets. We called in fire, called in helos [helicopters], called in mortars, had rockets fired at us. I probably expended over 350 rounds of high explosive incendiary tracers, not counting armor-piercing rounds that I had on board my vehicle … you name it. We unloaded shell clear several times."

The fighting was intense for Carpenter, who found himself and his wingman in a "killbox."[26] "We were so far ahead of the company doing recon that we were the only two within five klicks [kilometers] of the company and they had a 50-cal attached to the back end of a regular Toyota pickup truck. At the end of the road, they had holes in the side of the road with people in it and RPGs, covered with blankets because they learned through the previous war that [we] had thermals, that we could see heat signatures. This [happens] towards nighttime so we are in thermal mode … and they realize, 'Well, they're [using] thermals.

We covered up the heat signatures, they can't see us.' And they were right, we couldn't. We were up in the middle of this road, all of a sudden this 50-cal starts laying waste towards our vehicles. People pop up out of these holes with RPGs shooting at our vehicles, some bouncing off, some going right over the top of us. Then, to make matters worse, they had mortars set up, and they started dropping them on us. My wingman's vehicle had all eight tires blown off, my 25-millimeter chain gun broke and was down, so communication was destroyed due to the amount of damage done to the vehicles. But we were still firing everything we had and finally the company caught up with us, surrounded us, and protected us until we could get out of there."

Carpenter remembers the fatalism that overcame him while he was in the killbox. "When my vehicle's weapon went down, my main weapon, as soon as it wouldn't fire anymore and I tried everything I knew how to fix it, it was automatic, 'I'm dead.'" He continues, "I'll put it to you this way, most people get a sense of being afraid of dying and adrenaline kicks in so on and so forth. I didn't have that fear because I had realized at that point in time I was dead. I just wasn't dead yet. I knew I wasn't making it through that, there was no way humanly possible I should have made it through that. Because of that, I literally had a gray spot of hair, like in the middle of my head, come up within twenty-four hours. I literally freaked out. Well, I wouldn't say freaked out because I didn't lose composure, but my body's chemical imbalance or whatever just went, so I got gray hair automatically from that, that one night. I realized right off the bat that I was done for, that I was not going to survive that, and I'd come to terms with that. I was okay with it, but I was still doing my job for everybody else that was in big [trouble]."

Carpenter would have many more such experiences over his three tours. He describes with unusual calm being "literally blown up" from a wedge of land mines. "I had three land mines go off underneath my vehicle that were triple stacked, one, two, three [stacked] on top of each other. When they're done like that, they make what's called a wedge. Imagine having the explosive power of one, but now it's times three in directly to where one's pressured. They're all three pressurized so when one goes off, the rest of all the pressure is relieved from bottom to top. So one blows off, hits the bottom part of the second one and hits the bottom part of the hole, comes back up. Well, now it's magnified because two went off. Two hits three hits one, and one hits the ground, Bam! Bam! Bam! You're just multiplying the explosive power at that point in time. Thank goodness Iraqis are stupid and put the hole too deep. Otherwise, I would not be here today. But it blew the tires off my vehicle over 150 yards. I mean, we're not talking little tires, either. We had vehicle damage, and I happened to have attached 25 millimeter cans to the outside of my vehicle to help protect myself from any explosions from the bottom side, and even then I still had shrapnel go right over the top side of my helmet and it took pieces out of my helmet. But the explosion itself caused one Marine, his brain to shift in his head. Another one's arm got ripped out of its socket, the driver took shrapnel to the face, and it broke my spine in two places." Carpenter wouldn't learn about the damage to his back until he returned from his tour. He just knew that he was in pain. He was back in the field four days later. "My Marines said they needed me. I was chief gunner for an entire company."

Carpenter dealt with his emotions during tours by staying "pissed off" and "locked and loaded.... You've been eating sand nonstop for God knows how long. You haven't slept in four days, you're tired and you're hungry. You haven't had the warmth of a bed or your wife in how long? You've got somebody going 'Lah, lah, lah' in front of you and all you want to do is rip his tongue out and fist-fuck him with it. And so you just take all that anger from all these situations, having flies constantly bothering you. You haven't changed pants in three weeks, much less what you have on underneath them. Your feet are rotting off underneath you because of how many miles you've put on them and you're just pissed. I mean, there's nothing else to explain about it, so you take all that anger, all that hatred, all that, and it's not hatred towards one person or one civilization or anything like that, it's a hatred of everything, but that's what makes a good Marine, a good Marine. A bitching Marine is a happy Marine. A Marine that doesn't bitch is the one you've got to worry about, because that means it's going inwards, not outwards. And as long as it's going outwards, they're healthy. They're not thinking internally. They're not thinking about themselves and how they're feeling." For Carpenter and others, the externalized anger felt during combat is what kept him alive. He adds, "[The Marine] goes and does his mission and comes home alive. He doesn't turn his gun on himself."

Carpenter's back would be only one of many injuries he would sustain in Iraq. He had surgery for his shoulder after pulling the 25-millimeter chain gun out of the vehicle while caught in the killbox, but he also suffered from severed fingers, shrapnel, Traumatic Brain Injury, and PTSD. "I was told I was stationed at Camp Pendleton and shipped to Iraq to do tours in Iraq. I think I was stationed in Iraq and did tours to America. If you did the math, I did three combat tours in four years … but at least after the third one I became an instructor. So while they were trying to fix me, I got to teach Marines what not to do and what to do in those stressful situations. My goal was to save lives, as many as I possibly could."

After he returned to the States, Carpenter's legs locked up on him during a three-mile run after his reassignment as Marine instructor. His lifelong goal of becoming a career Marine was about to end, but he didn't know it. He was yet to have the MRI that would reveal his broken back and the spinal surgery that would follow. "So they do an MRI and that's when they realize, 'Oh, he's got a bad problem! Let's stop doing this to him.' Not to mention I'd already had enough, and I'd said, 'The next doctor that touches me, I swear to God I'm going to kill him!' And they had a good feeling I meant exactly what I said. I didn't care about rank at that point, when you hurt me that bad." So I'm over there [the school of infantry] and I'm teaching and going through physical therapy, too. And they find out I've got this problem with my back and they put me on morphine and everything. They ask me how I was doing what I was doing. They couldn't believe that somebody could go through that amount of pain and not be psychotic due to it and I said, 'Because I was trained better than this.' So I knew how to deal with pain. Pain is weakness leaving the body, so I sucked it up and dealt with it until they finally realized that I had a bad injury."

Today, Carpenter continues to live with severe pain. "Even still to this day I wake up and my pain level is an 8 out of 10 to start the day. Usually I can get away with a 9 out of 10 at the end of the day." His legs continue to drop out from under him with no warning. He has difficulty walking and shakes when does. Like Mayfield, he finds sleep elusive, but he has no regrets. "Let me put it to you this way. I could've started crying out of the blue and nobody would've considered me weak, but it wasn't a matter of disappointing somebody more than it was of myself. I had high expectations of what a Marine is, was and should be.... But at least while I was there at the school, I was able to help Marines, and that's what matters most."

Like so many who have shared throughout the interviews, Carpenter dreaded demobilization and viewed it as only prolonging a soldier's return to friends and family. Hyperaware of the stigma associated with admitting trauma, Carpenter wanted to go home as quickly as possible. But he also understood the need for transition as well. "I tell you what. This is what happens.... They put you in an area for two weeks where you can get recivilianized, where you're around people again, not in a combat situation. They're [detoxifying] you from war and during that time they put you in large groups of everybody you've been in combat with and ask you, 'Does anybody feel suicidal?' You are going to answer that? Or, 'Does anybody feel that they're going to have a problem?' I mean, 'I'm going to have to stay here longer or you can send me home now to my wife or girlfriend. I'm fine.' So that's what you go through.... That is one thing that I would love to see changed.... Nobody in their chain of command needs to be in that room because that's more stress! They don't want to look weak in front of their peers and especially the person that they're trying to please above all things." Carpenter is convinced that while the transition phase is needed, the absence of command being present would lead to fewer suicides and problems. Soldiers would be more willing to open up about their problems.

Like Mayfield, Carpenter continues to have difficulty talking to civilians about his war experience. "And it's not the civilians' fault, it's the fact that they haven't been there, they have no idea how to deal with me when I get upset, whereas military members can diffuse the situation.... I could sit here and run you through pictures that I've got here of combat situations, of explosions that I've got on camera and other things. And you would still not have a clue if you've never been there." For Carpenter, the only people he can talk to remain his "brothers in arms." He admits he is easily agitated and has a low tolerance for small talk. "I think PTSD comes from people that are in high-stress jobs within the military that have seen more than their fair share of combat and then have no place else to go back to. You take a tiger and you put him in the wild, have him in the wild, he's happy, he knows how to hunt, he knows how to do his job to survive. You take him and put him in a cage, part of him dies. Put a military member back into the civilian populace, it kills him because they don't have that high intensity that they're so used to."

In theory, the social psychological payoff for edgework leaves one with the sense of "finely honed skills and experience of intense sensations of self-determination and control,"[27] especially if individuals can *believe* they control the outcome of the risk pursuit with their own skills, strategies, and tactics. Moreover, edgework of any type is necessarily temporary and not meant to be sustained over long periods. Finally, reluctant edgework that occurs in combat is visceral—the body acts and feels. The notion of a "soldier's switch" and an emotional shut-off is not realistic, and the "Shoot, smile, shoot" phenomenon can be maddening over time.

Voices from Combat: "Regular" U.S. Army

Army Specialist "John Doe" served in Iraq in 2008–2009, the last "leg," as he calls it. Although "John" provided consent for the study, I chose to assign him a pseudonym after he withdrew his interview for the Library of Congress. John was trained as a forward observer but wound up serving as a gunner stationed out of Camp Liberty. The airport was secured by the time his unit flew into Baghdad on a C-130. John kept to himself most of his tour, although he liked the structure of military life. "I never really got into the whole group thing, go hang out with everybody, it just wasn't me. I had one or two close friends, and we just, you know, shoot the shit, talk about back home what's going on with them, what's going on with me."

Growing up in a military family, John felt more prepared than many in his platoon. When he was young, his father would come into his bedroom, rip the sheets off his bed, and tell him to remake it or clear off his dresser, telling him to dust and clean it the "right" way. He distinguishes himself from other recruits, declaring, "You do have people that are better off lifting heavy objects than deciding where to place them. But at the same time you have a lot of people that go and get an education and automatically become officers.... I ran into some great officers, I really have—officers that were leaders. But I ran into a lot more bad ones that were just thankful because of their position. We have a saying, 'Any officer in a uniform is a waste of uniform.' Some of the things you hear out of these guys' mouths just because of their rank—it's kind of the whole power trip.... Some days I could get better information [briefings] off Yahoo, like no joke."

Rules of engagement were problematic for John's unit as well. "When we first got there, we were told we haven't dealt with a VIED [vehicle improvised explosive device driven into convoys].... They haven't dealt with those, one of those, in a year and a half. Well, we had eight of them within three months by the time we were leaving and our tactical training and procedures, our escalation of force, our rules of engagement never changed. Did we go by those? No. When you go outside the wire—we did what we had to do to get back alive because obviously the guy sitting in the swivel chair wasn't doing what we were doing." He was outside the wire often. He ran approximately ninety missions in a turret behind a mounted M-2.[28] Most of them were night missions.

John's patrol got stuck with "shit" missions more often than not. "Sometimes we'd be three days on, one day off. Sometimes it would be every other day, but most of the time we got picked for all the shit missions, the shit detail, because we had our stuff together. So all the difficult long ones, we pretty much got, and we were the clip with the most ran missions out of ten other clips [logistic patrol]." He did not mind the missions so much in the beginning. "You go on your mission, and sometimes you get back by 4 or 5 a.m. and sometimes you get stuck at a FOB [forward operating base] because you can't make it back within curfew. Sometimes you make it back right at curfew, where everybody's coming out and you're coming in. I remember we did that one time and it was unreal because it looked like New York City, only with cars that barely ran and donkey carts pulling the propane tanks and everything else.... During the day you can see this and that, but then at night you can't see anything. So if you're going from night to early morning and like, you start seeing everything, you're like, 'Whoa!' All these parts of the city and there's trash mounds and stuff like that which you can't see because it's behind buildings.... We went out with the attitude that if anybody was going to engage us, that would be their last time. Every night, and we did have some close calls, we had vehicles that wouldn't do as advised and so you do warning shots and things like that. And sometimes they would escalate from there, and sometimes they wouldn't. Sometimes you would neutralize the threat, sometimes you would destroy it."

For John, structure was good in theory, but the missions became problematic after eleven months. "It's really good until it's one of those redundant, like, 'Wait a second, we've done this every day for the past year. Can we please do this?' It's actually great to be organized, but the best definition I can give you for being over there and doing what we did is purgatory because you did the exact same thing every day not knowing the outcome. And that is the definition of insanity. It is repeating the exact same steps, the exact same routine, hoping the outcome was going to be something different. If you can compare it to insanity, then that's what my job [was], insane."

John describes his emotional state during his tour as mostly that of anger. He found that physical workouts helped him cope. "I actually had my dad send me a speed bag. Then there was a heavy bag at the gym. After I worked out, we'd do, my battle buddy and I, J. T., who's like the best friend in the world.... We'd do intense workouts man, like every other day. Full body, you know, negative failure workouts and then

I'd go hit the speed bag or the heavy bag for about 20 to 30 minutes afterwards. That's kinda of how I released it [anger], really. He and I, we were into the same things so we'd both convert that anger and that negative energy into positive energy by making us more physically fit. So that was like the best way to deal with anger there."

Much of John's anger was directed toward his command leader, but he still struggles with it. "Before I left, as an individual I was more emotional and compassionate, and now that I'm back, I'm not as much. It's coming back slowly but surely.... I learned a lot, a lot about the military, about the Army, about myself, about my family, about my friends through this deployment, and as much as I hated this deployment, I'm grateful for it. You get kind of calloused at times, you do. I'm not going to tell you that you don't, because that's the first thing that happens is you get calloused. Then you get the same monotone, the same face.... You know, I always [would] laugh because our commander and the people who are in the compound most of the time go into Cinnabon and Burger King and crap like that and would come by with it and be like, 'Why don't you smile?' And so many times I'm thinking, 'Well I'm not eating Cinnabon every day and sitting in a swivel chair and making decisions.' It's kind of ironic—he makes three times the amount I do and I'm over here working my ass off, risking my life when the only thing he has to worry about is incoming, which I still have to worry about!" The last straw for John occurred after a serious incident debrief, when his commander "actually left me high and dry." In the end he was awarded by a "full bird" colonel and the command sergeant-major but not by his own captain. "I guess that's the price you pay when you deploy with someone you don't know."

Like Mayfield, John returned with no casualties in his unit, but there were problems. He had attributed the pain in his back to carrying his Kevlar and an M-4, but it worsened when he returned. The medic in his gun truck had helped him through with ibuprofen, but now he needed to have a doctor at the VA hospital look at it. "Have you ever been to the Department of Motor Vehicles?" he asks rhetorically. "It's like that, only times fifty! I just want somebody to punch me in the face whenever I walk in so it's not that bad. I actually had to switch care providers because the doctor they assigned me to just wanted to give me pain pills, just wanted to dope me up, and I was like, 'No, not doing that.'" Not long after the back trouble, John received a diagnosis of PTSD and the results were similar. He saw a social worker at the local Veterans Administration hospital with the hopes of getting some relief. "She wanted to send me to a psychiatrist for medication, and I was like, 'I'm not going to do the whole medication bit.' I believe you're supposed to go through life conscious. If I assigned a pill to everything, then I would no longer be me, I'd be whatever I take. I'd be a zombie or, you know, I'd be extremely mellow because of pain killers. And it's sad because some people go into the VA and don't know, like what's going on, and so they do what they're told. It's like, 'Okay I'll take this [pill] this time, this [pill] this time.' And I see them since they got back and like, 'Whoa! That is not who I endured a deployment with. That's some dude in his body because he's all doped up!' And like I said, he doesn't realize."

His choice to "remain conscious" has been a positive move for John, but he still fights his "demons." He can't be in rooms with large or noisy crowds. He still struggles with sleep and is aware of his body's "fight-or-flee mentality." "God, I'd love to leave the hypervigilance behind. There's nothing worse than standing at a gas station and having somebody stand too close behind you. You're just thinking, 'What's this dude's problem? If you stand any closer, I'm going to punch you in the throat,' because that's what goes on in your head. Definitely hypervigilance. . . . I have to make myself tired in order to focus, so it's weird. Some of the dreams. . . . I don't like having them, but I'd much rather deal with them than have them covered up with dope." He pauses. "War is purgatory. It's hell. It's everything nasty and everything vicious and everything manipulative, all rolled into this pill that you have to swallow every day and think of how you participated in it. You know, I mean, how does one justify strapping oneself with C4 and ball bearings and running at you? How does somebody justify loading a car up with bulk explosives and driving at a convoy? How does somebody justify cutting off your head? I don't know. I know that everything I did over there, I had to be accountable for all my actions. I had to explain to them and I did to the best of my ability and I received awards for it." He laughs, then with more than a little sarcasm adds, "That's the best part, receive an award for it!"

Still proud to have served, John has begun to question the politics of war in Iraq, especially as he prepares for another tour in Afghanistan. He says he wants to be remembered for speaking his truth. "I feel here lately, the past two or three years just as this whole war has drug on, I feel like it is more so political sacrifices, you know? Because when you give somebody a weapon and you teach somebody how to use it, and you send them somewhere, and all you're doing is providing security for a nation whose government has fallen because you took their leader out of power? I mean, I can understand sending a message on what happened on 9/11. I can understand that. We did that years ago, believe me! You have no idea what it's like driving through a town that's been blown up and people are still living in it. It's ridiculous. That's why it's important for veterans to share their stories, so that other people understand that there are consequences to their actions and we [veterans] are ones that get to hold the memories."

The Long Road Home

Sergeant Lisek, also "regular Army," enlisted in 2000 with the hopes of becoming an Army Ranger. Like Carpenter, however, he found his career cut short because of the injuries he sustained during service. Lisek almost died September 11, 2004, after being hit with an IED. The medic who loaded him onto the helicopter for evacuation told Lisek's mother that Colonel Abrams and Lieutenant Colonel Valesky pinned his Purple Heart to his pillow, believing he would never make it to Landstuhl Medical Center in Germany. Lisek woke up from a coma on October 13 to find himself at Walter Reed Hospital.

During our interview, I notice that Lisek struggles with speech and that his ability to stay on task during the interview is evident. Sergeant Lisek was my first introduction to TBI. Several times throughout the interview he finds himself lost in the conversation, assisted by his wife, who informs me that Lisek is suffering from a severe Traumatic Brain Injury. The fact that Lisek is alive today is nothing short of a miracle. In any previous war, he would have probably died from his wounds.

He arrived in Iraq in March 2004, stationed with Charlie Company at Camp War Eagle, Baghdad, near Sadr City (formerly known as Saddam city, then as Al Tharwa). Day 1 in Iraq was hell for Lisek, whose unit experienced an ambush during their first patrol. "They had put tires out there and lit them on fire at the crossing. So we couldn't go down the alley or turn down the roads. They had parked cars there and we tried going through it. Then we got on Delta Street, trying to get down to it, then to Bravo Street. Our Humvee didn't even make it halfway down Delta because they were throwing Molotov cocktails at us. I got hit in my vest with an A-K round. It didn't go through because it hit my radio and then it hit that plate [pointing to his chest] that's in there. We lost all four tires that were on there. We were riding on rims." Lisek also received a surface wound to his arm. Pointing to the visible scar, he describes how the medic in his unit stitched him with a rainbow knife and fish wire.

"We did night patrols," Lisek struggles but continues, "We walked through.... I mean they had those date trees. We got ambushed when we was walking through there. And I seen that green snake. So I killed him. That was probably the only snake I seen over there. They got them camel spiders. Oh, my God, they're so big. They're huge. We'd have tower duty. That was life for the War Eagle, Camp War Eagle. You'd take your team and you'd have two guys in each tower and you'd walk back and forth, spend about 30 minutes for each for about 24 hours. Then your team would get five hours of sleep. Then as a platoon, you'd go out. And you'd stay out. Then, after you raided houses and got in firefights and you didn't have vehicles, you'd come back."

"We did everything you see on TV," Lisek says, becoming agitated. "But reporters are a bunch of bullshit. Liars—they lie. Oh God, do they lie. And they're always in the way." His attention returns to his unit as he recalls one of many attacks his unit received. A fellow soldier, named

Chapman, was in the Bradley just in front of Lisek when it was hit. "We spun around and they dropped the ramp and I got out with my team and we pulled Chapman out of that Bradley and I was trying to hold his leg together for him but you couldn't.... He lived, but he's missing his right leg. Like here down [pointing to his knee on his leg that was not amputated]. That would, I would say, would be, well that day after we, after we took Chapman to the aid station and then we watched Chapman get on the helicopter and take off, we went back out to the school and as we was heading down to Bravo Street to recover the Bradley that was destroyed there. We got to about Alpha and then, 'Boom,' and I thought, after the smoke cleared, I thought I was dead."

Lisek often walked beside the Bradley vehicles in his battalion. "We'd go as a whole battalion. We'd take Charlie Company and all three platoons would go out there in their Bradleys. And the infantry, the guys that aren't mounted, we'd walk behind the Bradleys or we would walk out to be a guinea pig, I guess, so those guys would come out and try and fight us.... I don't know, there's a lot of stuff that you do over there, but it's your job, so you just roll with it. We got constantly, got mortared at our base. Our base was Camp War Eagle, but everybody else in Iraq called it Camp Dirty Bird because that's all that happened. I'd say maybe a week, combined, from the time that I was there, in those seven months or however long I was there—I would say a week, combined, not five days straight but like one day out of a month, we didn't get shot at. Well, during Ramadan they'd claim, 'Oh we'll not do anything to you during Ramadan. Cease fire, cease fire.' Oh, whatever. They lie. They're conniving people. I don't like them. I won't trust a Muslim. I won't even go near one. I won't even let a Muslim doctor work on me."

Lisek's anger is palpable but also understandable. He was in Sadr City on April 4, 2004, during what has been dubbed "Black Sunday." "After April 4, you had to split your guys up cause, and give away to other platoons, so the guys that you trained with and all that.... We lost a lot, especially Alpha company. On April 4 they lost a lot. A lot of people got wounded that day. There's a book on the First Platoon's mission, Lisek explains, referring to Martha Raddatz's *The Long Journey*

Home.[29] "They didn't, I don't know why they wouldn't interview any of the other people that was there, why they just did it on one platoon's side, you know?" Lisek's unit had tried to get to Alpha Company but the fighting was too thick and their Bradleys were destroyed and ammunition was "cooking off" everywhere. "So, we were trying to get there to rescue their platoon but we couldn't. . . . and unless you get shrapnel and like you're, like what happened to Chapman [the soldier he had tried to help] and almost everybody else, I mean you just get shot—who cares? Sergeant Shane got shot through his armpit and [it] went through and you're dead, just like that."

Like thousands of his fellow soldiers, Lisek suffers from both signature injuries of the wars in Iraq and Afghanistan. Lisek looks on as his wife describes the barrage of injuries he sustained, leading to over twenty-six surgeries and still counting. "He has seven screws that are holding his skull together," she explains. "The whole side of his left skull shattered into his brain. They had to remove pieces out of his brain matter. The brain matter that surrounds your brain to protect it, there's a certain percentage of that, that's gone." She points to Lisek's left leg that is amputated just above the knee, adding, "His right ankle was broken. His neck is fused by two cables, his left leg amputated above the knee. His back is broken in three places, one arm is paralyzed and the other is full of metal plates." Lisek interjects, "I would say that, I'd say I been blown up about 80 times. You just get blowed up over there. And for so long, they weren't big enough to kill you. I mean, they were, but you can drive through having your ears bleed and your nose bleed." The blast also "shattered his face," his wife continues, pointing to the disfiguring scars. "All his sinuses had to be reconstructed. The only teeth he has are the front five or six on the bottom. The rest, we're in the process of replacing at this point. He's had to have metal screws surgically implanted into his jaw bones for us to attach his teeth to. His jaw was broken in several places."

Lisek's wife describes the hell her family suffered waiting for paperwork to clear.[30] It took two years for Lisek to receive his full disability and begin treatment with a psychiatrist for mental health. Both Lisek and his wife are grateful to the psychiatrist who saw him for reevaluation. She remembers their conversation: "He said, 'Do you know what your options are?' I said, 'Yeah, my option is that I have to pay for him to have medical care.' I said 'I can't afford this. What else can I do?'" He explained the benefits available to Lisek and from there they were able to receive treatment, including family therapy.... Now we know that there is a problem and we know how to handle it. And they've also ... we've gotten many places and support groups that we can go to. But the VA, no one ever made us aware of this. No one ever told us any of these things."

Losing Faith in the Mission

Army Sergeant George served with the 82nd Airborne during the early phase, just after 9/11. He still has fond memories of attending Airborne school and getting to jump out of planes, a dream come true for George, who would go on to serve in special operations in Afghanistan. When he graduated from basic training, he was still invested in the Army and considered himself in a committed relationship to his military life, despite the experiences he witnessed in basic training. However, a sense of betrayal would grow as the wars dragged on.

George's first tour was in Uzbekistan, but it was short, only two months. He was transferred in the summer of 2001 as part of the push to Bagram Airbase, part of U.S. efforts to establish the main hub of operations in Afghanistan. George supported the efforts in Afghanistan in the beginning, believing they were truly fighting a counterinsurgency war. His small unit was on the move often. "In special operations, you don't just go and sit there for eighteen months, which is kind of how the normal Army works." He compares the operations in Afghanistan to Iraq and later years in Afghanistan. "We usually knew exactly what we were going to do before we even went over there. We went all over the world doing different things. We didn't just go to Afghanistan." Outside the early battles with the Northern Alliance in Tora Bora, combat was mostly light in the early phases, with only "sparse pockets" of insurgency. Now the insurgency movement has grown well beyond the initial years, a problem George attributes to the occupation of Iraq. Although Afghans were well armed, a leftover from the Soviet invasion, there were few IEDs in Afghanistan in the early phases of the war, but after the invasion of Iraq the insurgents in Afghanistan began using them as well.

Having served in military special operations, George is hesitant to talk about specific combat incidents, places, or names of organizations beyond acknowledging the presence of the CIA. "There is one incident I'll tell you about," one that left its mark on him, creating a sense of moral anguish that he struggles with still today. "There are many layers to this war that people don't understand yet," he continues. "Some kind of contact had been made [between insurgents and military] and it was just two people. They had run into this building. And there was no telling who else was in that building. There were lots of people in that building, actually. But a group of Rangers had gotten ready to go into the building and they were kind of stacked up on the wall and someone threw a grenade over the top of the wall from inside the building. And it landed pretty close to, I think it was either a lieutenant or a captain with them and they just jumped on him and tried to cover him up.... But there were a couple casualties from that grenade. So they called in air support and leveled the entire building! It was two Apache helicopters, they just Winchestered everything! Afterward, I wound up carrying two body bags full of body parts back to Bagram Airbase just to try to figure out who we had just killed. That was the only reason—just trying to figure out who was just slaughtered.... It's like [military policy], just kill them all and sort it out later. So we'll never really know who was in that building." For George, the carnage of possible innocent civilian deaths was disproportionate to the assault. He began to question the missions, the strategies, and when he did, he was met with hostility by command.

George describes early operations in Afghanistan as a nomadic war of counterinsurgency, but it changed significantly after the invasion of Iraq. In his previous tours, there was little concern for regulations. The counterinsurgency war model was necessarily less formal—soldiers wore wrinkled and dirty uniforms, grew beards, and focused on staying on alert and inconspicuous. On his return for his third tour, there was an established Army presence. Soldiers were wearing "starched and pressed uniforms" that "make you light up like a light bulb on infrared radar.... It just turned into a different war," he says. For George, the military presence in Afghanistan had turned into "a dog and pony show." During his first two tours, military policy was specific, with instructions not to pour concrete barriers or teach locals how to build long-lasting structures. In other words, it was understood that they were there on a temporary mission and this was the message they wanted to send to the Afghanistan people. "There was a real push for a light military footprint," George recalls, and "long-term occupation was not the goal." But when he arrived for his third tour, military installations, concrete barriers, and buildings for military training were being set up. "It was no longer a nomadic war." The atmosphere was markedly different. "This is when it really changed for me," George remembers. "This is kind of when I got my heart broken. Again, like I said, it was a relationship."

George was disillusioned in August 2002 when he found a memo that called for the invasion of Iraq. "That's when the strategy changed," he explains. Military presence was transforming from a "light and mobile and flexible" war against terrorists to an occupation. "I had been on the Afghanistan/Pakistan border and I had just come back to Bagram Airbase for a bit." It was at Bagram that Sergeant George would learn of the growing attention to Iraq. "There was a memo that everyone was passing around and this was like, August 2002. And the memo called for the mobilization of 500,000 soldiers, sailors, airmen, and marine for the impending invasion of Iraq. And that was alarming to me because we hadn't even come close to winning this war yet! So like, how were we going to start another one?"

Disillusion with the military and its policies deepened when he returned home on leave in the fall of 2002. "This is when it really changed for me. This is when I really got my heart broken." After having seen the memo months in advance, he returned to "watch our government use our media to talk this nation into going to war after they had already issued the order to do it. It didn't matter what they were actually saying. None of it was relevant. They had already made the decision to do it. So this huge dramatic theater just unfolded in front of me on the media—this idea of an 'axis of evil' or this idea of them having some kind of 'weapons of mass destruction' or 'Al-Qaeda in Iraq,' really?"

Edgework and Its Consequences

As these stories reveal, returning veterans who have experienced combat trauma have to make sense of the paradox of military service, "non-standard combat," and episodes of reluctant edgework. Some return and find outlets to tell their stories to those who understand and move toward healing. Others keep it bottled up. A smaller percentage return to find they can no longer live in civilian society, so they go back again and again to a regimented structure that guarantees them episodes of edgework. But each time they return, they know the odds are stacked against them. Loss of empathy is more likely to occur after extended exposure to combat as soldiers learn whom they can and cannot trust. Time blurs the mission, rules of engagement change, and loss of life creates a new understanding. As we have seen, normalizing the word "kill or be killed" does not necessitate an understanding of its magnitude, because the broad range of emotions that make us human doesn't disappear. Rather, vulnerable emotions are pushed back during combat but not erased. For some, they can be unpacked on return to civilian life; for others, a scar forms over the heart and veterans become trapped in a reality that cannot be easily expressed or understood by those who have not experienced war.

Many still deal with the disillusion of arriving in country to find those they anticipated would welcome them increasingly turned against them. Others become disillusioned with command, or the seeming disregard for civilian lives by the enemy or fellow soldiers, and some begin to question the war itself. Moreover, many return from service to find themselves, like those whose testimony we have heard in this chapter, dealing with the heavy moral weight and aftermath of war. Regardless of their political views, they served to the best of their ability. None questions this service, although some do resent the politics that sent them to war—only deepening the paradox of reluctant edgework and the true meaning of warrior.

These experiences raise important questions for society as a whole. Reluctant military edgework is not a psychological state of mind, but rather a condition of war. Moreover, with technological advances, more people now survive war than in any other historic period. Physical wounds can be handled by medical teams on the ground. Soldiers can be airlifted to surgeons at nearby hospitals before being brought back to military hospitals in the United States. Medicine is readily dispensed for anxiety, depression, and loss of sleep during service and is available upon return. Soldiers who have a diagnosis of PTSD are welcomed back for more tours. But we have to ask on behalf of today's soldiers: Just how many times can a soldier be exposed to reluctant edgework before he or she succumbs to war trauma? How many times should one's brain be exposed to Traumatic Brain Injury before a soldier begins to lose his or her ability to function in everyday life? The military does not know the answers to these questions, yet many are allowed to return again and again for multiple tours.

Episodes of edgework that occur during combat become surreal and the memories of combat make their way into the bodies, hearts, and minds of those who return. Adding insult to injury, soldiers who seek help are often stigmatized, creating a huge barrier to healing. Perhaps Edward Tick aptly describes it when he argues that the underlying conditions of Post Traumatic Stress Disorder are those of a national disorder that soldiers "imprisoned in their private terror" must carry so that "the rest of us along with our leaders" can "perpetuate the public fantasy of our own innocence." If Tick is right, then the signature injuries of those returning from war may mirror our nation's own "soul sickness."[31]

I turn next to female soldiers. Their experiences are shaped against the backdrop of military masculinity and can result in a very different type of war trauma, but one that can lead to Post Traumatic Stress just as easily.

CHAPTER FOUR

Sister Soldiers: Women and Military Service

A
ccording to the Department of Defense, women constitute 14
percent of all active duty armed forces and 11 percent of those
deployed to the Middle East. Since the 1994 reversal of the
"risk rule" by the Department of Defense, women have been assigned
as combat pilots and military police and serve on combat ships. More
females have served and died in Operation Iraqi Freedom and Operation Enduring Freedom than in all previous wars combined. Although
there is some evidence that gender boundaries have blurred in recent
military culture, women are still prohibited from some areas in the infantry, field artillery, Special Forces, and the Forward Air Defense. As
I mentioned in the introduction, this policy may be changing soon. As
of now, women continue to be trained and placed in support positions,
but it is important to note that despite the military's restrictions, female
soldiers are often pulled into combat in both Iraq and Afghanistan.[1]
Female soldiers find increasingly that, like their male counterparts, they
have become reluctant military edgeworkers.

Even with these changes, the presence of women in the military is
still considered problematic to some and the debate continues.[2] A recent
report of changes in physical training exercises at several sites (e.g., Fort

Sill, Oklahoma, and Fort Jackson, South Carolina) prompted a firestorm of reactions from both males and females on a local news website.[3] The majority of those who posted comments to the thread viewed the changes as a feminization of training. When a female wrote in about her experiences at Fort Jackson, stating, "We did everything with the males and everything they did," she was quickly criticized with comments like, "You did everything with the males. You just did not have the same standards. You have more time for runs. You have less sit-ups and less push-ups [than men]. I guess you forgot all that information!" Another responds, "Let's face it, women do NOT belong in combat positions.... they aren't made for it." One post was a hybrid, reading, "Get rid of the gays also. Let's get tough."[4]

Paternalistic views such as these often came up among males around the issues of either combat or workloads, leading one to ponder whether there will be significant resistance to General Casey's recent announcement to consider removing the ban. As Specialist Harper explained during an interview, "I think seeing a woman hurt is a lot different than seeing a guy hurt. It makes you want to go help them a lot more. Just, I don't know, it's a lot easier if you've got a mission you've got to walk past, if you've got to walk past a guy getting hurt, that's a lot easier than walking past a girl getting hurt." Harper attributes this to being raised "taking care of girls." He wasn't keen on working with females at his base, either. "I don't know," he explains, "my job was kind of a male-heavy job, so, a lot of manual labor and stuff, so I kind of didn't like working with females. That means more work for me. No offense or nothing."

The continued resistance raises an important question: What does it mean to be a female in today's military? Research suggests that stereotyping and marginalization of women combine with sexual harassment and sexual assault to create specific challenges for today's sister soldier.[5] As revealed in their narratives of basic training, women are acutely aware of their gender as problematic within the masculine ethos of military culture. But women serve proudly in spite of these challenges. Some encounter the vehement disapproval of male counterparts and others maneuver the system, unaffected for the most part.

Military life is a mixed bag for women. The hostility may represent a small percentage of males in the military, or it may remain a larger issue. Like homosexual males who serve in the military, females may challenge some military identities that are opposed to all things feminine.[6] But these stereotypes, while real, sometimes fade during actual service. As the following interviews reveal, there is a wide range of experiential knowledge to be gained from women's perspectives of military life.

Voices from the Not-So-Margins: Afghanistan

Tech Sergeant Douglas enlisted in the Air Force in 1991 and served two deployments in Operation Enduring Freedom, Afghanistan (2001/2002, 2002/2003). Douglas arrived in country after a brief stop in Oman. The flight to Afghanistan revealed to Douglas just how marginalized she was on the all-male flight. During the long flight, Army Rangers and Navy Seals were not allowed to sit in the same row of seats as her and they were forbidden to talk to her. "It seemed like every time I went in and out of anything, everyone stared at me, just, 'Where is she going? What is she doing?'" Douglas recalls. Most of the social life took place in their tents and because she was not allowed to interact with the Rangers, she often felt isolated. "I wasn't allowed to socialize with the Rangers, or they weren't allowed to socialize with me, we'll say.... So as far as having a social network, I didn't have that there."

After she arrived at Bagram Airbase, Douglas worked with males who were unclear about her duties and resentful of her presence in their units. "I worked with the Navy Seals, the Army Rangers, and other Army units that we're not really allowed to talk about. And most of those people never work with women and my job was to do stuff with them. I trained with them, but they weren't prepared to have a living area for me, a restroom, shower, so I had to wait for that stuff to get done. Once we had decided and they understood I wasn't living by myself in a tent and that they were sharing one with me, I was able to go up to Bagram and I shared a tent with guys. I got to shower once every three days.

They would have to post Rangers outside the tent for my half hour so that nobody else would go in there."

As the only woman in her forward unit, Douglas was well aware of the stigma associated with her gender. She was not only working in a masculine military culture, she was serving in a country that was protective of its own rigid gender roles. "I had one Navy guy ask me one day what it was like to have 300 sets of eyes on me because I was the only female. You know, we'd go running in our shorts and stuff and the locals would go in and out because it wasn't a closed area at that time. I had people staring at me everywhere I went. They hadn't seen Western women. They hadn't seen—obviously my legs were showing because I was running. I was just like, 'I ignore you guys. I do my job. I ignore you guys, that's all there is to it.' But it was hard in the sense that I had to prove myself every time.... It was very isolating," Douglas remembers.

Douglas stood out everywhere she went. "It's not just people walking down the street staring at you, it's 300 type-A trained killers staring at you, so it was very intimidating and I had to, like I said, not just do my job well, but I had to do it better and I had to prove myself to them that I was worthy because most of them have never ever even worked with a female before and here I was on their turf." She understood their resentment of her presence, though she didn't condone it. "For them, you know, they had trained fifteen years to get to do a war or do a tasking and I was on their turf and possibly in their way. I was excess baggage to most of them."

It would not be until Operation Anaconda that things would settle down for Douglas. Still, she was heavily scrutinized by the males in her unit, a process that has been identified as a form of gender harassment and hostility in which males generalize isolated mistakes to all women in the military.[7] "Until I had to do my job, they didn't understand why I was there with them.... There were times where they had missions where they would go on, and I trained to go on missions, and they had one that a lot of people know about. It's Operation Anaconda, the Roberts' Ridge.[8] They went on it a couple of days before and this one guy, he was showing me, I was getting ready to go on a mission with them and I had my belt ready to rig into the helicopter and he was saying to me on one side of the room, 'Hey, don't do it like that. I know that's how we're supposed to do it all the time but I almost got stuck in the helicopter and got killed yesterday. Do it this way, because I've figured it out.' And I'm like, 'Okay.' Well, across the room, unbeknownst to us, were the Ranger battalion commander and the command sergeant major watching, so all they needed to see was the Ranger correcting the girl. All of a sudden I wasn't going on the mission and they were yelling and I was like, "But I have to go on the mission. It's my job. Who else is going to do it? Nobody else knows what my job is.' It ended up going up to the two-star general and everybody outside tents in the dark waiting to go on the aircraft arguing outside. Finally, I was going. My general was just like, 'That's what she's here for. She's going.' So I got to go but right when we were getting on the airplane, the intel [intelligence] they decided was bad and the whole mission got canceled. That happened to me a couple times."

Before Anaconda, Douglas was glad that part of her job as a personnel officer was slow to start and still unknown to her male cohort. She was not only assigned to account for where soldiers were but also to account for the wounded and fallen soldiers. She remembers well the first death she encountered. Her job was to provide information to her general about the status of wounded and dead. So Douglas spent hours at the three hospitals, U.S., Spanish, and British, where U.S. forces were taken when their own beds were full. It was lights-out time on base, so she used a head lamp to maneuver between hospitals to get to the wounded. She remembers turning on the lamp to scope out her navigation, turning it off and running 50 feet or so, then repeating the process. She collected information from the hospitals about the wounded and the dead. "So after doing all that, my general is [still] wanting to know about the status of our forces and I'm not even at a point where I can tell him. The Doc, he says, 'Hey, now that we've got everyone else taken care of, are you ready to go into this other tent?' Okay, well, it was the morgue. So we spent about two hours in there going through seven body bags figuring out what everybody's, you know, scrapes, wounds, lacerations, taking all of their personal effects off of them and labeling them." Douglas grew up with race horses and remembers having to deal with putting down horses and following the veterinarian around the farm. She felt this work prepared her for dealing with the presence of blood and death, but this was different. "We did all the easy ones first," Douglas explains (those who could be easily identified), "and then we got to the last one, which was [the first casualty from Operation Anaconda] and the Doc asked me, 'Are you sure you want to do this? You can leave.' And I was like, 'No, this is my job, I'm going to stay.' And they opened up his body bag and he had his head cut off. And that was just one of his wounds, but that's probably the hardest day."

Douglas stayed up all night typing the report of the dead and wounded and was just about to make it to her tent for some much needed rest when a male soldier intervened. "I was headed back to my bed and the light was coming up at that time. This guy walked up to me and he says 'You have dirt all over you,' and I didn't really hold my composure really well and I started telling him how it was somebody's blood and he was sleeping and he wouldn't know. But then I went and I got like three days of sleep I think and I was fine." After that, Douglas remembers, the males in her unit began to relax a little over her presence. Taking care of the fallen soldiers gave her presence at Bagram credibility in their minds. "After Anaconda and after doing my casualty [job], it was kind of a blessing in disguise for me in that it let them, them being the guys that I worked with, they actually got to see what I do. They didn't just think that I went to the gym and walked around the jock. They saw that I was there for a purpose and after that they started talking to me and letting me hang out with them and be their friend. And when there were missions going on, they knew that I was there for them, that I wasn't going to hinder them in any way. They didn't make me feel ostracized anymore."

During her second deployment, Douglas missed a training flight because she had been sick. She had gone to the gym to work out when the call came. The helicopter had crashed and her fellow soldiers died. "At that time we didn't have control over that hospital because Bagram had grown so much so we had to work with the conventional forces on clearing us an area. They put our guys into the morgue so for about four hours me, the chaplain, a representative from their unit and one other person from our unit sat in this room with these guys.... I was just sitting there because we were just waiting for something to happen back at Fort Bragg so we could say, 'Do this, do that, and release the message' so they could notify the families. So we're sitting there making sure other people didn't come in and mess with anything and find out who it was because it wasn't releaseable. And it wasn't until hours later when I was sitting there that I just realized I would be laying there with them if I didn't go to the gym that day, so that was pretty surreal for me."

For Douglas, there were no illusions about war. "I don't have rose-colored glasses thinking that I'm never going to be involved in a war." In spite of the isolation and resistance from her male comrades, Douglas is proud of her service. "What I like about it [the military] is I've gotten to see the way it's shaping the world. I was in Kabul the day that women got to go to school for the first time, you know? So I got to see the women going to school and that was something that we did. I've seen the ruins of the Taliban with their black flags hanging with holes in them, like you picture old pirate flags. But they're now banned and people are trying to make their country a better place, you know, rebuild their cities, their towns, their villages. I've seen a market that they just throw things on the ground to now where they actually have a building to put their market in. So, I mean, there was a reason for it."

Staff Sergeant Hewitt was in the Army Reserves when her unit was called up to serve in Operation Enduring Freedom, Afghanistan. Her unit arrived in country in April 2003, but Hewitt was trained as a combat engineer, mechanic. She had already dealt with being a female among a largely male group when she trained as a combat engineer. She remembers the scrutiny she received as one of only a handful of females. "Working on the equipment, I had to crawl up and down, you know, to get in, and they would be watching us like, 'Do I ask her if she needs help, or not?' I've been doing this for years. 'I know what I'm doing, so when you give out assignments to work on vehicles, don't overlook me,' because they did. Don't be the, you know, don't let me be the last one to be picked, which they did, you know don't give me some pansy change a light bulb, which they did, and it's like, come on, you know, just because I'm a female doesn't mean I can't do that. So I guess it's more or less being a mechanic and a female because where I was as an engineer, there were never any females, one or two tops. So I've always been outnumbered and everything but I've adjusted and I've accepted, and I've brought up my own morale."

Although Hewitt was trained as a combat engineer, she worked in the mailroom at Bagram Airbase. At first, she felt discriminated against: "I felt gender discrimination because we couldn't go out to the forward operating bases and it's like, 'Well, I have the same MOS [military occupational specialty] as them. I can do the same job as them, yet you're restricting me from doing my job,' which is going out there to work, carpentry, electricians, and plumbers, and I was like, 'I feel discriminated because I can't go out there and do my job I was brought here to do.' But the guys—they did. They got to go out and do that, but I couldn't. The females didn't. And there was like three of us that had the MOS to do those things. You know, for a while it really set bad, left a bad taste in our mouths. You know, it's not fair."

Hewitt remembers that the unit they replaced from North Carolina had experienced a huge "blowout" over female presence that caused morale to "go to pot." She explains the base was simply not prepared for women. "She was the only female. She had no privacy. It wasn't equipped. They're saying it wasn't equipped for another female to be out there. She would have to have had a separate place to use the restroom if she needed to clean up. Not if that was out there! ... So at that point they stopped—no more females going out to the forward operating bases." Her commander "counseled" women on why they could not go out to the forward operating bases. Her response was, "I told him, 'This is so wrong and you know it's wrong because you bring us here. You're actually cutting into your manpower because you won't let these qualified females go out there and do their job.' He's like, 'Yeah, I know, but it came down from the commander of the post.' So you can't get around that."

Hewitt took the rules in stride and came to see her role as a mail clerk as an important link between soldiers and their families. "Well, the guys in my unit, they went out to the forward operating, forward fire bases, and the females, because they had a previous incident with another unit, they wouldn't allow the females to go out because of the living conditions, limited privacy for females, not equipped to handle females, so the females stayed in the rear and the guys went out to the forward operating bases with the special forces.... I worked in the post office and that was different because when we went there I was thinking there at the forward operating bases, they're going to have something to remember. It looks all exciting and everything, and I'm thinking, 'I'm just here in the post office chunking mail.' After about a week of doing that, I realized I have the most important job. Besides food and medical, mail was the most important. It was like their lifeline back to their country, their home, and at that point I realized that just because you're not on the front lines at the forward operating bases where the other guys are that you're back here because they also need their mail. I was helping get their mail out and at the end of the day when I go back to my unit if any mail came out afterwards, I would bring it to them and get mail out and everything so the mail was a very important aspect of it."

Although she never experienced direct combat, Hewitt and her unit experienced plenty of incoming. Mortar rounds and IEDs were commonplace near the airstrip. "Normally [when] they fired it would [be to] try to destroy the airfield because that's where the trafficking and food and more troops and everything came in. So they would aim more for the airfield on our end. That's about as close to firing as it got." Minefields were also common, left over from the Soviets. She remembers hearing them "going off left and right." The stress did build over time and Hewitt found herself losing weight, unable to eat. Once she returned to the States, she tried to get her sleeping patterns back down, avoided newspapers and television reports of the war, and noticed that she was different. She had a strong support network when she returned. "It's not that it changed my behavior actually toward my family," she explains, "but it changed my thinking, the way things are done. And it impacted me as to how important, even though I didn't think I was doing anything that important, my family thought it was. And you know, my friends thought it was. But because you're in harm's way, it does. It's changed your thinking about everything. It's kind of hard to put into words where and how, but it does. It changes you as far as your everyday life."

Voices from the Not-So-Margins: Iraq

Army Sergeant Bonham served in a communications unit in Iraq in 2003. She was close to the end of her active duty and was surprised by her orders to deploy. "I didn't think I was going and the stop-loss people were the last to find out. . . . I was seriously pissed off," she remembers. "I did not want to go to war. I did not agree with the war. I didn't like the, I didn't understand the reasoning behind it. It sounded to me like a bunch of B.S. Most of the time I was in the military I tried not to pay attention to politics or what was on the radio, but I was starting to get out and it was interesting to me. So I was paying more attention this time and probably shouldn't have. But no, I did not want to be there. It wasn't something I really wanted to be a part of, and I felt like, I really felt like it was a matter of fear. The American people were just scared and it was a matter of, 'Do something. Do anything,' because they were just too scared at the time. . . . When I went to Kosovo, it was totally different because I felt we were doing something worthwhile, and this [Iraq] I felt was exactly what it was, preemptive."

Sergeant Bonham's unit was stationed at Camp Udari in Kuwait, waiting for orders to move up to Iraq. "We sat around Udari waiting to get gassed, essentially. We were just sitting there. At first it was really freaky, because you know the alarm was sounding, like, 'Oh my god that's a gas alarm and it's for real.' But eventually people got used to it." Bonham remembers, "We spent a lot of time sitting." They were experiencing a build-up at Camp Udari and Bonham was made sergeant of the guard. Entry into the gates for guest workers and returning troops was confusing enough, but the lack of firepower "was laughable," she remembers. "I was in a real division, so I had my ammunition and everything and I was a sergeant of the guard for a group of National Guard soldiers. They all had one bullet apiece. And one of them actually pulled his gun, his weapon. He actually pulled it on one of our, the United States Army vehicle, because it was coming in the wrong gate. You don't do that, you know? And the guy jumped out of the car and started screaming at him. He's [the National Guard soldier] refusing to put his [weapon down]. I was just like, 'Oh, my God.'"

Bonham's job was to make sure supplies for communication got sent to Iraq from Kuwait. "They had me stay back because I was stop-lossed and they didn't know when the stop-lossed people were going to be leaving.... And they, we had one soldier in our company, this female soldier, and her platoon hated her. Her sergeant was kind of a jerk. He didn't deal with her real well, she was older. She was twenty-eight at the time and I was twenty-one. And they didn't want to deal with her, so they wanted to leave her. In order to leave her, they had to have a female NCO, and since I was stop-lossed, I was a good candidate for that. So I stayed with her and that other team of people. We would drive down to a permanent base in Kuwait and get our supplies. Sometimes, we would usually do it in Kuwait. We would go down there and get the supplies arranged there on some convoy there or arranged on some convoy in Udari, things like that."

"I didn't mind being held back with that little female that they didn't like," she goes on, "but I had a suspicion that my commander had a crush on me and that he was afraid something would happen to me. He just got really weird and protective of me," Bonham explains. "People are kind of flirty [in the Army], you get used to it." Bonham didn't experience gender discrimination during her tour in Iraq, but her experience in Kosovo with a sergeant was very different. Happily, she found closure when she ran into him during a trip to Iraq and he apologized. "I had one sergeant and I knew him. I was his soldier for years, probably two years, which now doesn't seem like that long, but at the time two years seemed like a long time to have a certain sergeant to me, and I remember the day he got me as a soldier. I walked by the office and he's like, 'You're going to give me that little thing?' Well, you know, he was ex-infantry and actually signal hadn't been open to women that long. Signal's not one of the female-intensive jobs. It was more physical than administration, but that guy I had a lot of problems with, and mostly he just didn't recognize the things I did as the same as what a guy was doing and it lasted for years. One day a new soldier came in and he came in from a division that wasn't really a deployable division, so it's a lot different for them. They don't train the way we do. And this guy had longer time in service, but he hadn't had as much time in the job. I was a specialist, promotable at the time, and I had a team. He wanted to lead the team even though he had just got there. He hadn't actually been to the field and my sergeant let him and he screwed up. So after that my sergeant told me, 'You know, I finally realized you never let me down.' And I didn't. I never let him down. I never was drunk and needed to be covered for on a day. I never got arrested. I didn't make him look bad. Then one day when we flew up to Iraq to bring some laptops, I went over to headquarters when I saw him. He brought me over, introduced me to his soldier, a female soldier, and he told me, 'You totally changed how I am. I was such a sexist jerk to you and I'm so sorry.'" Bonham learned a lesson from her experiences, "One thing I got being a female in the military is it's not good enough just to be good enough. You've got to really strive."

Sergeant Bonham was later moved to Iraq, to wait along with others who had been stop-lossed to go home. "That was where they were doing it from. I know, weird," she explains. It was spring 2003 and Bonham had little to do once she arrived in Mosul. "The first four days are horrible when you're signal, but then after that it's really pretty relaxed. Plus, we're the people with the phones and the Internet, so it was pretty cushy. I didn't have a bad time at all up there." She remembers their military presence as welcomed by the locals in the early phase. "It seemed like a more relaxed [atmosphere]. People were more hopeful while we were there. But that was in the first few months and everyone was really excited. They rolled right in. I don't think they started getting the resistance yet. I heard things started getting worse when they switched out with the Marines who came in next, and that happens to be around the time they found Uday and Qusay [sons of Suddam Hussein] and that kind of stuff started happening, things started getting more turbulent."

Sergeant Bonham considered herself one of the lucky ones. She was leaving Iraq as things were tightening up. "We were mortared once, just at Mosul, and they hit the air strip there. It's really funny because at that point, even though we hadn't been mortared a lot or anything, we'd have the big, you know, 'trying to gas us or trying to missile us while we're at Kuwait' but when we were in Iraq and they tried to mortar us, it was just that time when I was there, and like I said, they hit the airfield. And they came in and had everyone put the Kevlars on and lay on the ground. So basically, everyone, at that point, they don't care that much, so everyone just laid down and put their Kevlars on and went to sleep. The next day they had everyone do sandbags," Bonham remembers. "The very next day it kind of started getting locked down."

Army Reserve Specialist Ferretti had a very different experience. She also served twelve months in Iraq in 2003. Her specialty was carpentry and masonry, a nontraditional field for women in the military. She remembers the first mortar attack on her camp occurred within their first month in Iraq. "It wasn't someone from my unit, but it was someone that I saw get hit with shrapnel and later I found out that that individual died." Ferretti was surprised by her reaction to the attack and remembers it as surreal. "It was almost like it didn't really happen. My reaction to it was like I was watching a movie and not like I was actually there, and not like I was in actual danger myself. Because I was, I was close enough to see someone get hit with shrapnel and yet it didn't occur to me that I could get hit with the same shrapnel. I didn't react the way I thought I would."

Ferretti remembers that rules of engagement compounded and sometimes hampered soldiers' ability to defend themselves. She recalls working tower duty during November and December of 2003. "I had the midnight to 8 o'clock in the morning shift and it was bitter cold," she explains. "It was colder than any cold I've ever experienced over here. I had eight layers of clothing on and I still was shivering cold. I got shot at in the tower, but I never did see the source of the shooting, so I couldn't fire back because of the rules of engagement. I also couldn't call for helicopter backup because I couldn't determine who shot at me. They couldn't just go shooting randomly, either."

Ferretti often found herself in convoys where the truck in front or behind was hit with an IED. Like her male counterparts, she remembers feeling helpless "because we'd have to come to a halt and put parameter security on our convoy and we couldn't move forward and try to give backup support to the convoys that were being hit. So we felt kind of helpless that we couldn't do anything." Like her male counterparts, she knew the hypervigilance that came with realizing "that if it's your time, it's your time, and no matter how much skill you have, no matter how prepared you are, you just never know when one of those bullets might come to you. You worry about the guy next to you. You worry if they're going to get hit. You worry if it is going to be your convoy that gets hit next. How much devastation? If you have enough people, enough ammunition do you have enough energy? Can you withstand how long it might take to stop the fire? Because sometimes we had to stay still for several hours waiting on the convoy in front of us to clear the fight and it was tiring to just pull security, not shooting at anyone, so I just worried that I wouldn't have the strength to withstand and endure a firefight." Ferretti found reluctant edgework exhausting. She compares her own experiences to those of the males in her unit, which meant that processing her emotional reactions after firefights was a lonely enterprise, representing the gendered division of emotion work in military culture, where emotions are linked to disruption and are deemed inappropriate. "And guys don't generally talk about their emotions as much. They seem eager to shoot. That's what they said while we waited. They just were saying, 'Give me my turn, let me shoot.' They seemed more eager to experience, I guess, an adventure is how they looked at it."

Like Douglas, Ferretti found that her own unit was resistant to her presence at first. "The guys, they had their camaraderie. They got together and hung out and had their little pack and I didn't have any other females in my platoon, so I either hung out alone or I had to hang out with other females." She later began to make friends with males from other platoons because being around those from her own unit was often "just awkward because during the day they sometimes were very harsh to me and I didn't really want to be around them." Ferretti believes her military occupation specialty (MOS) also caused her to stand out. She continues, "Well, being the only female in a platoon full of men and our MOS being one that is mostly male dominated, it was quite different being the only female in that guys either treat a girl like a sexual object or like their sister. It seems like they don't know how to treat a female as a co-worker, a soldier. It's different because you are living with these people. You're working with them, seeing them day in, day out. They are your family. They are the people you hang out with after work. They're the people you talk to when you have issues, but yet you're still a female. You're different than they are. And at times it was hard to show them how to treat me because I didn't want to halt production or hinder the mission in any way. But sometimes treatment was inappropriate or unfair or unjust and there's just no way of measuring that, really. I think that perhaps as a female we are a little bit more sensitive to the way we're treated than men are, but that doesn't necessarily mean that we're wrong for being sensitive. It's just how we [women] are."

These perspectives often surface among women in discussions of combat, perceived by many males as their domain. For some males, the growing presence of females diminishes the symbolic import of the masculine warrior (i.e., women and children constitute the "innocents," as one veteran describes). A male soldier explained after an interview that the presence of women in a war zone was especially hard for him. If there is a female casualty, "we are more upset because she should not have been there in the first place." Females are keenly aware that this is a common view and acknowledge that gender influenced not only their boot camp experiences but their specialization and service assignments as well, where their struggle to be accepted often followed them into combat.[9]

Army Specialist Little enlisted just prior to September 11, 2001 at the age of 18. Like others, Little had to contend with some resistance from her male comrades. "We had some men that thought that girls shouldn't be in the military: 'It's not tough enough anymore,' 'I wish I'd joined the Marines because girls are girls,' and you know they were very sexist about it." Little didn't give it much thought during the missions, though. She signed up to be a mechanic and after two years in Germany found herself driving a truck in a convoy from Kuwait to Iraq. Her unit moved into Iraq out of Camp Pennsylvania immediately after Bush declared war. "We left from Kuwait on the 18th and it took us two days to get to the border, which was March 20th at 1 o'clock in the morning. So that was when we went into it."

Specialist Little describes numerous times when her unit was being fired upon, although they usually arrived just after firefights. She remembers the carnage that remained and the civilian bodies that her unit came across. "We had to stop on the side of the road right next to the car that had burnt, maybe a day before. And a burnt body was hanging out of it. And to this day, I would never forget that smell. There was actually two burnt bodies, but we could only see one because they didn't want us to get so close to it. It's a haunting memory." Little explains.

She is also haunted by a chance encounter her unit had with a small group of Special Ops soldiers. They had stopped at the airstrip to gas up their vehicles. Each one was dressed as an Iraqi civilian and they chatted about their relative missions ahead, each dreading the days to come. The next day a sand storm hit, turning the "sky orange," Little remembers. "Then it got pitch dark, pitch black at 3 o'clock in the afternoon. Even a flashlight wouldn't help–it was so dark. And that lasted for two days. And after that went away, we found out the Special Forces guys hit into that, you know the dust storm and everything. And out of nowhere, these Iraqis invaded and killed them. It just sends a sense of, 'I just saw them!' It's like, 'How can that happen? We just saw them.'" Little, who had prided herself on not showing emotions as freely as her female comrades, adds, "That was the first time I actually cried because it was like, 'That could happen to me." There were plenty of times where we were just out in the middle of nowhere and we could have been invaded because we didn't know this land and they did!"

Little also remembers feeling helpless during the attacks on her convoy with the nonfiring weapon she was issued. "The first time I was shot at," Little remembers, "I was driving one of our maintenance trucks. And really didn't even know I was being shot at. We heard the pops from the weapons. And my sergeant that was sitting in the passenger seat got his gun out and he was going to start shooting because we didn't know where it was coming from. And we were the very last vehicle. So it was like, 'Oh, my gosh, what do we do?' So we kept driving on. Nothing was hit, thank goodness. But it was a very terrifying moment, to sit there and drive and think, 'Oh, my gosh, I'm driving and I can't reach for my weapon.' The whole time I was in Iraq, my weapon was broke. It was missing a part to fire. They had supposedly fixed it before we left, but it wasn't fixed [laughs]."

"Black Jack" [pseudonym] was diagnosed with PTSD after she retired from the Army, but she was not diagnosed by a VA doctor. Rather, she saw a private physician who diagnosed her with PTSD. She served two tours, both in Iraq and Afghanistan. Like Bonham, she didn't experience combat other than the occasional mortar round on her unit, but her military service took its toll. Black Jack's diagnosis resulted from the stress of working under a difficult commander who belittled her constantly and often took credit for her work. The stressful working conditions combined with being on alert near a combat zone and sent her spinning downward into a dark hole after she returned home. She was bitter and described herself as angry all the time, as opposed to her former optimistic self. She isolated herself for a full year after coming back, even considering suicide at one point. After she'd been back for a full year, she began treatment and group therapy.

Like other females, "Black Jack" encountered male resistance. "I definitely came into contact with men who felt that women shouldn't be there. And you know, everyone has their viewpoint, but even in the group I was serving with, there was definitely that attitude that women shouldn't be there.... Well, not everyone was vocal about it, you just knew. Even some of the guys that were the most pleasant, they were gentlemen, I found out later didn't think women should be there."

For "Black Jack," realization of her marginal status was gradual, but by the time her unit was deployed to Iraq Black Jack knew what lay ahead. "It started with, for example, I guess during premobilization, before we ever left the States. The company or the first sergeant may call a formation, and because the males and the females lived in separate living quarters, oftentimes the males would not relay that information down to the females. And we missed, or we'd run up late to the formation. Now it didn't matter that it wasn't our fault, it was just that perception, 'Here's a rag-bag of women running up at the last minute.' It didn't matter that it wasn't our fault."

Conclusion

As these experiences reveal, female soldiers face unique challenges. Not only are they sometimes placed in reluctant edgework conditions which can lead to trauma, they may also face these conditions against a backdrop of hostility from within their own ranks. But what these oral histories further reveal is that time in the field can blur these differences and those who serve can become "brothers and sisters in arms." It is important to note that males are hardly a monolithic group and some are supportive of their female comrades. Some of the males in these accounts came to appreciate their sister soldiers.

Army Reserve Captain Decoster found that female coworkers provided an advantage when responding to combat stress. "I think one of the advantages was, I think the dynamics changed when we worked with groups of soldiers, especially after a significant event, the loss of a soldier and a serious IED or RPG blast—that sometimes the soldiers would respond differently when there was a female on my team.... I think some of the testosterone was balanced out by having a female there, and maybe they were a little more genuine as opposed to keeping their game face on for the other males on the team."

In *Masculinities* (1996), Robert Connell states that hegemonic masculinity is established when there is a link between cultural ideals and institutional power.[10] Others have further delineated masculine hegemony as having an external and internal component.[11] External components of masculine hegemony are embedded in institutional practices, such as the military policies described earlier that restrict women's participation and, until recently, silenced expression of nonheterosexual orientation. Internal hegemony plays out in our everyday interactions through hostility, scrutiny, valorization of heterosexual prowess, and sexual harassment.

While women gain some of the symbolic resources of military service that set them apart from civilians (e.g., patriotism, sense of duty, honor, sacrifice, strong bonds) and gain much of the material benefits of military service (e.g., pay, retirement, GI bills), they are more often blocked from obtaining the ideal warrior identities available to their male comrades.[12] This leads some males, especially younger males, to express their felt ambivalence toward females. For example, Sergeant Hurt states, "I hate to say it, I don't want to make it seem like I'm looking down on somebody who served because if you've been over there, you've been over there. But there's two different worlds between if you're combat arms, cavalry scout, infantryman, or if you're a cook or supply or whatever. Like I said, I don't want to seem like I'm downgrading them, but Iraq's two different places depending on which sort of thing you're doing. I mean, I lived in sector for five days out of every week, so that's not the same as someone that literally spends an hour of their day outside of concrete walls, you know what I mean? It's kind of hard to make that comparison so if it's a female, she probably wasn't living the same kind of world I was. I don't want to sound like I'm running them down, like, 'Oh, you didn't serve,' because that's not the case at all. God knows there is plenty of supply people that got killed over there, but realistically it's a different world depending on what you're actually doing."

While it is true that support personnel who do not engage in direct combat are less likely to obtain the esteemed status of warrior and may be looked upon as "pogues" (person other than grunt), it holds true for many female soldiers who found themselves in combat as well. Males experience subordination during basic training but move forward with the possibility of having their masculine identities affirmed and legitimated. On the other hand, females experience subordination starting from their entry into military service and it appears to follow many from boot camp to combat zones and back again.

Not surprisingly, female soldiers are more likely to experience PTSD from harassment or sexual assault than from combat, a diagnosis restricted by the Department of Veterans Affairs to combat until only recently. The women interviewed here are unique for their ability to perform their duties under the conditions they described. To claim sexual harassment is a murky and risky enterprise when it occurs in a male-dominated organization. Most of these women simply shrug off their experiences and move on. Some resolve their experiences through perseverance, as seen in their accounts. Some receive apologies from males who become self-aware of their abuse. Others keep it to themselves, and some even turn upon other females—masculinity is practiced by both males and females. "Black Jack" didn't report the abuse until the end of her deployment and even then she was left "out to hang" by others in her unit who also experienced the abuse. She did receive an apology from her comrades after the fact.

These women are similar to their male counterparts when it comes to reasons for not reporting the harassment they experience. Like males, they fear being stigmatized, being removed from their units, or "hindering the mission," but they also fear retaliation, which some warn may lead to further sexual assault. Research now reveals that women are said to experience the same rates of PTSD from sexual harassment as men do from combat.[13] Adding insult to injury, they know that if they complain, they may be removed from their units for their own "protection" or they may be punished or at the very least seen as "bitches" by their male comrades. Interestingly, the Department of Defense only retains paper records of substantiated reports for two years. After five years, the records are erased from the Discrimination and Sexual Harassment (DASH) database.[14]

Military sexual trauma (MST) is another subject, indeed. Congresswoman Jane Harman stated in 2008 that women who serve are "more likely to be raped by a fellow soldier than killed by enemy fire in Iraq."[15] In a 2006 survey of gender relations among active duty troops, 7 percent of females reported unwanted sexual contact at U.S. military installations. Among the 24,600 surveyed, 29 percent reported attempted rape and 21 percent reported having been raped. But among both active duty and reserve, 79 percent of this group said they did not report it because of possible retribution or being labeled as "trouble makers."[16] For female soldiers it remains a taboo subject because it essentially occurs within a "family" unit. The Pentagon reports that in 2008 approximately 3,000 women were sexually assaulted, an increase of 9 percent over the previous year; among those serving and Iraq and Afghanistan, the number rose to 25 percent.[17] For reasons similar to those reported for gender harassment, assault victims fail to report the offense, and "over twenty percent of those who do file reports opt for a 'restricted' mode that precludes official investigation."[18]

None of the women interviewed said they had been sexually assaulted, although some spoke "off the record" about incidents. They knew of stories of rape in their units. Two interviewees who chose not to have their interviews put on repository with the Library of Congress spoke openly about sexual assaults, though they did not report having been a victim of sexual assault. They were warned by other women, however, and described the practice of not drinking water after dark for fear of using the latrines and of being harassed or verbally assaulted by males in their units. They knew of instances where women who complained about discrimination then became victims of assault. These issues are discussed in greater depth by Helen Benedict in *The Lonely Soldier* (2009). Benedict describes the experiences of women soldiers in Iraq as a "private war" of harassment, abuse, and sexual violence, a common side effect of all war.[19]

The masculine military culture that presides over all branches of the military continues to perpetuate an essentialism that renders the perceived feminine (homosexual and female) "other" against a backdrop of institutionally sanctioned heterosexual manhood. This goes far in explaining why females who encounter expressed resentment choose to grin and bear it; why an NCO could joke about women and homosexuals for reportedly years before being fired for it (e.g., Captain Honors); why those who experience sexual harassment or even assault don't want to disrupt their units and be labeled troublemakers; why males who experience combat trauma don't want to be seen as weak or associated with feminine stereotyping.

Because of this, military culture must necessarily reflect on its own cultural lag or soldiers (male, female, gay, and straight) will continue to be harmed. It turns on all soldiers who are emotionally wounded by war, devalues felt emotions, and simultaneously marginalizes the feminine. As the next chapter reveals, this plays itself out in discourse surrounding PTSD, but as chapters 6 and 7 illustrate, there remains hope for those with emotional wounds of war, and potential still exists to "unlock the iron cage"[20] of masculinity for all veterans.

CHAPTER FIVE

Military Masculinity and Combat: The Perfect Storm for Post Traumatic Stress Disorder

Some events are so emotional as to leave a scar upon the cerebral tissues.
William James (1890)

Trauma and the Body

Thus far I have described a military culture with remnants of a masculinity ethos that impact not only the training of soldiers but also their service experiences. Oral histories from both male and female soldiers reveal that the gender stereotypes found in the culture at large are perpetuated in military culture, but this is unfortunate because all soldiers are harmed by these sanctioned standards. Basic training highlights this problem, but we also see evidence of it during their military service. On the other hand, these oral histories reveal that some of the emotion norms or feeling rules that are attached to traditional masculinity—being "rational, tough, indomitable, ambitious, competitive, in control, able to get a job done, and ardently heterosexual"[1]—are not realistic and may even harm soldiers both during their time in the military and on their return to civilian life. This will be addressed again as we look closer at the stigma that combat trauma carries, especially for male soldiers who seek or don't seek out mental health, but first I want to discuss what occurs to the body when it experiences trauma.

During the heated moments of reluctant edgework, felt trauma has a physiological component, and when the body is put in a position of being scared "out of its wits" the response is not bound by gender norms. To use a personal example, I was washing dishes at the kitchen sink a few years ago when my husband sneaked up on me. I didn't hear or see him coming from behind. When he reached out to touch me, he was met with a loud scream, a jump, and a slap on the face. By the time I realized it was him, I was in tears and barely able to catch my breath. He was stunned by my response. I was revved up and furious for having been scared. I calmed down after a few seconds and realized there was no real threat, but I was still angry for having been startled. What he encountered in that experience was not my thinking brain. Rather, the startle response came from my emotional brain, which reacts to stimuli at a rate that is approximately 80,000 times faster than our rational brains.[2]

Everyone can remember a moment like this. We've all had similar experiences where we found it took several minutes or longer to calm ourselves after being startled. When we experience this sensation, we are in the middle of what Daniel Goleman, the author of *Emotional Intelligence* (1995), calls the *amygdala hijack* process. Imagine being a soldier in Iraq or Afghanistan, where the amygdala gets hijacked time and time again and it is a matter of life and death.

Whereas the brain stem is often referred to as the reptilian brain that regulates basic bodily functions (blood flow, breathing), the limbic system (or survival center) rests at the top of the brain stem. It includes the hypothalamus (our body's thermostat that regulates hydration, temperature), the amygdala (storage box for basic emotions), and the hippocampus (temporal blueprint of experience, i.e., memory). This region at the top of the brain stem, sometimes called our midbrain, activates our autonomic nervous system (ANS), our body's response to stimuli and arousal. We can think of the midbrain as the information processing center or the liaison between the body and the cerebral cortex (rational brain or center for reason). It is like a bouncer at a popular night spot—nothing gets to our thinking brain without going through this process first.

In *The Body Remembers* (2000), Babette Rothschild discusses the psychophysiology of traumatic memory. "As the stress level increases," she states, "hormones may be released that suppress hippocampal activity, while the amygdala remains unaffected"[3] and can lead to the type of memory distortion in the hippocampus that is often associated with PTSD. When individuals experience a perceived threat by the amygdala, real or imagined, the autonomic nervous system (ANS) is activated. Under normal conditions, the hypothalamus activates the sympathetic nervous system (SNS) and the survival mode kicks in. Hormones are released, preparing the body for fight or flight. When neither of those is perceived as an option, the body may experience a "freeze" effect. Ideally, when this occurs, the parasympathetic branch (PNS) is activated, causing the secretion of the hormone cortisol to inhibit the alarm, a vital response to recovery from a traumatic event.[4] Our heart rates and breathing slow, and we often feel a sense of fatigue afterwards.

When soldiers speak of being exhausted after an edgework episode, they are illustrating their body's ability to produce cortisol. But recall the inability to turn off the "soldier's switch" from chapter 3. Time takes its toll on the body if this process is repeated.[5] What can happen over time is if the hippocampus is suppressed continually, the brain begins to respond as if it is under constant threat, even if the event occurred months or years before. This is because those who have experienced severe amygdala hijacking may be unable to slow the chronic state of activation of hormones by either the sympathetic or parasympathetic branches. Under these conditions, the body may vacillate among episodes of fight, flight, or freeze.

Soldiers largely remember these experiences, as First Lieutenant Doss put it, as "a whole gamut of emotions, basically being out there—adrenaline flowing one minute. The next minute you're tired, want to fall asleep, but you can't do that." The word *surreal* is often used to describe the sensations. Many remember it, as Mayfield did, as an exciting though ephemeral moment. "There was a feeling of, 'Man, that was cool!' There was exuberance and a massive adrenaline rush that was, I mean, man, I never experienced anything like that before because you were scared but never felt so alive." But as Mayfield aptly states, "You can only live with the adrenaline high for so long and then you crash. And when you crash, it is a bad crash."

Military edgework pulls the body into action, and it is only afterwards that the self interprets what the body has done. In his *Philosophy of the Act* (1938), G. H. Mead explains that one can "distinguish very definitely between the self and the body. The body can be there and can operate in a very intelligent fashion without a 'self' involved in the experience."[6] Complete absorption in combat is to be expected, and those who experience reluctant episodes of edgework *must* be able to retreat and reflect on the experience. Otherwise, they may indeed get their thermostats stuck.[7] Losing control over one's body and emotions is humiliating under any circumstance, but it is especially problematic when masculine composure is in high demand.

Army Sergeant Hurt learned during his extended tour in Iraq that each soldier responds to edgework differently. "You never really know, it's funny, stateside you hear certain people, the most blustery people in the world, I'm [going to] get over there and kick some ass and take names, and you never know who's what until you're in that situation." He recalls one soldier under his command, "always talking about how he couldn't wait to get into it, couldn't wait to get into business. First time he gets shot at, he drops down into his turret and starts crying. I'd say that's the biggest surprise—no matter what someone's personality is, no matter how tough you think they are or how weak you think they are, everybody becomes who they really are when you get into that situation. [Combat]'s not always what you think it's [going to] be. I had two different soldiers I thought would do great in Iraq, and both went AWOL during their leave [be]cause they couldn't take it anymore." Hurt explains: "People change" in combat, "but until you watch someone else die and your truck gets blown up, you can't say what you're afraid of."

For Sergeant Hurt, the most surprising thing about combat "was seeing how people were modified as people as the year went on, because you change, there's no way not to, really."

As humans, we don't just have a bodily response to trauma—we also interpret the experience through a variety of filters, including socially prescribed emotions, such as embarrassment, guilt, or shame. And it often requires emotion work to realign ourselves with the given climate. For example, one soldier recalls joking around to ease the awkwardness felt after a firefight. "A lot of the incidents, the moment they happened, they weren't funny at all. But everybody, 30–45 minutes.... Then you could start kind [of] making fun of [each other]— 'Well, you were hiding under the table.' 'Well, you were curled up like a little girl in the corner.' Well, you went screaming across the field over there.'"

Just as military edgework occurs on a continuum, if the experiences occur often enough without release or are extremely severe, the body may find itself struggling with hyperalertness or arousal. Another possibility is that the body's hormonal release gets depleted and over time stops working. As some studies reveal, severe stress can cause the hippocampus to malfunction or even atrophy, leading to memory loss and long-term synaptic changes associated with memory.[8] When this occurs, the body may experience adrenal burnout that can be masked by many things, including depression and even chronic fatigue.[9] Finally, for some who experience severe trauma, the results can lead to addiction and substance abuse and a need to either experience more adrenaline or self-medicate to calm it.

The masculine emotional orientations specific to the military (i.e., sanctioned aggression through expressed anger, shaming, deference, and domination) combine with episodes of reluctant edgework to create the perfect storm for soldiers who experience combat trauma. We label this trauma to the body a "psychological" condition (PTSD), but it has real consequences for the moral and potentially stigmatized self. Thus, PTSD is far more than a physiological/psychological condition, it is also a moral condition. Without serious attention, returning veterans will inevitably "collapse under the crippling effect of carrying the moral and spiritual burdens of a nation."[10]

Diagnostic Frames of the Signature Injuries of War

Most military service members who return from Iraq and Afghanistan won't experience the signature injuries of war, but it is important to note that the number of those who do is now at epidemic proportions. Studies estimate that approximately 20 percent of those who experience a traumatic event will develop PTSD.[11] An estimated 300,000 returning veterans are suffering from PTSD or severe depression. These rates should not be surprising given the nature of repeated and reluctant edgework conditions of combat in both Iraq and Afghanistan. In their 2007 study, *The Invisible Wounds of War*, the Rand Corporation estimated that of those deployed in both Iraq and Afghanistan, 14 percent are currently affected by PTSD while only half seek treatment,[12] prompting the U.S. Military Mental Health Task Force to claim that "without a fundamental realignment of services, this situation will worsen."[13] If we pause to consider the ripple effects of this phenomenon, it is astounding. As a nation, we will have to acknowledge, sooner or later, that in addition to those directly impacted, all of us will at some point work with or personally know someone diagnosed or yet to be diagnosed. In other words, the signature injuries of war, Traumatic Brain Injury and Post Traumatic Stress Disorder, are now America's diseases.

Traumatic Brain Injury and PTSD

In addition to PTSD, an estimated 320,000 have experienced a probable Traumatic Brain Injury (TBI) during deployment, yet 57 percent of those reported they were never evaluated by a physician for brain injury.[14] Although TBI is not a new phenomenon of war, it is certainly not a surprising finding for troops who encounter suicide bombers or drive in convoys through streets littered with improvised explosive devices. As Sergeant Lisek attests, soldiers can continue to perform their duties with their nose or ears bleeding from concussive blasts. Because more lives are saved in the current wars, the number of troops returning with neurological damage from improvised explosive devices is more pronounced. Traumatic brain injury remains underdiagnosed, in part because upper military ranks have been slow to recognize it as an injury and, reportedly, some simply don't believe it exists.[15] This may begin to change as the Army experiments with a "simple blood test" that should be able to identify mild cases of TBI.[16]

Those who experience TBI often display symptoms very similar to those associated with PTSD. But they are very different conditions. Mild traumatic brain injuries often affect the brain's frontal lobe, which in turns guides our behaviors and decision-making processes. When the brain has been traumatized in some way—for example, from a concussive blast—then simple tasks such as keeping up with a checking account, deciding what to wear, and remembering names or phone numbers become problematic. These impaired tasks can lead one to feel irritability and depression, which are then connected to diagnoses of other psychological conditions. As with PTSD, soldiers suffering from TBI may find that their relationships begin to deteriorate. Some self-medicate with alcohol or substance abuse, further masking their condition. A recent report revealed that 43 percent of troops binge drink and one in four admit to driving drunk.[17]

Dr. Gregory O'Shannock, director of the Brain Injury Association of America, describes the difference between the conditions this way: "Fundamentally PTSD is a psychological disorder where you remember too much (reliving the experience, feeling emotions of guilt and shame), whereas TBI is a (physiological) disorder where you don't remember enough."[18] Many soldiers with TBI display symptoms such as difficulty with balance and dizziness. They are likely to experience headaches, lightheadedness, or other neurological conditions that may be masked while they are deployed, because in daily military life much of one's day is already highly structured. The frontal lobe damage is not as evident. Once they are home, those close to soldiers with TBI may begin to notice slight changes in their ability to perform everyday tasks. I argue that the frustration of being unable to control the body and mind affects veterans with TBI in ways very similar to those being diagnosed with PTSD, hence the confusion in diagnosis. For both signature injuries, the ability to find continuity between the body and mind creates a moral wound and a stigmatized self.

History of Diagnosis and Stigma

In every society, illness is shaped by "cultural and moral values."[19] Similarly, the history of Post Traumatic Stress in combat is both morally and ideologically situated. In wars of the past, the labels "soldier's heart" and "battle fatigue" were used along with "hysteria" to describe those with invisible wounds. "Shell shock" in its earliest use was a precursor to the TBI diagnosis because it originally described injuries of concussive shock from explosives. Later this would become synonymous with more stigmatizing diagnoses such as "war neurosis."[20] Those who were emotionally or psychologically harmed by war but had no physical evidence of injury were often labeled cowards or malingerers.[21] Shaming was suggested by one prominent psychiatrist as a way of reestablishing courage for battle.[22] The shaming of soldiers who experienced combat trauma would provide a moral grammar, one used to mask the reality that no warrior returns from battle unharmed.

By World War I, large numbers of soldiers were returning disoriented from explosive blasts and combat trauma, but their stories soon gave way to the culturally prescribed discourse of gallantry and stoicism. British soldiers were executed for desertion if they were too traumatized to return to the front lines. The stigma of war trauma began to influence military procedures by World War II, leading military psychologists to attribute "invisible war wounds" to those they perceived as predisposed to mental illness. A large-scale screening process was implemented to weed out those who might be psychologically unfit for duty, resulting in the rejection of approximately 1 million men for service.[23] Still, the military reported high rates of "psychiatric casualties."

In 1941, American psychiatrist Abram Kardiner published *The Traumatic Neurosis of War* after working with returning soldiers from World War I for several decades. Kardiner began to establish a list of criteria that pointed to conditions of war rather than predisposed psychological disorders. By 1952, the term *gross stress reaction* became codified and made its way into the first version of the American Psychiatric Association's Diagnostic and Statistical Manual of Mental Disorders. Accordingly,

> Under conditions of great or unusual stress, a normal personality may utilize established patterns of reaction to deal with over-whelming fear.... When promptly and adequately treated, the condition may clear rapidly.... If the reaction persists, this term is to be regarded as a temporary diagnosis to be used until a more definitive diagnosis is established.... This diagnosis is justified only in situations in which the individual has been exposed to severe physical demands or extreme emotional stress, such as in combat.... In many instances, this diagnosis applies to previously more or less "normal" persons who have experienced intolerable stress.[24]

Finally, soldiers could be given a diagnosis that would potentially lead to compensation. However, by the publication of the second manual in 1968, the term *gross stress reaction* had disappeared from the DSM-II, leading many who worked with traumatized veterans to resort to diagnoses that were not combat related and thus not eligible for compensation. Soldiers returned to experiencing stigmatization and a "spoiled identity"[25] if they sought help for combat trauma. Diagnoses of character disorder implied preexisting conditions that were inherent in the soldier rather than the circumstances of war.

It would not be until long after the return of thousands of Vietnam veterans and the efforts of political action groups such as Vietnam Veterans Against the War (VVAW) that a diagnosis would be agreed upon and the unofficial "Vietnam syndrome" would give way to a psychological mental health discourse, that of Post Traumatic Stress Disorder. After complaints from thousands of Vietnam veterans that mental health professionals were still focusing on preexisting conditions such as childhood trauma, the mental health community finally stepped up to the plate and the moral grammar of war shifted from "cowardice" to "victims of military strategies," guerrilla warfare, and the insanity of war itself.

After the My Lai atrocity of March 16, 1968, the VVAW grew rapidly. Among its many political positions was the claim that brutal military policies and poor leadership had psychologically traumatized returning soldiers. Soldiers began to tell their stories of reluctant edgework in combat, of killing not just enemy soldiers but women, children, family pets, and entire villages. Soldiers recounted being forced by commanding officers to kill innocents and disregard rules of conduct. As they revealed the hell of war, Americans had no choice but to listen and try to understand how good soldiers could be caught in such webs of atrocity. Some blamed the soldiers themselves, viewing them as vicious sociopaths. Others came to understand that the image of the righteous mythic warrior is an illusion in the fog of war. The moral grammar that had held sway for generations unraveled in the public and political arena. In its place was the growing awareness that war is never a noble enterprise and that those who carry the burden of battles become victims of war themselves.

Regardless of the cultural shift and the increase of medical models to explain the wounds of war, many veterans would wait decades for acknowledgment of their suffering. Many suffered over their adult lives before acknowledgment of the effects of Agent Orange[26] and a variety of other conditions, including PTSD, would be forthcoming. Indeed, some from the Vietnam era have only recently been awarded compensation for their emotional and psychological wounds. Notions of masculinity remained a major barrier for male veterans, especially because a mental health diagnosis was still associated with "all things feminine."[27]

Finally agreed on by the mental health community and acknowledged by the Veterans Administration, PTSD made its way into the DSM-III in 1980 and the diagnosis was revised in 1987. The DSM-III-R detailed the essential feature of PTSD as a psychological disorder that develops "following a psychologically distressing event that is outside the range of usual human experience. The stressor producing this syndrome would be markedly distressing to almost anyone, and is usually experienced with intense fear, terror, and helplessness. The characteristic symptoms involve re-experiencing the traumatic event, avoidance of stimuli associated with the event or numbing of general responsiveness, and increased arousal."[28]

The latest DSM-IV-TR (2000) now defines the essential feature of PTSD as the result of experiencing, witnessing, or being "confronted with an event or events that involved actual or threatened death or serious injury, or a threat to the physical integrity of self or others. The person's response involved intense fear, helplessness, or horror." The latest description also states that traumatic events of "human design" may be more severe and last for a longer duration. Examples include being kidnapped, being taken hostage, terrorist attack, incarceration as a prisoner of war, concentration camp; some witnessed events such as the death of another because of violent assault, accident, war, disaster and the unexpected witnessing of dead bodies or body parts.[29]

To receive a diagnosis of PTSD requires that the traumatic event be reexperienced in some way, either through recurring or intrusive recollections, distressing dreams, or "reliving" the experience through illusions, hallucinations, or flashbacks. Other ways that it can be reexperienced include feeling intense psychological distress over cues that symbolize or resemble an aspect of the trauma. In addition, the person diagnosed must demonstrate persistent symptoms, such as avoidance of the stimuli associated with the trauma in three or more of the following ways: efforts to avoid thoughts, feelings, or conversations associated with the trauma; efforts to avoid activities, places, or people that arouse recollections of the trauma; inability to recall an important aspect of the trauma; markedly diminished interest or participation in significant activities; feelings of detachment or estrangement from others; restricted range of affect (e.g., unable to have loving feelings); and a sense of a foreshortened future (e.g., does not expect to have a career, marriage, children, or a normal life span).

Symptoms of PTSD are now described as (two or more) conditions that last more than one month in duration and impair one's social or occupational performance. In addition to those listed, other examples of symptoms include sleep disorders, outbursts or uncontrolled anger, irritability and/or difficulty concentrating, hypervigilance and/or exaggerated startle response, memory loss, an unrelenting "survival mode" response, depression, problems with intimacy, suicidal thoughts, revenge fantasies, and nightmares. Interestingly, the revised edition of the DSM-IV cautions practitioners to screen for those who may attempt to fake their symptoms, stating "malingering should be ruled out in those situations in which financial remuneration" is considered.[30]

Military Mental Health

According to the Army's 2006 manual, *Combat and Operational Stress Control*, an "event is considered potentially traumatic when it causes individuals or groups to experience intense feelings of terror, horror, helplessness, and/or hopelessness." Expressed "guilt, anger, sadness, and dislocation of world view or faith" are defined, as "emotional/cognitive responses to PTEs (potentially traumatic events)."[31] Enough traumatic events and expression of these responses can lead to a diagnosis of Combat Operational Stress Reaction (COSR), which then may lead to Post Traumatic Stress (PTS), and/or finally, Post Traumatic Stress Disorder (PTSD).

As part of its effort to keep "boots on the ground," the U.S. military now hosts "combat stress detachments" in Iraq and Afghanistan as part of an effort to "help soldiers cope with psychological problems and finish their deployments."[32] According to the military, this effort has been successful. The placement of mental health officials in Iraq and Afghanistan has reduced the number coming home and remaining in theater by as much as 95 percent, according to a study by the Walter Reed Army Medical Center.[33]

The intervention model has been criticized by a growing number of mental health practitioners—including the American Psychological Association, the National Association of Social Workers, and the American Psychiatric Association—who view it as "patching up" soldiers only to send them back to suffer potential further injury, mental and/or physical, and unethical by most standards.[34] Although in-field mental health responses may provide temporary help for those seeking treatment during deployment, the executive director of the Gulf War Resource Center considers the deployment of mental health during combat "a Band-Aid over a gaping wound that may need really a different kind of attention."[35] While useful to the military in keeping an all-volunteer military staffed, advocates argue it may be counterproductive, leading to an even more troubled population.

Those who serve in combat stress units admit that stigma is even more prevalent in country. For example, Army Captain DeCoster of the 113th Combat Stress Control Company in Baghdad (2006–2007), explains, "We saw it as a challenge where people don't go to mental health because you'll be, for lack of a better word, you'll be a 'pussy' if you go to mental health." Choosing not to seek treatment is like the diagnosis itself, both morally and ideologically situated. Males especially are reticent for fear of being dubbed a "pussy" by their peers. For soldiers who are physically wounded and removed from their units guilt and shame are inevitable, but, for those removed for psychological wounds, the shame is often unbearable. Research of depression among men reveals that not only is it often not tolerated, it also can lead to punishment by other men.[36] Thus, a mental health diagnosis is still associated with moral and/or psychological weakness.[37]

Army Major Taylor worried for his unit. He feels the Army has learned much from earlier wars, but he also is concerned that the stigma remains. "I can't speak on behalf of the entire Army, but we pretty much, you know, came home and Desert Storm and marched in a parade and were told to go have fun. But the Army learned a lot from that. The debriefings, the first-time home in particular, with chaplains and, and psychiatrists or psychologists—they try to identify those that we thought needed that type of stuff, we being the senior officers and noncommissioned officers of the unit. By the time we did OIF-III, in 2005 and 2006, we realized that everybody needed to be screened by a professional."

Major Taylor viewed the efforts of combat stress units as a positive move by the Army but adds, "The biggest problem is it is a male-dominated organization, the Army, you know? A lot of times males don't want to tell anybody they need help because that's a sign of weakness, in people's psyche.... So there's a lot of—long story short—a lot of people fall through the cracks because of that, at least in my opinion." Major Taylor's comments reflect the socialization into military culture that leads to self-censorship, the results, Connell suggests, of a military that combines middle-class masculinity (technological savvy and dominance) with working-class masculinity (physical prowess, endurance, and combative solidarity).[38]

While there is now widespread consensus and growing attention given to PTSD and TBI, veterans understandably remain reluctant to seek mental health services for fear leadership will retaliate or see them as weak. However, we live in an age of medication—we can take pills for most ailments, including overall malaise. Many opt for medication to help them cope and stay with their units, and apparently military doctors and psychiatrists are more than willing to accommodate. *Time* magazine reported in 2008 that military doctors were prescribing an unprecedented amount of antidepressants and sleeping pills to active duty military. The article, "America's Medicated Army," describes the overabundance of Prozac, Zoloft, and Ambien doled out to keep troops functioning. "Data contained in the Army's fifth Mental Health Advisory Team report indicate that, according to an anonymous survey of U.S. troops taken last fall, about 12% of combat troops in Iraq and 17% of those in Afghanistan are taking prescription antidepressants or sleeping pills to help them cope." The article also cites a 2005 warning from the U.S. Food and Drug Administration that adults who are being treated with antidepressants "should be watched closely for worsening of depression and for increased suicidal thinking or behavior."[39] Twenty percent of Army soldiers who committed suicide in 2007 were taking antidepressants.[40]

In addition, there is rising concern about the availability of opiates for soldiers in Iraq and especially Afghanistan, the world's largest producer of heroin. Some estimate that as many as 30,000 veterans are being treated for opiate addiction. Dr. Jodie Trafton, a VA health-care specialist in Palo Alto, California, was cited in an article by filmmaker

Shaun McCanna, who describes the availability of heroin for U.S. troops just outside the wire of Bagram Airbase, in the makeshift shops at the "Bagram Bazaar" prior to 2007. While the shops have since been raided, McCanna claims the drug is still readily available and brought to the base by runners. VA officials are starting to acknowledge opiate addictions, McCanna reports, but the problem has been slow to reveal itself. Gulf War veterans are reportedly just now being seen for heroin addiction. McCanna says, "The VA has recently seen a surge in cases from the first U.S. war in Iraq. For the first few years after a conflict, it's hard to gauge the number of soldiers who've developed a substance problem." Young soldiers are especially hesitant to seek treatment. McCanna quotes Dr. Trafton as stating "usually people don't show up for treatment till much later."[41]

Sharing of prescription drugs and abuse of over-the-counter medicine is also said to be increasing. One explanation for the rising tide of substance abuse is that the shortened amount of time between deployments does not give soldiers the opportunity to "reset" and recover before they are sent for more tours. For some, medication becomes a way of numbing out the stress of combat and the extended hypervigilance without having to be subjected to the label that accompanies a diagnosis. Soldiers admit that if they seek a diagnosis for mental health, they may be subject to shame and guilt by command. Besides, receiving a diagnosis of PTSD does not keep soldiers from being redeployed, a common practice in the military. Rather, many return for additional tours along with their prescribed meds. Others take extreme measures that result in serious consequences, adding insult to injury.

For example, when Arkansas's First Cavalry Brigade returned for a second deployment in 2008, Specialist Eric Jasinski refused to go. During his first deployment as a military analyst, his tour was extended to fifteen months. During that time, 487 soldiers in his unit were killed. Jasinski was already being treated for PTSD when he received his paycheck and learned that his Army contract was extended from February 2009 to March 2010 ("stop-loss"). When his unit was called up for a second deployment, he reported to his redeployment and stated that he was diagnosed with PTSD, was on a host of medications, and did not feel he could function in Iraq a second time. The response was that he could take his medications with him. Jasinski had been depressed, was abusing alcohol, and was self-medicating in addition to the prescribed drugs (Zoloft and Trazadone) to a point of self-destruction. He said he used the drugs in combination with alcohol to numb himself and told his mother as he sat, packed to leave for his second deployment, that he would rather die than return to Iraq. Jasinski's mother told a reporter that after witnessing her son's internal terror, she discouraged him from reporting to duty. She questions the policy of sending soldiers with PTSD back to war, stating, "There is something really wrong with the system. When you got a soldier that comes back, is diagnosed with PTSD, and you're gonna put him on drugs and they're gonna send him over there with a gun."[42]

Eric Jasinski joined the military after 9/11 declaring that "being a soldier was all I ever wanted." He lived with the knowledge of possible punishment for his AWOL that turned into "desertion" after thirty days, expecting to be caught and imprisoned for a year. When his unit returned from their second deployment, Jasinski turned himself in, reporting to Fort Hood. Jasinski faced a court-martial and spent twenty-seven days in the Bell County Jail along with a stripping of his rank. He continues to attend group therapy for his PTSD at Fort Hood Darnall Army Medical Center and is currently waiting for news of his request for medical retirement. He recently sent a letter to his lawyer, James Branum, to be shared with others. This is the full letter, verbatim:[43]

> Since entering the jail I feel my mental state is greatly declining. I do have access to my medication (zoloft, seraquil, periactim, ambien) but even my medication is beginning to have no effect. Even after taking a seraquil all day and then taking 200 mg of seraquil and ambien, I still can't fall asleep. I sleep on and off throughout the day and night and when I am in isolation mode (I suffer from severe anxiety and social isolation from chronic PTSD), I cannot get any privacy to wind myself down. The thin plastic mattress on my steel bunk makes my insomnia that much worse.

When I am taken out of jail back to Fort Hood for any appointments I am led around in handcuffs and ankle shackles in front of crowds of soldiers in the offices I am going to, which is overwhelming on my mind. My guilt from treating prisoners in Iraq sub-human and I did things to them and watched my unit do cruel actions against prisoners, so being humiliated like that forces me to fall into the dark spiral of guilt. I now know what it feels like to have no rights and have people stare and judge based on your shackles and I feel even more like a monster cause I used to do this to Iraqi people. Even worse is the fact that this boils down to the military failing to treat my PTSD but I am being punished for it when I got to the R&R center on Fort Hood on 8 April because I felt like I was entering a crisis that landed me in the mental ward, on Fort Hood for 21 days in December 2009. I was told to wait until Monday 12 April and not do anything dumb by a psychiatrist. I feel as if I am being a threat to others or myself and still the Army mental health professional blow me off just like in 2009 when I felt like I had no choice but to go AWOL, since I received a 5 minute mental evaluation and was stop-lossed despite my PTSD, and was told that they could do nothing for me. The insufficient mental evaluation from a doctor I had never seen before, combined with the insufficient actions by the doctor on 9 April show the Army is not trying to make progress. The Army is simply trying to label us as outcasts and put together useless programs for public relations just like Vietnam.

I have tried to "do the right thing" as those in the Army say and all they do in return is destroy me even more mentally and publicly say that they are going to look out for me while behind closed doors the exact opposite is happening. The Army works off of a "good ole boy" system and I have fallen out of the graces of the machine. So I have been tossed in the trash just like the brave and honorable resisters of Vietnam. The machine never stops and it never changes.

Respectfully,
Eric Jasinksi—IVAW member

The masculine ethos that soldiers internalize during training continues to play itself out regardless of rhetorical efforts from military brass to diminish the stigma.[44] Jasinski, who voluntarily turned himself in, is not the first or last to be stigmatized for his condition. Associating inability to perform in combat with shaming was brought to public awareness long before Jasinski's case. In September 2004, Sgt. Georg-Andreas Pogany was charged with cowardice. Pogany "was shipped back to the United States to face the cowardice charge, the first such case since the Vietnam War. Conviction on the charge can result in the death penalty." The charge was dropped when it was discovered that Pogany had been prescribed Larium, a drug used to fight malaria (known side effects are hallucinations and panic attacks) by his military physician. Even though the charge was dropped, the event itself sent a clear message to troops: "Don't report mental health issues." Sergeant Pogany was discouraged to ask for help because of how it might affect his career.[45] No wonder veterans are afraid to seek help—the stigmatization continues to be a barrier.[46] This concern is also echoed by Army Lt. Col. Charles Engel, of Walter Reed Medical Center, who states, "Many people are reluctant to seek specialty care. In the military setting, there's a lot of concern that if they visit specialists, it will affect their careers."[47]

A soldier discharged from the armed services for mental health has genuine cause for concern regardless of what top military officials are saying. Loss of security clearance is a fact of military life for those diagnosed. Many report that seeking mental health could damage their military careers or bring about stigmatization by leadership and fellow soldiers. One study revealed that only 23 percent to 40 percent of Marines and soldiers with PTSD actually sought out mental health treatment.[48] This may help to explain why so many military psychiatrists in the past have found themselves caught between a diagnosis and a restrictive military structure whose "mission is to 'preserve the fighting strength.' This usually means: retain men in the field....Therefore one of the important functions of the psychiatrist is to *not* diagnose, for the mental illness diagnosis is likely to result in limited duty assignment or discharge from the service."[49] The military needs to retain its voluntary fighting force but apparently, as seen in the case of Eric Jasinski, it is willing to take what it considers "damaged goods." Very few soldiers, however, take extreme measures. Instead, most who suffer from combat trauma go undiagnosed, raising important questions for the large number of troops returning from service.[50]

National Guard soldiers are considered especially vulnerable. A study by the Department of Veterans Affairs reported that 58 percent of those seeking care from Operation Iraqi Freedom and over 70 percent from Operation Enduring Freedom were not active duty soldiers but rather Guards and Reservists.[51] Ironically, this population is less likely to be referred for treatment.[52] They receive less training prior to service and are often returned to civilian life with little time for decompression, expected to pick up where they left off and get on with their "normal" lives. When they return to families, jobs, and communities, their combat trauma is invisible, and unless a soldier self-discloses his or her diagnosis, co-workers, friends, and family may be unaware and further complicate the situation for some. On the other hand, self-disclosure is a risky choice. A Veterans Affairs transition officer for returning soldiers reiterates concerns for National Guard units during an interview: "In my opinion, the Guard was just not designed to mobilize like they're mobilizing.... How can you expect that Wal-Mart stocker? You know, yes, he wanted to be a weekend warrior. He wanted to help his town if there was a tornado or a flood or something. He can sandbag. But he wasn't planning on being there to defend our country and possibly kill somebody."

National Guard units wait ninety days before receiving their post-deployment individual training (IDT), leaving them to fend for themselves if they are experiencing trauma. But efforts to gain better access to soldiers once they return are hampered by more than simply the masculine ethos and stigma; returning veterans lack knowledge of available services and military bureaucratic regulations. A mental health worker for a local VA hospital expresses frustration with the regulations: "We know there are veterans out there who do not know about the VA, who do not know how to navigate the VA. A lot of these veterans are young. The VA is sort of their father's or their grandfather's hospital, so they don't quite feel like they belong here, I guess. We know they're out there and what we want to do is find them, find some way to let them know that we're here, and let them know what the VA has to offer them.... A lot of our soldiers are Army Guard soldiers, so when they come back from deployment, then for ninety days the Guard just kind of has a hands-off policy. But after ninety days they have a debriefing scheduled, so we get on the agenda for the debriefing schedule."

Ninety days can be a lifetime for a veteran who is dealing with war trauma. A lot can happen in three months—marriages can deteriorate, road rage can escalate, sleep deprivation and depression can worsen. A VA counselor explains why it is so important to reach veterans when they first return: "Anywhere in Iraq appears to me to be, or Afghanistan, but especially Iraq, [it's] a dangerous place. IEDs make it [Iraq] a very dangerous place. They get mortared so the body just goes into that sort of hyperalert, hyperawareness. It's like a colleague of mine tells us that your thermostat gets set 'up here; most of us are down here,' and it's hard to bring that thermostat back down. We find that when they come in they're not sleeping. Also the other major thing is irritability; they're irritable. They're prone to angry outbursts, and again it's that hyperarousal, to some degree." For some, extended service or repeated tours result in a changed worldview. Sergeant Hurt echoes what so many soldiers have said upon return: "Well, I'd say I definitely became a lot more cynical for sure. I guess it's even now. I've been out of there for a year and a half. Even now, it's still a lot of stuff about daily life pisses me off. I've got a real short temper. Even now, a lot of things just, it seems like a lower level of importance. Yeah, it's important that I pay the rent on the first of every month, but to me that's a trivial thing. You know what I mean? It's kind of hard to explain, I just view things through a different lens than I did before. It's a lot harder to take trivial things and give them the importance that a lot of people do. I'm a lot more cynical, a temper, just, I think like basically the way I view the world and people and interactions with people probably changed the most."

A VA nurse who screens for possible PTSD during routine check-ups with returning soldiers explains, "I've had people that, they don't want that connection [PTSD] because they're afraid they won't be able to get a hunting license.... because they want to go back to Iraq or they are a police officer here and they are afraid that's going to affect their job, or they are afraid their family's going to think they're crazy. You know, there are lots of reasons people don't want to have a mental health diagnosis." Some become discouraged by complicated bureaucratic protocols and view the procedural obstacles as especially injurious.[53] Ironically, as more veterans return in need of services, the number of uniformed mental health workers has dropped in the last year from one counselor per 668 troops to one per 743 troops. Reports indicate that mental health workers (and other medical personnel) are leaving the military because of the strain and fatigue of caring for soldiers.[54]

PTSD in Context

In the spring of 2007, I directed a thesis project to examine the academic literature surrounding PTSD over a sixteen-year span (1990 to 2006). Graduate student Joshua Rohrich's research project entailed sampling two major academic online databases: Ebsco: Military and Government and PsycInfo (the central database for research literature in psychology and psychiatry). Keyword searches included the phrases "ptsd" or "posttraumatic stress disorder" or "post-traumatic stress disorder," which were then combined with "military" or "combat" or "soldier" or "veteran" or "war."[55] From January 1990 through January 2007, 1,077 peer-reviewed articles were published or cited in the two research engines. A sampling of the articles revealed that research discourse for PTSD fit into three broad categories, or what sociologists David Snow and Robert Benford define as discursive framing. These include *diagnostic* frames that identify a problem and its causality; *prognostic* frames that suggest possible solutions, strategies and target populations; and finally *motivational* frames that compel others to take some form of action.[56]

Initial findings from this project reveal that more research is needed. A large number of articles combined one or more frames, suggesting causes, interventions, and treatment along with a call to action. However, among those articles identified as diagnostic frames for PTSD, Rohrich found that two trends emerged. Articles attributed military PTSD either to conditions of combat or to preexisting attributes of PTSD populations. A significant number of articles of military-related PTSD did attribute causality to conditions of combat.[57] However, among those that attributed PTSD to a preexisting condition, a majority of the authors were affiliated with the Veterans Administration and the Department of Defense. This body of work focused on a diagnostic frame that continues to associate combat or military PTSD with individual attributes and/ or family of origin that predisposed them to PTSD, such as preexisting psychopathology, race, ethnicity, parental alcoholism, childhood abuse, character and/or personality traits.[58]

Sociologist Wilbur Scott explains, "When the war ends, the patriotic service remains 'priceless'—that is, it cannot be reimbursed at 'market-value,' while medical care and compensation for veterans carry specific price tags and compete for priority in limited budgets."[59] At the same time, the number of compensations for PTSD grew by 79.5 percent between 1999 and 2004 (from $1.72 billion to $4.28 billion).[60] Perhaps these numbers are what prompted a VA official to send an e-mail in 2008 discouraging VA health-care workers from "giving a diagnosis of PTSD straight out." Instead, he wrote, "Consider a diagnosis of Adjustment Disorder, R/O [rule out] PTSD."[61] Veterans' advocates describe this as an institutional effort on the part of the military to block benefits to returning veterans.[62] In addition, mental health workers within the military voice concern over the 6,000 U.S. soldiers discharged with "personality disorders" and the other 40,000 U.S. troops discharged for "misconduct." They argue that many of the conditions (e.g., substance abuse, uncontrolled anger, physical aggression) that lead to discharges are, in fact, masked symptoms of trauma and stress-related conditions of war. "Even though they have this new regulation saying they can't kick them out for personality disorders, they can still kick them out for misconduct. Everything they say, they have an escape clause."[63]

As a sociologist, I find writing about PTSD to be a moral dilemma itself. As sociologists, we are in the business of examining how social processes work in order to understand who benefits and who loses from structural arrangements. As the foregoing trajectory of a diagnostic frame for PTSD suggests, a label of cowardice gives way to a victimization discourse that lumps combat trauma with a wide variety of conditions and glosses over wide differences in experiences, leaving the body out of the discourse for the most part. Most sociologists who study traumatic memory focus upon the far-reaching effect such claims-making processes have and its consequences for both individuals and the culture at large.[64]

A specific criticism among sociologists of the diagnosis of PTSD and the rhetoric surrounding diagnosis is that it is used as an affective solidarity-building device at the expense of understanding the consequences it has for social control and the creation of stigmatized "troubled identities."[65] As a Walter Reed clinician suggests, "At some arbitrary point, stress becomes trauma, a response becomes damage, the temporary becomes enduring, and the subjective ("I feel stressed") becomes objective ("You have PTSD"). Then the power to define what's happened shifts from the person to the mental health provider."[66] Some note that the growing standardization of PTSD is a result not of disease, but of "politically charged alliances" that allow "professional associations and therapists" to build "clientele and careers" on the backs of those who are unable to fend off labels.[67] These criticisms of diagnostic trends raise important questions as to how mental health is socially constructed and spread throughout discourse.

I acknowledge that the generic terminology that groups a variety of symptoms and experiences together detaches the meaning of trauma from the context in which it occurs, but it does not negate the reality of trauma. Thus, while I agree wholeheartedly that discourse such as that provided in the diagnostic criteria glosses over distinct differences and renders the physiology of trauma silent, my aim here is to show that regardless of what they are called, the edgework conditions of combat create deep emotional wounds that require healing for many.

I, too, am troubled by the overreaching diagnosis of PTSD for returning veterans. However, my fear is that it transforms the result of military training and the conditions of war into a pathological model that focuses on the victim rather than the circumstance and prohibits discourse that incorporates the need for a new moral grammar. War is pathological, not the soldiers who experience it. The language of PTSD is itself pathological, encouraging a view of individuals who have encountered the brutality of war as somehow damaged. In other words, we treat the symptoms of war, not the causes, and we are doing a poor job of that. Is it no wonder some do refuse medication and diagnosis on return to civilian life? They want to understand their lost innocence. Returning veterans know the military is engaged in doublespeak in its own discourse surrounding PTSD and TBI—agreeing that traumatic events cause conditions, all the while stigmatizing those who seek out services. Mental health officials with the VA try to minimize this stigma, but they too realize that veterans are caught in a military culture that is predominantly masculine.

Soldiers are deemed either self-reliant heroes/antiheroes or traumatized victims.[68] In truth, it is the nature of warfare that leads to an understandable psychological response such as PTSD. The moral ambiguity that accompanies urban combat, combative solidarity, accidents, attempts to out-terrorize the terrorists, episodes of reluctant edgework, accountability from the bottom up, and unclear missions combine to unravel the warrior.[69] As Edward Tick puts it, "Modern warfare damages and destroys the youth and his character and threatens him with annihilation at the very time rites of passage are supposed to mature him in psychologically nurturing, socially useful, and spiritually enlightened ways."[70] Perhaps this explains why so many young soldiers feel older than their years.

The felt ambivalence of those who recognize the need to heal veterans but challenge the diagnostic frame is understandable. Tick points to this in his discussion of combat-related PTSD, arguing that it also has a "helpful and constructive side" if it sheds light upon the wounds of war. "If understood in its mythic context and social functions,

[PTSD] is an alarm system sounding a warning through survivors that the social order is breaking down and the savage breaking through."[71] Tick quotes the ancient poet Pindar of Thebes: "'War is sweet to those who have not tried it. The experienced man is frightened at the heart to see it advancing.'"[72]

Military Masculinity, Edgework, and Shame: The Perfect Storm

In combat, not having the "switch" on can get one killed or can lead to serious mistakes. Not being able to turn off the "switch" when danger is no longer apparent is equally problematic and can lead to judgment by others and a negative moral evaluation of oneself. The potential for dehumanization becomes very real as well. A young Army sergeant recalls during an interview, "I probably shouldn't say this [laughs], but they put him on the hood of the Humvee and drove him up to the headquarters like he was a deer, like a guy who drives a deer on a pick-up truck." Equating an insurgent to an animal hunted for sport and expressing humor in it reveals the moral and emotional wounds that force expression of combat edgework into a masculine emotional framework. As this young soldier ages and reflects on his experiences, this memory may return as trauma. Vulnerable emotions such as fear, grief, guilt, or shame are suppressed or repressed in the retelling of something that *outside of combat* would be deemed despicable and repugnant. Both psychological and psycho-physiological explanations assist us in understanding these conditions, but a sociological approach may help us to consider the deeper meanings these experiences hold for returning veterans.

Sociologist Peggy Thoits notes that the ability to demonstrate a competent identity carries with it "social rewards—reflected in self-esteem, approval, prestige, power over others, financial remuneration, and so on."[73] Soldiers are keenly aware of the military's institutional narrative that equates emotional difficulty during readjustment with weakness. In chapter 2, I argued that hazing rituals (shark attacks and getting smoked) include shaming but are understood by males especially as a proving ground for masculinity. For others, it was simply tolerated. I also argued in chapter 2 that military training requires full commitment to the soldier identity. During times of peace, soldiers may better negotiate this process. However, combat and its episodes of reluctant edgework create a deep and lasting gap between soldier and citizen, one that is difficult to bridge for some on return to civilian life.

Sociologist Arlie Hochschild explains how, like our actions, our emotions provide a signal function. How we label and interpret our feelings is influenced by previous interactions and the contexts in which they occur. Sometimes we alter our emotional expressions during interaction according to what is called for in a particular situation. Other times we resist, but there are consequences when we do. Our primary emotions are indeed biologically based. For example, when we are afraid, we may literally feel "butterflies in our stomachs" and adrenaline surges. When we are deeply sad, our hearts may truly feel physiological pain. Thus, the ability to suppress particular emotions or muster up others, what Hochschild deems "emotion work" or "deep acting," can be tentative, depending on the degree to which the body is involved.[74] Our biologically based emotional experiences are then interpreted within a moral framework of what sociologists describe as "secondary" or socially constructed emotions, those that arise from deference and social control (e.g., pride, shame, and guilt).[75]

A more phenomenological view of this effect is offered by sociologist Norman Denzin in *On Understanding Emotion* (1984). Denzin acknowledges that emotions are embodied processes that are given moral value. He identifies four categories of emotions that are not mutually exclusive: *sensible feelings* (those located in the body), which Denzin associates with biologically based experiences such as hunger or pain; *lived feelings* (not located in the body but understood as the body's unitary expression), such as fatigue, sadness, and even nausea; and *intentional value-feelings*, moral values given to both sensible and lived feelings that can be expressed to others but are seldom "perfectly felt or realized by the person."[76] Examples include feeling sorrow at a funeral or reacting in anger at an assault to self. *Self* and *moral feelings*, the final category described, can bypass bodily sensations. In other words, they need not be felt physically, nor can they be "directly produced by the person."[77] Rather, they arise out of "intentional reflection of the self as an object of consciousness—for example, shame." Denzin adds, "Moral (or spiritual) feelings encompass the totality of the person and are not given through body states, external values or sensible feelings."[78] Soldiers who experience symptoms of PTSD or TBI are vulnerable to moral feelings that lead to a loss of self dignity either through self imposed shame or labeling by others as "damaged goods."

The masculine ethos turns on male soldiers when trauma is present because it cannot be understood outside a military narrative. Intolerance for weakness among deployed soldiers remains a hallmark of military culture, regardless of policy efforts. Tick adds, "Many veterans who cannot get on with life are boy-men stuck in the psychic war zone, lost in an incomplete and horrific rite of passage."[79] Not surprisingly, many express a desire to return to military duty and a setting where their accumulated experiences and emotions are understood and accepted.

Continuity is important to our sense of self, sociologist John Hewitt explains. It "is the feeling that one's experiences of self make temporal sense" or that changes in the self can be "sensibly" accounted for.[80] Recall the discussion of the "hijacked" brain earlier. The ability to place a beginning, middle, and end on trauma can be inhibited when the body experiences severe and/or repeated trauma. Integration, on the other hand, implies that one's "activities, thoughts, and feelings fit together into some more or less coherent whole."[81]

When continuity is prohibited, either by the body's response to trauma or through a loss of identity, feelings of disconnect may become too deep to bridge. Sergeant Reinold illustrates what many veterans are saying upon return: "I feel like I don't belong outside the Army. I don't think I could function out in the civilian world. 'Cause everything makes sense here in the Army. Out there it doesn't, you got to pay your taxes and do stuff like and people get frustrated because they have to stand in line at the grocery store, or get mad because they've got a flat tire, want to commit suicide because a girl leaves them or something. They just don't realize how good they've got it, you know?"

The Shame-Anger Spiral

Sociologist Erving Goffman's attention to embarrassment reveals that, as social actors, we are all vulnerable to both esteem and disrespect from others, real or imagined.[82] Shame is similar to embarrassment in that it can be found in social situations where deference is either bestowed or withheld. In the military, rank is nonnegotiable. It determines deference. Chapter 2 revealed that early phases of military training are built on the concept of erasing old identities through a host of "degradation ceremonies."[83] Recruits are subject to repeated rituals that demean, embarrass, humiliate, and shame in order to build a soldier identity that leads to obedience to command, discipline, and the proud status of soldier. When soldiers cannot live up to the illusory warrior archetype, they often feel they've fallen short, and too often agents of social control (command, fellow soldiers) and even well-meaning social support groups (mental health, family members) allow this process to occur.

Sociologist Thomas Scheff connects micro-level emotional processes of shaming with deference, adapting Cooley's (1918) concept of the "looking glass self," the notion that our perceptions of ourselves are the result of social interaction and perceived judgments by others. Like Cooley, Scheff assumes we are always in a state of self-feeling, particularly that of pride or shame. Self-monitoring is inherent to social life. Mutual respect and solidarity lead to pride and other positive feelings. But, Scheff adds, "when there is a real and/or imagined rejection on one or both sides (withdrawal, criticism, insult, defeat, etc.), the deference-emotion system may show a malign form, a chain reaction of shame and anger between and within the interactants."[84] When shame goes unacknowledged—and Scheff argues it typically lies just below the surface of awareness—it can be a force for alienation and breakdown of social relationships. Conversely, Scheff argues, acknowledged shame can lead to healthy reconstruction of our social bonds, but when denied or repressed, it activates what he calls the "shame-anger" spiral that reveals itself through interpersonal and group interactions. According to Scheff, the process begins early in male socialization, but it occurs at individual, group, and even national levels.

In addition, Scheff explains that "overt undifferentiated" shame creates painful feelings, but the real source is hidden or unknown to an individual or group. "Bypassed shame," on the other hand, is evidenced by hyperactive behaviors that attempt to avoid painful feelings, leaving shame not only unacknowledged but often externalized as anger toward others. Embarrassment, while a more immediate reaction to a particular exchange, can lead to shame over time. Similarly, sociologist Susan Shott views shame as a particularly important indication of social control.[85] It can be seen as the label given to physiological arousal that others or the self interpret as "deficient behaviors" and/or having behaved "incompetently."[86]

Guilt, on the other hand, results from a sense of having failed to live up to moral codes. "Survivor guilt" is a significant experience for some. One veteran returned home to be married on leave and during his leave a member of his unit was killed. He cries as he tells of the death: "I wish I had been there for my unit when that happened. I should have been there." Among those who experience combat trauma, survivor guilt often combines with shame. The stronger the social bonds, the greater the vulnerability to these emotions in combat.

We all tend to avoid both shame and guilt where we can, but when we are placed in conditions where we can't escape the feelings, we internalize them or are triggered into defense mechanisms such as repression, displacement, and anger. When the object of our anger is more than we can control, we project it on to "safer" objects, such as persons of lower status. More often, though, we internalize the shame, which then takes on moral self-feeling. Indeed, a 1992 study of Vietnam veterans diagnosed with severe PTSD employed the Internalized Shame Scale (ISS) and found that internalized shame was a "central affect" of self-feelings related to PTSD.[87] An additional study found that "guilt over the death of a friend" in combat was "significantly correlated with PTSD."[88]

The paradox deepens when veterans return home. During combat, hypervigilance and anger are normalized, even encouraged. When soldiers return home, however, the very emotional expressions that became a way of dealing with combat turn on them and become a diagnostic signal for PTSD. The emotions deemed necessary for combat edgework become "embodied thoughts."[89] Sergeant Reinold recalls waking up to find his hands around his former wife's neck. "My wife would be reaching across me to get a glass of water and I'd wake up and I'd be holding on. She said I'd jump up and grab her arm and stuff and act like I was about to kill her and stare her in the eyes. And I don't remember any of this, but she'd wake up with these big bruises on her arm."

Soldiers return home with little time allotted to their own emotional and moral processing. For some, the vulnerable emotions turn on the self (e.g., depression, suicide) or lead to more extreme edgework (e.g., alcohol or substance abuse, thrill seeking); for others, it results in externalizing anger (e.g., domestic abuse, road rage, or murder). The potential for internalized shame or externalized anger is real. Once the feeling becomes entwined with adrenaline surges from experienced episodes of edgework during combat, it takes on new meaning for those experiencing it. Again, combat is visceral—the body acts and feels. Moral feelings about the body's inability to be fully in control demand release sooner or later and can contaminate relationships once the soldier is home. Symptoms of PTSD are also symptoms of internalized shame that result from the symbolic meaning that is placed upon one's physiological response to trauma and a moral interpretation of that which leads to real or imagined stigma.

As a PTSD diagnosis reveals, trauma sometimes cannot be delinked from the physiological arousal. Similarly, there is also a biological reaction to shame that is eerily similar to PTSD. In *The Shame Response to Rejection* (2005), Herbert Thomas writes that shame remains one of the most painful emotions one can experience; responses to shame vary according to the level of rejection experienced, whether it occurs unexpectedly, and whether others have witnessed the shaming. Like Scheff, Thomas views anger as the "shame response" but addresses the physiological/neurological aspects as well, stating that the shame response "acts as a traumatic event, a wounding as it is located, or stored, in a specific area of the brain," the same process as that associated with PTSD. "When stimulated by an additional increment of pain, the energy stored in this area can be automatically and rapidly discharged."[90] Babette Rothschild also addresses this issue: "Many who have suffered trauma feel much guilt and shame for freezing or 'going dead' and not doing more to protect themselves or others by fighting back or running away."[91] Understanding the physiological response is the beginning of "self-forgiveness," Rothschild argues. Psychologist David McMillan adds to this argument, describing shame as the "most difficult of our emotions to manage. Too little creates meanness and sociopathic behavior. Too much creates self-hatred and poisonous, blaming, projective defenses."[92]

Soldiers experience shame not only when they feel they have not lived up to the warrior ideal and/or are stigmatized by command or fellow soldiers —they also are shamed. When society is apathetic or understates their trauma by placing it within a constraining discourse, we lose the overall understanding of what constitutes war trauma, and the result is cultural ambivalence or possibly even cultural amnesia, as I posited in the introduction. In *Waking the Tiger* (1997) Levine and Frederick discuss the "cowboy logic" that those who experience trauma must contend with—one of denial accompanied by comments like, "Pull yourself together," or "Grin and bear it. It's time to get on with your life."[93]

As illustrated earlier, well-meaning mental health officials are constrained by medical models that don't get to the moral symbolism that trauma holds for its victims. Yet as Levine and others argue, although physicians and mental health workers don't speak about the moral conditions of trauma, they work with these conditions continually. As one VA mental health counselor describes it, "I've had veterans tell me that they feel like they've lost God, they've lost their innocence in some way." After serving two tours in Iraq, Army Major Taylor describes his own moral struggles. "I'm a Christian" he says, "and sometimes there are things that go through your mind, that you ask yourself, 'Am I? Am I [a Christian]?' You know, 'Is this okay? Is this morally right?'"

For some, the warrior myth unravels completely. Sergeant George didn't renew his contract. He didn't talk about war. He even withheld from others the fact that he had served three tours in Afghanistan. He simply wanted to forget. He viewed his commitment to the Army as a "relationship" but lost faith in both the war and the media as time went on. "The warrior ethos," he now believes, "is this collection of ideas and principles that they try to instill, but in all reality the training regime that we go through is designed to turn people into sociopaths, to disregard human life with a complete lack of empathetic understanding of the enemy, their culture, the language, food, clothes—why they greet each other the way they do. You know, we're not taught any of that. We're just taught to kill the people, but we weren't really told why we needed to kill them or taught to have pity or mercy or understand exactly who is on the other side of that weapon. So if you're just killing somebody to kill them, that *is* sociopathic behavior. But this government doesn't want warriors. They want soldiers and people that will follow orders."

Rites of Passage and the Journey Home

As the stories of veterans throughout this book show, some hold mental health professionals suspect and prefer talking to empathic others or chaplains to help them heal the deep emotional burdens that accompany them home from war. Some seek solace in religion, others in substance abuse, some turn against the military all together. What they all share, however, is the weight of combat and a deep knowing that they can never be the person their friends and families sent off to war.

I borrowed from anthropologist Victor Turner in my earlier discussion of the symbolic importance of rituals and rites of passage when I described the transformation that occurs in basic training. In traditional societies, rituals of significant import provided warriors with purification rites of passage on their return, to welcome them home and back into community.

Over the past years, talking with veterans has taught me that such rites of passage cannot occur in today's military culture. Too much is at stake, whether it be an institutional acknowledgment of the policies that send soldiers back into battle after being diagnosed with trauma, an admission of the fundamental incongruence of rigid rules of conduct imposed upon a military that is fighting guerrilla warfare, or a revamping of the military rites of passage that emphasize traditional masculinity. All this is too deeply embedded in military culture to expect healing within its own institutional structure. The services provided are greatly needed, but our veterans are in desperate need of rituals and rites of passage that cleanse the moral and deep emotional scars of combat. It is up to us to honor these veterans by creating within our communities, outside the margins of military life, deeply symbolic rites of passage, if we are to heal our nation's wounds of war.

Such rituals need not glorify or render any particular war "just" or "unjust," but they must honor the veterans who fought them. In the next chapter I introduce a program called Vets Journey Home, a nonprofit organization that has developed a deep rite of passage for veterans of all wars, one that provides a safe container for healing the broad range of emotional wounds that soldiers bring home and welcomes the act of telling of one's story to other veterans who can truly understand and contribute to the soldier's journey home.

CHAPTER SIX

History of Vets Journey Home

C hristan Kramer received his orders for Vietnam in 1967 at the
age of 17, just weeks away from his eighteenth birthday, and went
straight from the eleventh grade to basic training. While the war
was heating up in Vietnam, he was "freezing his butt off" in Kentucky
at Jungle Training. Before he left for 'Nam, Christan had a short leave
and returned in January 1968 to say goodbye to friends. He would have
five months in Vietnam before they graduated from high school. Most
replied with, "Oh, you're going to Vietnam? Cool! See you when you
get back. Hey, look at my new car! Hey, did you know me and Suzie are
dating?" He made the mistake of stopping off to visit his sister who lived
in the Haight Ashbury district of San Francisco, not exactly a welcoming
community for soldiers about to head off to war.

General Westmoreland had just come back to the States to tell
Congress things were "looking good." Meanwhile, the Tet Offensive
was about to begin (January 1968). Christan left for Vietnam on a commercial plane but had a quick stop in Hawaii, just long enough for him
and the other soldiers to take in the beauty of the islands and feel the
weight of war looming over their young shoulders. They were no more
than an hour into their flight to Vietnam when the flight commander
announced, "I've good news and bad news. The good news is today you
are not going to V-F-Nam! More good news—today will count as part of

139

your tour." Christan remembers the cheers and then the overwhelming silence that followed. "Now, gentlemen—the bad news. We're going to Clark Airbase in the Philippines and we're gonna put you on a military transport because Tan-Son-Nhut Airbase (near Saigon) is under siege and we can't land a commercial plane." However, they could land a C-130 military plane. "We came in hot," Christan remembers. The back door of the plane opened as it slowed and the soldiers were directed to grab "any duffle bag and run out of the plane to the nearest bunker." As they descended from the plane without weapons, jackets, or helmets, Christan was confronted not only with the chaos of combat, but with war's deepest and darkest emblem. "As I'm getting off the plane, listening to the explosions and small arms fire, the first thing I see is a row of body bags. I've got to run past a row of body bags to get to the bunker! Welcome to sunny Vietnam!" he remembers thinking to himself as he took in the unique smells of Vietnam, the humidity combined with rotting garbage and smoke, a sensory memory so many veterans share.

Sent to Long Bihn, waiting for his duty assignment, Christan was stunned by the presence of locals who worked on the post during the day. There was a common perception among the young soldiers, already on high alert, that many of the locals were the same people who shot at them at night. Some worked in the kitchen and laundry, others did cleaning on the base, but there was the constant question, "Is this the same person that was dropping mortars on us last night? Are they coming here for intelligence gathering?" Like those who serve in Iraq and Afghanistan, soldiers in Vietnam could not discern between "enemy" and "friendly." The black patches worn by many of the locals signaled they had lost a loved one, only increasing the overall concerns of soldiers. "Were they grieving for the enemy?"

Christan had been on base all of four days when he witnessed the first attack. Some North Vietnamese soldiers, or "Charlie," had penetrated the base and blew up an ammunition supply. He remembers the constant flares in the air, the "surreal" yellowish-orange lights that lit up the perimeter and cast shadows over the barbed wire to illuminate the 20 feet or so of cleared jungle outside the wire. Red flares, he remembers, meant "pucker factor," often combined with the constant roar from the gunships with their orange tracers. The building he was in literally shook as the sky lit up with flares and machine gun fire reminiscent of strobe lights. Still waiting for his duty assignment, Christan had not been issued a weapon, and now the 18-year-old soldier came to an understanding—he was "expendable." He remembers thinking, "Man, I'm not going to make it to eighteen and half."

By the end of his tour, Christan had served ten days short of two years to get an "early out" but explains, "A lot of my tour I don't even want to remember." He stayed in 'Nam in the hopes it would keep his brother, already stationed in Okinawa, out of the fog of war, but it didn't work—his brother was sent to Vietnam as well. Besides guard duty in his combat engineer company, Christan often had to drive outside the wire on engineering missions on the dirt-packed roads, fully exposed. His job was to go out to the forward operating bases in the jungle to inspect equipment, dozers, belly scrapers, and flat tires and build bunkers, military compounds, or villages. He remembers the bizarre experience of being shot at by snipers from the jungle, which was "close enough you could spit and hit a tree" while driving. And he remembers only too well the hypervigilance that accompanied him throughout his tour. He is still haunted by the images he saw as he drove through small villages with bodies piled on the side of the road, not sure if they were enemy or friendly, but it didn't matter—because the carnage of war would be burned into his memory for life.

Returning from Vietnam was not the homecoming he had hoped it would be. He stopped off to see his sister in San Francisco on his way home to "Milwaukee, the city that made beer famous," where he was still not old enough to go into a bar. "I know some guys talk about it and fabricate it," he explains of his experience in San Francisco, "but I was literally spit on and called baby killer, which hurt.... That's my reward for staying an extra year? Trying to keep my brother out and stuff, and I'm rewarded by that kind of a greeting?" When Christan arrived home, he returned to the same friends and family who greeted him with the same indifference as when he left. "Hey, have you been out west? You're really tanned," and "Hey, guess what, I married Suzie." The combination of leaving his fellow soldiers behind, the nightmares, the hypervigilance, and returning to friends who had gone on with their lives oblivious to what was happening in Vietnam led Christan to begin isolating himself. He started living on the edge, self-medicating with drugs, alcohol, and motorcycles. He didn't have a death wish, he remembers, but he was still at war. It was a private war with the demons who accompanied him home from too many months in Vietnam. He could not simply wish the flashbacks and nightmares away—something had to give.

On November 17, 1970, Christan Kramer woke up, rolled out of bed, and made a decision to live again. He stopped drinking and using drugs and sought treatment for his invisible war wounds. He was tired of self-medicating to cover his wounded soul. He wanted to help other veterans, but it would be almost two decades of experimenting with self-help groups before Christan would find a program that could be applied to veterans. Vietnam veterans were still falling through the cracks of the VA and soldiers were suffering from PTSD, depression, and substance abuse.

In 1987, Christan met Patricia Clason, co-founder and director of the Center for Creative Learning in Milwaukee. Patricia and her business partner Jay Edgar have been doing personal growth work with groups for decades, guided by principles of Gestalt therapy, experiential group work, psychodrama, and rational-emotive approaches long before the term "emotional intelligence" became popular.[1]

Christan enrolled in one of Patricia's Taking It Lightly weekend retreats. Although the curriculum was not designed specifically for veterans, it was an extraordinary healing experience for Christan and he realized Patricia's approach to group work could be applied to a weekend designed specifically for Vietnam veterans.[2] After several years of training and working as a senior instructor with Patricia through the Center for Creative Learning, Christan and Patricia established the Bridge Foundation, a nonprofit foundation to support Bamboo Bridge, an offshoot of the Taking It Lightly workshop but tailored specifically for combat veterans.

Patricia Clason is a civilian but grew up in a military family. Her father was an Army master sergeant who served in World War II and Korea as a medic. When I asked Patricia what prompted her to want to work with veterans, she explained that, like me, she too lived with the ghosts of war when she was growing up. She remembers going with her father to the local Veterans of Foreign Wars post for many gatherings, holidays, and "just hanging out." She especially remembers Memorial Days, because "the men would also be fall-down drunk by the end of the day, sitting around telling war stories." As a child, she made the flowers and wreaths that were put on the graves on Memorial Day. Her boyfriend in high school went off to Vietnam and she remembers, "He came back a different person." She lost another veteran friend to suicide when he returned.

Patricia lived in Milwaukee in 1967 when riots broke out and the National Guard was called in. She remembers, "The tanks went up and down our street. I remember sitting on the steps with my dad watching the National Guard convoy and having him say to me 'I pray to God this is the closest you ever get to war.'" Her father was a "proud man who carried a lot of pain but didn't talk about his military experience" with her. Patricia used to listen to "stories late at night when he sat around with his friends. I remember my uncle talking about how dad 'hit the ground' when the fireworks went off." Thus, extending the work she was already doing with her Taking It Lightly retreats to include veteran-only groups was an easy choice for Patricia. She knew intimately the trauma both experienced and caused by veterans who have not healed the invisible wounds of war. In 1993, Patricia and Christan began facilitating Bamboo Bridge weekends for combat veterans. The program continues today but has changed its name to include veterans from all wars, male or female, combat or noncombat.

The torch was passed to fellow Vietnam veteran, Gene McMahon, in 2005 and the program was renamed "Vets Journey Home." Gene served two tours in the Navy, patrolling the Cua Viet River in the demilitarized zone (DMZ). Gene, like so many veterans, carried the invisible wounds of war home with him. Like Christan, for Gene there were no "welcome home" ceremonies or parades, and he similarly kept his military service to himself for years. Gene writes, "For over thirty years I never spoke of my experiences and feelings about Viet Nam. I was a closet veteran. In early 1998 I met a Viet Nam veteran, a US Army ranger, Al Fletcher (Capt, USA retired) and he told me about the Bamboo Bridge, a weekend program helping Viet Nam veterans with their emotional wounds from being in combat. As he spoke, tears came to my eyes and I finally realized that I had been holding onto a lot of grief and anger over the years from my service back in the late 60's. It was time for me to see if there was a way to acknowledge and release them, to finally stand proud and tall to be a Viet Nam veteran." He adds, "It was not an easy decision for me because there was a part of me that wanted to 'let sleeping dogs lie.' I offered my small retreat center as a place where we could hold the first east coast Bamboo Bridge. Thanks to Christan Kramer and Patricia Clason (co-founders of the Bamboo Bridge), Al Fletcher, Bud Leazenby, and Jeff DuVall, I finally got my chance to be welcomed home and be honored for having served in the military for the first time in my life."[3]

Vets Journey Home can be described as a self-help program or personal growth retreat but it is distinct in its mission to heal veterans from the wounds of war with the aid of other veterans. Within the self-help community there are various social networks; crossover between programs and philosophies are easily found. This has been the case for Vets Journey Home and the popular ManKind Project (MKP) and New Warrior Training Adventure (NWTA). It is no coincidence that the work done by Patricia Clason and Christan Kramer paralleled that of other self-help groups during the same period. For example, both Christan and Gene are graduates of MKP and both have been involved with groups associated with the men's movement.[4] Patricia is known to many as the "grandmother" of NWTA, which is affiliated with MKP. There are only a few degrees of separation between the seeds of this movement and Bamboo Bridge, given their therapeutic focus on accountability, emotional healing, and their roots within the movement community, but the healing modalities and therapeutic models differ in important and significant ways.

Both Christan and Patricia explain that one of the most important distinctions between such programs and the structure of Vets Journey Home is one of confrontation versus gentility. When I asked for further clarification, Patricia shared an e-mail correspondence from a Taking It Lightly graduate who wrote about the distinctions between it (the instructional blueprint for Vets Journey Home) and programs such as MKP or Women Within (the female counterpart to MKP). The reader, she explains, could easily replace the title Taking It Lightly with Vets Journey Home. I took the liberty to do so and with her permission reproduce the correspondence here.

I was asked by several people to talk about the differences between these programs. I replied that the programs are complementary. It is important to work on men's or women's issues within these gender specific programs. However, the greatest benefit I received from working with VJH has been the opportunity to work on my issues that cross gender lines. It has been an opportunity to emotionally experience women/men at the very deep level of emotional being that I've come to expect out of life, where I am interacting daily with both genders....

The nature of NWTA or WW, as men or women only weekends, does not provide the opportunity to learn with the other gender at a deep emotional level. VJH is an opportunity to work on emotional issues at a deep level with in a safe, gender-neutral context. Also, VJH does not rely on a mythopoetic or archetypal story. VJH heals in real time, with ordinary consciousness. It does not rely on trance and ritual to effect change. As a result, participants are left with the gloriousness of having achieved change and growth for themselves, rather than the experience of having something "done" to them, as in an initiation performed by a group. Both experiences have value and have their place in the healing process.... For some people it is important to do their work in a same sex group first. For others, it is not.[5]

A significant amount of sociological criticism has been rightly aimed at popular men's groups that challenge the traditional masculinity ethos for falling short of the mark. As sociologist Michael Schwalbe aptly states in *Unlocking the Iron Cage* (1996),[6] the causes of emotional grief for males in American culture are not "mysterious," as the popular men's movement icon Robert Bly argues. Rather, men suffer because "of the actions of other men."[7] What I have learned from both male and female soldiers confirms this. The biological essentialism that drives the ideology of exclusionary groups hampers serious consideration of male privilege as it impacts on women.[8] Both respectful and critical of the men for their overgeneralizations from personal experience, Schwalbe writes, "The men seemed to believe that if *they* didn't have power over women, if *they* didn't feel like powerful patriarchs, and if *they* didn't seem to have privileges relative to women, then all the feminist clamoring about men's power was wrong or exaggerated."[9]

From conversations with numerous MKP participants, it appears that Schwalbe's criticism is fair in so far as well-intended "warriors" push and shove their way with highly confrontational "guts work" that celebrates yet another form of masculinity. Fortunately, this is not the case with Vets Journey Home. The term *warrior* is seldom spoken and when it is, it refers to soldiers of all branches, male and female.

One link between Vets Journey Home and programs such as the MKP is that both models draw from and modify the earlier models of existential encounter groups. However, whereas men's groups are more likely to draw on offshoots of Jungian psychology and mythology to confirm their masculinities, Vets Journey Home draws on a hybrid of other healing modalities, such as rational-emotive therapy, emotional intelligence, and psychodrama.[10] Some who lead the weekends are informed by their understanding of the "shadow work" of self-help icons such as Cliff Barry but do not impose this framework on the program for veterans.

Thus, while I have never heard a VJH staff member criticize these programs—quite the contrary, many facilitate MKP or WW retreats— the differences cannot be overstated. Moreover, confrontational "guts work" can traumatize or retraumatize an individual. In the case of those who have been diagnosed with PTSD or TBI, the results can be lethal. Without a student-led orientation (i.e., allowing the participant to choose from a variety of role-play scenarios) in a nurturing and gender-neutral setting (possibly excepting veterans who have experienced sexual trauma) that is absent ideological dogma, Vets Journey Home would fall short of its goal to heal veterans from the emotional wounds they bring back from war. Unlike the other programs, which are very costly, VJH is free to any veteran who wants to attend. This is an important distinction and one that minimizes class bias and the exclusion of potentially large numbers of veterans. The gender-neutral approach also ensures that women are not marginalized for serving in support roles. Finally, there is a strict nonpolitical stance toward any war or administration. These are the characteristics that render the program so effective and appealing to all veterans.

VJH weekends take place in several locations throughout the United States and are taught by a community of veterans and veterans' advocates. They are specifically designed to include civilians as well and are staffed by volunteers. On their website (http://vetsjourneyhome.org), the program is described as a "large community of volunteers, both veteran and civilian, who desire to serve those who served our country, by offering this compassionate and welcoming retreat, where any story is heard without judgment."

Instructors for Vets Journey Home are not therapists or counselors per se, although some do have professional credentials in therapy and counseling. They are certified instructors who have attended personal growth programs and have been trained as facilitators for the course. While therapists often refer clients to VJH to help those who are "stuck" or not making progress, the curriculum is designed to complement, not replace, one-on-one therapy and/or group counseling. This is made clear both to participants and the therapists who refer veterans to the program.

Perhaps the most significant aspect of the program is that from the time they arrive at the welcome reception until they say their goodbyes at graduation, veterans are told continuously by the staff of volunteers (veterans and civilian) that they have come to staff the weekend in order to honor them for their military service and that this is *their* weekend, *their* welcome home! And as many veterans have shared, it is the first true welcome home they have received.

In the next chapter, I describe what transpires during a Vets Journey Home workshop by reconstructing three specific VJH weekends: a retreat in the early winter of 2010 for veterans and their spouses (a new addition to the VJH program); a weekend in the late summer of 2010, primarily made up of veterans who experienced military sexual trauma (MST); and finally, more typical for VJH, a weekend in the fall of 2010 that included veterans with a wide range of experiences.

CHAPTER SEVEN

"Welcome Home"

Anyone who says that Houston never gets hit with frigid weather has never heard the phrase "Blue Norther." The wind howls outside our rustic meeting room on the Gordon Ranch outside Houston. After a few greetings, the meeting starts around 10 a.m. once the staff members have arrived. It is Friday and the instructors, Patricia and Carl, along with David, our supervisor, are about to assign staff members with duties and discuss the logistics for the weekend. I'm told by several members of the all-volunteer staff, "Get ready, it's going to be powerful." It's my first time to staff a VJH weekend and I'm feeling anxious.

Rituals are built into the program at every turn. The meeting opens with a "blessing," a Native American prayer, given by the designated "elder" for the weekend. Notebooks are passed out to the staff. Inside each notebook are the program, a list of what to do and not to do, a mission statement, "agreements," and job duties. For example, my duty assignment for this weekend is to be facilities assistant; my job is to help keep the meeting room clean and ensure that bathrooms and water supplies are kept stocked. Next, we do a check-in, starting with David and moving clockwise around the circle. Each person is asked to say something brief about why they are here and provide a "feeling state." For example, "I'm David and I'm the supervisor this weekend and I'm here to serve Carl and Patricia and make sure they get what they need to have a smooth-running program. I'm excited and honored to be here to serve these veterans and their spouses. I'm feeling like a lot of good work is going to be done this weekend. I'm feeling blessed to be here, but I'm also feeling anxious about it because it is our first VJH with spouses. And I'm in!"[1]

After check-in, the meeting gets down to business quickly and we are reminded by Carl and Patricia to keep our focus on the participants this weekend. Because we will possibly be asked by a veteran or a spouse to participate in a role-playing exercise during the emotional process work tomorrow, Carl tells us that if we find that we are "not comfortable with the requests," we are given permission to state, "I am not available to do that." During the staff meeting, boundaries are set. Patricia adds in a serious tone, "We are not here to do our own work." Each volunteer is told to choose a buddy for the weekend "because we need to know where you are and if you have emotional processing to do, you may need to excuse yourself, but you will want to tell your buddy so that someone always knows where you are."

Specific phrases are repeated throughout the staff meeting, such as "I'm in," "intentionality," "hold the energy," and "pray into the process." They are used to create both an emotional and a spiritual focus on the participants ("students"). The aim for the weekend, we are told, is to provide a safe container for the veterans and their spouses to come and tell their stories, to experience emotional process work, and possibly role-play around the issues that they have come to work on. Next, we are briefed on each veteran attending, such as branch of service and where he or she served. On this weekend there will be veterans attending who served in Vietnam, Bosnia, and Iraq. "The students will guide us," Patricia explains. When I look puzzled, she adds, "The process work tomorrow will reveal itself through the students." We are reminded again not to intervene during process work. The more seasoned volunteers nod in affirmation.

Next, staff members are given the opportunity to volunteer to be a mentor for a specific veteran, someone who will ensure that a veteran is supported throughout the weekend. The job is to quietly observe the emotional process work done by the assigned "mentee" and provide affirmation and positive feedback at the end of the program.[2] On this weekend, everyone will be a mentor because the ratio of volunteer to student is equal. Groups are usually capped at ten, which means there can be as many as twenty-five individuals present on a given weekend.

After a short lunch break, we begin setting up the meeting room. Each weekend is designed similarly. Folding chairs are placed in a large circle, flags are put on the wall—OIF/OEF, United We Stand, POW and it begins to look like a meeting lodge for veterans. A camouflage uniform hangs over a window. Some of us are assigned to make posters reading, "Welcome Home," "We Support Our Troops," and "Thank You for Your Service." There is a celebratory atmosphere as we prepare for tonight's reception, when the veterans and their wives will arrive. Music plays in the background and there is laughter and joking among the staff. I think of a patriotic homecoming party minus the military brass band. But the mood shifts as the reception nears. Other posters are placed on the wall near Patricia and Carl's seats with phrases or lists of words that the instructors will refer to throughout the course of the weekend. For example, one that is referred to several times reads, "The mind believes what it sees, then sees what it believes."

At each VJH weekend a table is set up for "sacred objects." I watch as staff members place objects on it prior to the arrival of participants, who have also been encouraged to bring something sacred to them. I am struck by the photographs of loved ones, fallen soldiers, flags with signatures, medals, old love letters, family photos, and other memorabilia. In the center of the table rests a framed poster of the Vietnam Wall by artist Lee Teeter. In the photograph, a man leans forward with one hand against the wall. In the reflection are ghostly images of soldiers reaching out toward the man who appears to be grieving the fallen soldiers. An American flag sits next to the poster, folded in military fashion. The room feels especially somber to me now as individuals quietly place their items and walk away. The seriousness of the weekend begins to sink in.

As evening nears, greeters are assigned to welcome participants as they enter and finish up any last minute paperwork. Participants and volunteers are milling about the coffee and refreshments. The atmosphere is light with greetings, handshakes, laughter, and lighthearted conversation, along with several awkward moments of silence. It appears everyone is eager to get started.

At the start of each weekend, an empty chair is placed in the front. "This chair is put here for all the veterans who are not here tonight."[3] After the participants are seated, Patricia and Carl welcome them and ask permission from the veterans for the staff to be seated. Charlie, one of the staff members, walks over to the door and sits facing the group with his chair propped against the doors that lead into to the building. His duty is to be "door guard." Charlie could easily pass for a bouncer at a bar; he is a rather large and intimidating presence. The room is quiet for a moment and then Patricia explains that Charlie is there to "make sure nobody who is not part of the weekend is allowed into the room" and to "protect and make it a safe place for all." The ritual of guarding the door is highly symbolic, reminding veterans that "their six is covered."

A version of "I Get By with a Little Help from My Friends" plays softly in the background as we settle into our seats. Staff members introduce themselves in one or two sentences, such as, "I am here because I am the son of a Vietnam veteran and I came this weekend to serve you in any way that I can and honor you for having served our country." The veterans on staff include their branch of service along with where and when they served. Some reveal that they have attended a previous VJH and have come back to serve as staff. A few of the veterans appear more at ease hearing this.

After the staff and instructors have introduced themselves, attention turns to the participants. Carl speaks first. "Each one of you, whether combat or not, deserve to be here. You signed on the dotted line," he tells them, then shares a story about a veteran who attended a previous VJH weekend. The veteran had questioned his role as "just a mail clerk" but was assured by another veteran in attendance that getting mail was the most important thing for him and it provided him with a lifeline. Carl uses this story to assure everyone, regardless of their military service, that they deserve to be honored and welcomed home. Next, Patricia reads the "agreements" aloud and everyone is asked to raise their hand, staff included. Items on the list include, "I agree not to use alcohol or other substances during the weekend," "I agree to let a staff member know if I need to leave the building," and "I agree to honor confidentiality of others attending this weekend." After the agreements are read, Patricia continues, "Now we'd like to hear from you. Tell us a little bit about who you are and why you are here."

Responses vary from group to group but often include statements such as, "I came for more peace," "I'm here to learn how to cope with my anger since I got back," or "I've had trouble sleeping since I got home and I'm here to learn how to cope better." Others might tell something about their service experience. The instructors are also looking for feeling states from the participants at this point. One of the wives at Houston offered, "I'm here because I feel broken inside. I'm feeling a lot of apprehension." When participants respond with vague responses such as "I'm fine," Patricia probes deeper. After several participants introduced themselves as "doing fine," Patricia interjects, "I just want to mention to the group that sometimes when people say that they are fine, they are really feeling Fucked up, Insecure, Neurotic, and Empty.[4] So we discourage 'fine' because we want participants to be honest and clear about their feelings."

The evening opens with the topic of movies, prompting participants to think about how they live out the "movies" of their lives. Patricia starts the evening saying that early experiences in our lives get inside us as messages according to whether they are pleasurable or painful. Some are conscious messages, but most of the earlier life messages are subconscious. An example is used of a toddler chasing a bouncing ball into the street. The child's mother comes running out and grabs the child by the shoulders, shaking her, saying, "Don't you ever do that again!" As a toddler, Patricia explains, we are not likely to look up at our stern mother, her face contorted with fear, and think, "Oh, Mommy thank you for saving me!" Several laugh at the notion of any toddler having such a rational thought. She adds that what we are more likely to do is to make a subconscious decision that "fun is not okay" or that "when we play, something will go wrong."

Experiences that occur early on in our lives, she explains, are like scenes in a movie. They can later become beliefs that filter the rest of our experiences. Hence the saying, "The mind believes what it sees, then sees what it believes," Patricia continues, adding that emotionally charged experiences from our pasts begin to shape our expectations; thus, the goal of the program this weekend is to "support you in being 100 percent response-able for the movies you play." She then refers the group to possible movies we've created over time. Using a variety of anecdotal stories, she draws on the analogy, "When I do X, Y happens." For example, "When I get close to someone, they leave or die," a theme repeated often among combat veterans. Once the expectations are there, "we search for proof of that in our interactions with others."

Although we are not 100 percent responsible for what happens in our lives, Patricia continues, we are response-able for how we respond to what occurs in life. Sometimes we "wind up creating the results ourselves" or "mistake what is happening with what we expected to happen." Next, she asks participants to be thinking about a title for their movies and to reflect on how they watch their own movies play out in their lives. Do they sleep through them, eat through them, self-medicate, or simply "put up" with them?

Carl then steps up to list four primary emotions. He writes the words *mad, sad, afraid,* and *glad* on the poster. The design of the program is taking shape. They are teasing out participants' value judgments and beliefs about emotions and how those become messages we've internalized. The "emotional intelligence" framework is employed to foster thinking about emotional dysfunction and our ability to respond appropriately to our emotions. Carl asks the participants to help him rate these emotional states as either positive or negative. He places a plus or minus symbol next to each term, then adds, "Maybe as a child we learn it's not okay to be mad, or it's not safe to be sad, or maybe it is not okay to be afraid or, in some cases, even show an emotion." As I listen to Carl, I am reminded of the "soldier's switch" and the idea that emotions can and should be shut off in military training.

Carl prompts participants to offer their input. A Vietnam veteran in the group offers, "Boys don't cry." Another veteran says, "Men can't be afraid." Another offers, "Can't show emotions." After some discussion of the stereotypical rules about emotions, Carl begins to challenge these assumptions, adding, "Ever known someone who never gets angry, is always happy? What about someone who can't grieve?" Going down the list, he begins to provide a plus and minus sign for each feeling state. "Ever known someone who is never afraid or someone who is always trying to make you happy?" Several groan, apparently annoyed at the thought of such an encounter.

Next, Carl flips the poster paper and begins to draw a series of mountains. Adding some humor, he makes them snow capped and draws a few birds flying above them. We can't help but laugh at his crude sketch. These stereotypical perceptions, he continues, are "our values, beliefs or filters that impact our expectations." Next Carl draws a stream flowing down the center of the mountains. "The stream," he explains, "represents our emotions." He adds, "Our beliefs are rules that we put in place or are placed upon us and then become real to us." Rather than using academic jargon to discuss the alienating potential that accompanies "emotion norms," a topic I would have digressed into, accompanied with a boring lecture about institutional oppression, gender, and status, Carl equates these "filters" with boulders that dam up our felt emotions and cause them to build up internal pressure or leak out at inappropriate times. Patricia interjects, "And they can become land mines. And throughout life we get triggers that cause them to go off."[5]

Our felt emotions become "misplaced," "misdirected" or "buried," Carl explains. "How do you remove big boulders?" His rhetorical question is followed with, "You need help, don't you? These are big boulders and we need tools to move these because we can't do it on our own." Turning back to the participants, Carl says, "This weekend, the Vets Journey Home, we'll learn some tools to help you begin to remove these boulders. When we apply value judgments to our own feelings, we are obstructing the flowing stream of emotions." Patricia now asks the group, "What are your land mines or your triggers?"

When someone speaks up, Patricia listens attentively, restating what each person has said. A wife of a Vietnam veteran offers, "When he just shuts down." Another adds, "Mine is isolation, feeling rejected, abandoned." Another says, "When he breaks my trust." Patricia pauses, then asks the men for some response. "Drugs and being told what to do all the time, demanding." Others add, "I go ballistic," and "I feel helpless or hopeless, like I can't do anything to fix the situation."

As the evening continues, participants begin to open up and describe their movies, giving them titles such as "Abandoned," "Numb," "Age of Destruction," "Broken Dreams," and "Don't Rock the Boat." The discussion follows the design, which is to nudge individuals to acknowledge how they feel about the lives they currently live and become mindful of the choices they make. Other activities are built into the first evening to include rapport building and open communication among participants. During my first observation I'm astonished how quickly group cohesion develops, having gone from awkward silence and small talk to the sharing of deep feelings. Veterans are talking to other veterans about experiences and perceptions they have. Wives are hugging one another, a few of the men have hugged, and some have cried as they tell brief snippets of their war experiences. The evening ends with both staff and participants standing in a large circle. After a song is played softly and a brief blessing is provided from the designated elder, we adjourn for the evening.

Again, the pedagogy that drives the Friday evening activities is grounded in "emotional intelligence" or EQ, as it's sometimes called. The basic premise of EQ is that we are not always capable of distinguishing our emotions from our cognition unless we apply conscious thought to the process. Another premise is that our felt emotions are not inherently positive or negative but are rather tied to our psycho-physiological processes as "energy in motion." The goal of VJH instructors is to get veterans to think about how they respond to their feeling states. Based on this premise, when the analytical mind is engaged individuals can arrive at an optimum solution to felt emotional arousal.[6] Becoming mindful of the "movies" we play allows us to contemplate change.

Saturday morning begins early with a staff meeting in the bunkhouse. During check-in, staff share they are both "anxious" and "excited" about the day ahead. I'm anxious as well and so is my "buddy," a journalist from California who is also attending for the first time. We console one another about the pace of the weekend and our inability to break away and take notes. We also share quietly our felt apprehension because we have both heard from seasoned volunteers that today, "The rocket takes off!"

The morning begins with a blessing from the elder. Once in a circle, we hear a song about a veteran who has returned from war without a welcome home ("the day the band forgot to play"). Music is an integral part of the weekend, often used at the opening or the closing of an activity. It sets the mood for the day, reminding us all that war wounds the heart. An opening story is used to prompt the group to think about what happens when we run away from the things we most fear. The story goes: Lions have a unique way of hunting, one that seems counterintuitive at first. The female lions chase the prey, while the old male lion with the loudest roar waits, positioning himself so that when the prey runs away from the female lions they are unknowingly running toward the old lion. The toothless old lion greets the prey with a loud roar. Some freeze and others turn around, running straight into the pride of females waiting to catch them for a meal. Those who jump past the lion can escape peril. Carl follows the story by saying, "Today we encourage you to run into the roar. It is only a memory."

What follows is the storytelling phase that occurs on the Saturday of each program, during which the emotional process work is experienced. Participants are asked to check in with feeling states and the program shifts into group work, where a combination of Gestalt and psychodrama techniques are employed as veterans and their partners begin to share their stories one by one. Gestalt is a technique used in group therapy that includes focusing on one person's story while others serve as observers of the process or are drawn into role-play of some sort around a particular event or feeling that person is experiencing. Psychodrama is added to the mix as individuals are asked to perform a role after sharing their experience. VJH instructors will often offer a variety of role-play options to the individual or ask if they have a sense of how they would like to resolve a real-life situation they've encountered. Again, the purpose for using this technique in VJH is not to be confrontational (which can lead to retraumatizing) but rather to challenge individuals to move just beyond their comfort zone and to imagine a different ending to a memory or feeling that has them stuck emotionally.

While the program designs are consistent on each weekend, the stories shared by participants reflect the wide array of emotional wounds veterans carry—and in the case of the couples' weekend, their spouses as well. In the following sections I describe three VJH weekends: Houston (couple's retreat), Milwaukee (veterans and sexual trauma), and Mt. Airy, Maryland, just outside of Baltimore (combat veterans).

Houston

Saturday: After a break for lunch, the emotional wear and tear seems evident as I scan the group. Several of the veterans have shared their stories already and the wives especially look weary. There is a long hesitation when we return to the circle. Patricia asks for volunteers, but no one speaks. Rose, one of the participants, says she will do it but wants someone else to go first. Patricia turns to Julie, one of the staff members, and asks if she would like to share with the group what she is feeling. Julie and John, the couple who coordinated the event for the weekend, have been married since John returned from Vietnam. John has suffered from PTSD and was diagnosed a few years back. During staff check-in earlier in the day, Julie shared that her observations of the other wives on Friday night had touched her deeply. "I felt they were speaking my truth and I was drawn into the process." John, her husband, has attended and staffed many VJH weekends, but they have never done emotional process work together as a couple, she explains. Julie tells the wives they "touched her heart" the evening before and made her feel that she is "not alone as a wife of a vet with PTSD." She never got the opportunity to say what she would have liked to hear from John when he returned from war, referring to an exercise that took place on Friday evening between the veterans and their spouses. Patricia asks if she would like to have the opportunity now. "Yes," Julie says.

Two chairs are brought into the circle. Carl is standing to the left of Julie's chair, just behind her. Patricia stands to Julie's right and John's left, approximately midway between them. Their chairs are positioned the same way as the previous evening, with knees touching, and they are directed to face each other. Julie immediately leans forward and takes John's hands. Crying now, she tells him, "When you came home, your dreams became my dreams. I loved you that much. What I would have liked to hear from you was simply, 'Thank you. Thank you for waiting.'"

John is silent but begins breathing heavily, apparently trying to maintain his composure. Julie tells John that she still is haunted by holes punched in walls that she then would cover by hanging pictures. "There were so many holes to cover and so much pain." At this point, John begins to sob heavily and appears to be trying to catch his breath. Patricia gestures a staff member to come into the circle. It's David, the son of Julie and John, and he had been standing behind an empty chair watching the process unfold. David walks into the circle and places a hand gently on each of their shoulders. The image comes to mind of a loving parent, looking down at two children who have hurt each other, eager to see them forgive each other. It takes on even more meaning as Julie continues to share painful memories. David looks concerned for both his parents but later tells me that painful memories were stirred while listening to his mom. Growing up in a home with a father who suffered from PTSD was difficult for everyone.

John is now sobbing uncontrollably. David shifts to stand behind his father with his hand almost touching his father's back. Julie cries as she talks of being choked, of "walking on eggshells" when John would go into a blind rage. "I gave up my dreams and you were not the person I married when you returned." The other wives are crying heavily, nodding in agreement with Julie as she speaks. John tries to respond several times but chokes on his words and sobs more heavily. His body is shaking violently. As I look around the room, everyone is crying, including the staff. David and John remain silent and listen intently while Julie recalls the horrific memories of living with John's demons. Carl looks to David, moving his lips, and David nods, turning to his father, "Dad, what would you like to say to Mom?" Between sobs, John is able to say, "I am so sorry. I am so sorry that I hurt you and the children." He repeats, "I am so sorry." Finally, Julie grips John's hands close to her chest and says, "I love you and I will never leave you." She smiles and chuckles, adding, "We are old now and can relax." John smiles widely, tears still flowing, and they kiss.

At this point I look to David, who is wiping tears from his eyes but keeping his focus on his parents. He tells his father, "I am proud of you." Patricia speaks to the other couples, cautioning them to remember that when their partner shares their pain and what they lost, the other partner should not take on guilt and shame but rather listen and accept that this is "their truth." "Welcome home to your heart," she says to Julie and thanks John for allowing her to speak her truth. They hug each other and kiss once more as the room erupts in deep sighs and clapping. Staff members are looking at each other and smiling, exchanging hugs, and I feel as if I have peered into the window of a family that has lived with PTSD, but I have also witnessed an extremely powerful catharsis as well. There is a look of relief on both Julie and John's faces. David will later tell me he volunteers to staff for VJH weekends every opportunity he gets. "Dad's healing has been my healing as well," he explains.

I glance to my left and see that "Charlie," the door guard, is crying heavily but smiling. Charlie's father, also a staff member, is sitting just in front of Charlie. He stands, turns, and the two embrace. Charlie brought his father Tex to a VJH weekend a few years earlier. Now they come together to act as staff when the events are held in their area. Charlie was severely abused by his father as a child, but their love for each other now is palpable. "It's been a long journey," Charlie explains after years of living with his dad's demons. "Dad wouldn't be here if it weren't for VJH." Throughout the weekend, I watch as Charlie carefully tends to Tex, whose health is deteriorating. They hug often throughout the weekend, a testament to the power of forgiveness.

When we return from a short break, Rose is ready to share her story and tells the group that she too has been looking forward to the weekend. Wives are often left out of the healing process, she says, because "we aren't government issued," she says. "When Paul left for the war, he was my 'knight in shining armor,' but it disappeared when he came home. Paul was different when he returned." Having no family support, Rose was often forced to rely upon her mother-in-law, who treated her badly. She said she often felt dismissed by Paul and his mother, and her self-esteem bottomed out. "He was a different man," she says once more. She had "nowhere to turn" except to an aunt who lived several miles away. When she had all she could take with Paul, she would have to call her mother-in-law to take her to her aunt's house.

Rose begins to sob as she recalls "running away" from Paul's temper and treatment of her. She turns to Julie, "Oh yes, and we had the holes in the wall, too. I kept running away but had no support networks, so I always came back." She goes on: "There was never a place for my emotions because it wasn't about me. It was always about him, about the family, the children. We were poor, but I didn't mind. I fell into the role, nothing coming from anywhere. There were no solutions." As she continues, Paul lowers his head and closes his eyes.

Rose is tearful as she tells the group that she finally gave up one day and took her husband's pistol into the back yard. She remembers shaking as she tried to figure out how to use the gun. She wanted to shoot a hole into the wooden fence to see how big the hole would be so that she knew that when she pulled the trigger it would work. Several of the veterans in the room nod to one another as if they know the scenario well. "The gun was jammed, so I walked into the house and asked Paul to fix it." When he asked her what she needed it for, Rose responded, "Just fix the damn gun!" A fight erupted and somehow, as she describes it, Paul pushed her against the wall and broke her breastbone. "I've never felt such pain in my life," she tells the group. Paul then picked her up and carried her to the bedroom and threw her on the bed. "I thought I was going to die. I couldn't catch my breath." Rose is sobbing now. "And the only person I could call for help was my mother-in-law. How sick is that?" she tells the group, repeating, "How sick is that?"

"Rose, what are you feeling?" Patricia asks softly. "I'm feeling angry. I am angry for what we had and lost," Rose responds. "I am angry at my government for letting Paul down, for letting us down. I am angry at

God for letting this happen to us. I am angry that I had to take on the responsibility of his [Paul's] disease and he let me." Patricia probes after a short pause. "And I feel guilty for leaving my children, running away and leaving them with Paul. I was always, always running. I remember feeling like I wasn't important enough to bother with. We could not get rid of it, the PTSD. It didn't have a start and it didn't have an end. I wanted to run, I was just running, I needed to get away. We had a monster in the house." Rose looks down at the floor with her hands out, as if counting with her fingers. "We had it all, we had the road rage, we had no money, we had no sex life. It even affected how we disciplined the children."

Patricia: "So you are feeling angry, like you had no safe place to go, no way to have your voice, your needs met?" Rose nods, "Now I have triggers. I'm older and I'm tired, and the government doesn't support Paul or me. When you heal a veteran, you have only done half of the work. Until you heal the whole family, you're not done. In the end, that's all you have. All you have is your family and God." Carl adds, "Rose, what outcome would you like to place on this for you?" Patricia: "Would you like to say something to those who have hurt you?" "Where would I begin?" Rose chuckles. "Let's start with who you are angry with. We've got Paul, God, the government, your mother-in-law, who else?" Rose says, "Okay and I'm angry at my lost dreams."

At this point Patricia has Rose solicit participants to role-play government, God, mother-in-law, Paul, and her lost dreams. Patricia and Carl are in front of her now and the role players are lining up. They move back to stand to both sides. Carl notices that Paul is having a difficult time and directs David to stand beside him. Paul is beginning to slump in his chair and is crying now. T. J., the weekend's elder, is asked to play God and there is some laughter as he says, "Good choice." Patricia begins speaking softly to Rose, coaching her with words she might say to each role player. Rose is soft spoken and uncomfortable raising her voice, but Patricia continues, urging her say what she is angry about to each person. When Rose is directed to face "God," she backs away. "Oh, I could never be angry at God." Patricia: "Oh, yes you can! What did Christ say hanging on the cross? God, why hast thou forsaken me!" "That's true," Rose replies. "God, why did you forget about me? Why did you let me suffer so much?"

When Rose gets to the last character in the role-play exercise, it is her husband Paul. Carl steps in to assist her, but Rose's feet give out from under her and she is assisted to the floor. As he watches Rose fall into the arms of both Carl and Patricia, who hold her and then help her to the floor, Paul appears distraught. Patricia is now lying beside Rose on the floor with her arms around her, encouraging her to "let it go." "That's right, let it out," she tells Rose. She gently rocks Rose with her hands tightly around her waist. Other staff members bring jackets or sweaters to help cover Rose.

Lying together on their sides and rocking elicits the image of a mother holding and reassuring a child who has had a nightmare. There is a sweetness to the scene. Rose moans and the tears and sobs come in waves now. Patricia gently pats her on the back, saying, "That's okay baby, let it out." Another wave hits and Patricia encourages her to continue. "We are staying here as long as it takes." I look to my right and see that two of the male staff members are now positioning themselves behind Paul. Because of his health (Paul takes thirteen medications a day), there may be cause for concern if he collapses in his chair. Paul is now rocking back and forth in the chair that is too small for his large frame. I move to place my right hand on his shoulder, feeling sadness that he has to witness Rose's process. Paul maintains his balance and rocks, eyes closed and mouth tightly clenched. Paul was in an ambush in Vietnam and he is one of only two survivors. "We had them right where we wanted them," he had told the group, "right above us." Paul suffers from PTSD and was only recently diagnosed, after forty years of "hell," Rose tells me.

The room quiets and Rose and Patricia remain on the floor together. Eloise, one of the other wives, is gently rubbing Rose's forehead and Carol, another one, is at her feet. Three women have now silently kneeled down over Rose, smiling, and Rose begins to smile. I hear Patricia ask Rose if she can come up with a color to help her remember what she is feeling. She chooses turquoise. When Rose is able to stand, she is directed to a chair and both Carl and Patricia say that hugs can be offered by staff and participants. One by one, they approach her, asking, "May I share a hug with you?" After the process work is completed, Rose smiles and thanks everyone. Later she tells me, "I didn't know I had so much [pain] to let out."

After a break, Caleb, a veteran diagnosed with PTSD and TBI, speaks up. I am surprised when the soft-spoken young man tells the group he has "anger issues" that he can't control and that his "wife is afraid" of him. He tells the group that he was in Iraq and offers that he also has short-term memory loss that resulted from an IED that hit his Humvee. "I am not an emotional person, but sometimes I have trouble with—I get angry a lot." Patricia probes further. "I don't trust people. I hate people who are fake." Patricia probes to see if his thoughts are related to his service in Iraq and he confirms that they are. Caleb tells of encountering children while on patrol and then learning that he could not trust them. "It's like I don't know who the enemy is," Caleb adds, as if he is still at war. "There are so many selfish people. My wife, I have a love/hate relationship with her." Patricia interjects, "How long have you been married?" "Three years, and it's hard. The VA gives me drugs, but they make me numb." When Caleb returned to Iraq, "We got hit by multiple IEDs and there was a lot of religious stuff." While he talks, I am reminded of the many interviews with veterans who said the same thing. Caleb returns to his feelings again: "I get angry when people call me an alcoholic, my wife and my family. I drink a lot but I'm not an alcoholic. I don't like getting bossed around by my wife. Since the war, I can't express what I feel or what she needs. I have a problem with rage where I hurt people around me. My mom and dad don't want to meet my biological dad." Patricia probes. Caleb has a volatile relationship with his parents and has only recently met his biological father, but his mother and stepfather do not approve. "My stepfather is a preacher. My mom says I was a mistake. I was a lot of trouble when I was a kid. I can't blame them."

Patricia and Carl look at one another and Patricia turns to Caleb and asks him to look into her eyes. "You were not a mistake. Caleb, do you hear me? Look around this room. Everyone here [pointing around the circle while looking at Caleb] wants you to know that you were not a mistake." Several participants and staff members nod and repeat Patricia's statement, "Caleb, you are not a mistake!" Caleb continues, "I get angry. [Caleb's wife is nodding her head in agreement] I don't like being reminded all the time what I did wrong." Carl probes Caleb for some of the triggers for his rage. He responds, "Being told what to do, so many selfish people, crowds, traffic." "What would you like to get out of this process?" Carl asks. "What can we, what can this group offer you?" "I'd like to be able to communicate without it getting out of hand. I'd like to live again—feel things, express what I'm feeling." Carl repeats what Caleb says and adds, "You would like to not feel like your emotions are being dismissed." Caleb nods. Carl pauses for a few seconds and says, "I have an idea. Actually I have two ideas that we can offer. I'll tell you both and you can choose. We could offer you the opportunity to be born into a family of parents that love and support you, that want you, that don't see you as a mistake. Or we could provide you with role-playing and the opportunity to shout it out to those who have hurt you and you can tell them what they have done and what you need from them." Caleb quickly opts for the rebirth exercise.

He is asked to choose his old parents and his new parents. He asks Rose and Paul to role-play his mother and stepfather. He then asks John and Julie to play the role of his new parents. Carl and Patricia ask staff to prepare for the exercise. Patricia whispers something to Charlie; he exits the building and comes back a few minutes later with a mattress from the bunkhouse. Meanwhile, a staff member gets a prop from somewhere, a lamp that clamps to a chair, and positions it at the end of the mattress, near where Julie and John are placed. The staff members that are not participating in the exercise are asked to move to the end of the room behind Julie and John and to cheer Caleb on as he "leaves his old parents and is born into a family that loves and supports him."

I'm struck when several of the participants spontaneously get up and join the staff members. At this point, Carl says to Caleb, "Now this is important to the birth. We need to ask you: Do you want an easy birth, a medium birth, or a difficult birth? These people who are making your tunnel [six staff members are now bent over the mattress forming a human canopy over the bed], they need to know what you need from them." Caleb, now positioned in front of Paul and Rose where he will enter the birthing tunnel, responds, "Medium." "Okay, we make it a medium birth." Carl is looking at the staff bent over the mattress and they nod knowingly.

The lights are turned off and the lamp is turned on, reminiscent of a hospital birthing room. Those behind Julie and John are prompted to start cheering for Caleb. John and Julie start cheering him on as well. "Come to us, Caleb. We love you. You can do this!" Meanwhile Patricia stands beside Caleb and encourages him to talk to his current parents. Paul and Rose are instructed to role-play, saying, "You were a mistake. You should never have been born. We've done all this for you and now you want to betray us and go to him? How could you do this to us?" They repeat the same statements at Patricia's prompting, getting louder and louder each time.

Caleb is silent and Patricia instructs him to say, "I am not a mistake." Caleb's head is down and his stance is submissive. He speaks softly, "I am not a mistake," but Patricia presses him to say it louder. "Say it like you mean it!" she says more loudly this time. Then she models for him by screaming at Paul and Rose, "You're wrong! I am not a mistake!" She places her hand in the middle of Caleb's back and urges him to speak from his diaphragm, touching a spot near the top of his stomach. Caleb's body stiffens. His fists are clinched now and he is shaking. Standing next to Caleb, Patricia continues shouting at the old parents when suddenly Caleb roars, "I am not a mistake! You're wrong!" Patricia smiles and says, "That was great, Caleb. Now hurry, you can be reborn to parents that love you. Go! Hurry!" she says, pointing to John and Julie.

Caleb turns away from Paul and Rose, who are now silent. He drops to his knees and begins to crawl through the human tunnel with mild resistance from the staff members. Carl and Patricia begin shouting, "You can do it, Caleb! Look who is waiting for you!" The room is thunderous with shouts and cheers and Julie catches my eye, motioning for me to sit beside Caleb's wife, who is sobbing and appears troubled by the scene. I sit beside her and she whispers in my ear, "His parents have really hurt him." Then she is silent. Another staff member puts her hand on Jennifer's shoulder in support. Caleb comes through the tunnel and falls into the arms of John and Julie. Julie quickly pulls his head up to her chest and his body on to her lap. Both Julie and John hug Caleb and begin soothing him. "Oh, what a beautiful boy. We are so glad you are here. We love you. We are so glad you arrived." This is repeated as the room quiets. Caleb's body is stiff. He stares straight ahead for a few seconds, then relaxes into Julie's arms. Julie and John continue soothing him. Patricia motions for the room to quiet and there is silence except the soft-spoken affirmations from Caleb's "new" parents. Patricia tells Charlie to keep the lights off and allow Caleb "to soak up all this love."

Again, tears are shed throughout the room. Some staff members are whispering to one another and deep sighs are heard as everyone releases their intense emotions. I leave the room after Caleb de-roles with Rose and Paul and retreat from the building to gain my footing yet again. Caleb tells me the next day before the graduation ceremony that it was the most powerful experience he's ever had.

Milwaukee

By the time I attended the Milwaukee Vets Journey Home in August 2010, I had staffed three VJH weekends in both Houston and Maryland. In the spring I attended a trauma training seminar for practitioners outside Washington, D.C., and was beginning to think more about the relationship between PTSD and traumatic memory. I had just read Babette Rothschild's book, *The Body Remembers* (2000), along with Peter Levine's *Healing Trauma* (2005), and was especially grateful to have these readings under my belt when I arrived in Milwaukee. This VJH weekend was held for eight veterans, seven of whom had experienced military sexual trauma and all of whom had been diagnosed with PTSD.

As I stated earlier, military sexual trauma is especially painful because it is similar in some ways to incest when it occurs in a military "family." "Whoopie" (the name I gave this veteran for her strong resemblance to actress Whoopie Goldberg) served in the military in the late 1970s through the mid-1980s. She's been seeing a counselor for several years and was referred to VJH by her therapist. When she arrived at the Friday evening reception, she was especially reserved, though she didn't hesitate to tell the instructors, half jokingly, that she might "bolt any minute" and if she did, to "stay out my way." Her VJH "welcome home" was one of the most powerful welcome home rituals I've witnessed to date. As she later explained, "I've waited twenty-eight years to tell my side of the story." This weekend, she would be able to tell it to other veterans.

Stationed overseas in 1976, she recalls the day she met with her first sergeant. "I do not believe women belong in the Army, let alone military police," he told her, and "he meant it." Her job duty assignment as his secretary would have serious consequences. After several months, she befriended the first sergeant's wife, who confided in Whoopie that her husband was violent and abused her. She encouraged her friend several times to leave the abusive relationship, and finally "she took my advice and left and he was out for revenge." From then on, the harassment worsened. Whoopie's jovial demeanor begins to fade as she tells the story. She pauses for several minutes before she reaches back to her memories of the rape that resulted in the birth of her first child. "It started with small things at first," she remembers, "Pay check irregularities, eggs on windshields, flat tires" and more "verbal abuse" by her first sergeant.

"Every other Friday night a group of us would go to the NCO club, about the only thing to do on a Friday night," she chuckles. One evening she went with a group of fellow MPs, one of whom was a "poker buddy" of the first sergeant, and she suspects, one of the rapists. "Someone slipped something into my drink and the next thing I remember is waking up in the bachelors' quarters, being carried down the hall by two MPs, like a side of beef." Looking toward the ceiling, Whoopie continues, "I put sanity on hold for a while."

When she returned to the States, she was three months pregnant from the rape and was not sure who or how many had raped her. She couldn't report it to her first sergeant but did tell a social worker what had happened when she returned. The social worker tried to advocate for her, knowing it would be an uphill battle after three months and no physical evidence. When the social worker was fired, Whoopie sank into a deep depression. She felt alone again, tormented that she could not identify the rapist, or rapists more likely, and she regretted not going to the police, but "then again, the rapists were military police," she says with more than a little sarcasm.

After the social worker was fired, she checked herself into psychiatric evaluation on base, severely depressed. When she returned to base, Whoopie was six months pregnant and the same sergeant was now stateside and was her supervisor again. He gave a PT (physical training) test and she failed it. "I was six months pregnant and couldn't run two miles," she says, shaking her head and laughing. She wound up receiving an Article 15 from the first sergeant after she returned from maternity leave and "nothing ever came of" the rape. "So when you ask me about my service? No, I definitely did not get a welcome home. But I'm glad to finally tell my side of the story. Been there, done that, been screwed by the system. But today I can say I've forgiven them," adding that she does it not for them, but "for myself."

Whoopie's black hair is streaked with white and silver, revealing her years. Now a grandmother, she walks with a slight stoop and the help of a cane. When she has finished sharing her story, she smiles as she looks out above the round spectacles resting low on her nose and takes a deep breath, as if she has just finished reading a long bedtime story. I can't help but imagine how difficult it must be for her and her fellow participants to tell their stories of sexual abuse to a room full of veterans, mostly males, and more important, their own military "family."

Many of the participants during the day engage in role-playing to confront their rapists with empowering and dramatic scenes. Each individual is coached and provided with options for how they might engage the perpetrators and what they might say if they could go back in time and take back what was lost. Some choose "scenes" that involve kicking with props and pillows. Others choose to shout the perpetrator out of the room and take back their lost souls. As each role-play continues throughout the day, I am struck by the depth of support the veterans provide one another, both staff and participants. It is as if they are coming together for a family intervention against their military "brothers" who have harmed one of their own.

As the day comes to close, Whoopie is the last to share her story. Any objectivity I might have had as a researcher before this experience leaves me as I witness a ritual transpire that is both sacred and speaks to the depth of bonds between veterans. It unfolds as if it were planned months in advance. After she has finished, veterans in the room stand up and begin to form a single-file procession before her as if they had practiced for this ceremony many times. The image transforms immediately from that of a world-weary woman to that of a queen at her throne, flanked by two female staff members, one of whom is an art therapist and later tells me she has been working with Whoopie for some time on this very issue. She came to staff as a volunteer hoping to witness some closure for her friend.

Male veterans, perhaps a dozen, stand at attention in line. One by one they approach her, salute her, and bend down in front of her on one knee. Some take her hand, others remain at salute. Each of the men approach her tearfully, voices cracking as they try to maintain a formal military posture in front of her. They apologize, one after another, "on behalf of the U.S. military," some adding, "I would be proud to serve beside you," saluting her again. She receives each one, smiling through her tears and nods in acceptance of their apology as the procession continues. A Vietnam veteran on staff later tells me that he was especially troubled because Whoopie's rape happened on his "watch." He was still in the military when the rape occurred. The room is still now, minus the weeping of the other participants, no doubt moved by such a formal apology from their brothers in arms. By the end of the procession, Whoopie is rocking back and forth in her chair, crying and clapping her hands together quietly. She smiles wide and says, "I feel like I am home." I am frozen in my seat, awestruck by the support given by veterans to veterans and I try to imagine rituals like this occurring on a military base or within a group of soldiers at a VA hospital. "They can't," I think to myself. "This has to occur outside the military's sphere of influence" and, as this weekend reveals, in spite of it.

Mt. Airy, Maryland

What strikes me each time I attend a Vets Journey Home weekend is the bond between veterans that forms so quickly. The process seems especially remarkable among combat veterans, perhaps because their emotional wounds are so similar. Among Vietnam veterans, now in their mid-sixties, and Iraq and Afghanistan veterans, many still in their twenties, age difference seems to disappear as they open up to their fellow brothers in arms. Veterans voice a sense of relief in learning that others have been in combat. This may contribute to their instant connection to one another, which is often striking given their differences in age, rank, service, and political views.

On Friday evenings, veterans are asked to tell other vets what it is they would have liked to hear when they returned from service. One of the most common responses, especially for Vietnam vets, is "Welcome home," and "Thank you for your sacrifice." On a recent weekend, I was struck by some of the younger veterans who said they had wanted to hear, "Peace is on its way," "I understand," "We'll be here for you," "Wholeness is coming." I learned on this weekend that Iraq and Afghanistan veterans are exhausted from multiple tours and some feel "used up" by the military.

On Saturday, as veterans are asked to share their stories, Mark (named for his bushy eyebrows that remind me of Mark Twain), a Vietnam veteran, offers to go first. He is ripe to talk about his combat experiences. As he speaks, I realize that for Mark, Vietnam may as well have happened last year. His memories are fresh, his emotions raw. He enrolled for the weekend on the VJH website after hearing about it only weeks earlier through a friend who knew Gene, one of the weekend's instructors. I was not surprised to learn that Mark was only recently diagnosed with service-related PTSD from Vietnam. I have heard this from several Vietnam vets who found their trauma from war resurfaced after the United States went to war in Afghanistan and Iraq. This was equally true for Mark, but in his case the diagnosis has double meaning.

Mark is a clinical psychologist who has been working with clients for forty years while struggling privately with his own demons from war. He shares the humiliation that accompanied the letter he received just a month ago. "When I got the letter last month, I freaked out because it said 100 percent service-connected PTSD and I thought to myself, 'You're really messed up.'" Working in mental health for so long and then being labeled by his peers "just makes it worse," Mark tells the group. As he talks, I am reminded of research reports that I have read regarding vicarious trauma among military mental health personnel. I can't help but ponder the connection here. On the other hand, perhaps helping others with PTSD has helped Mark to function as long as he has.

Mark joined the Army after realizing that he could not gain his father's respect even after earning a graduate degree in clinical psychology. "I always thought I had to be smarter because my father liked smart people but even that didn't work." Because his father served in World War II, Mark is sure now that he suffered from undiagnosed trauma as well. Mark still struggles to forgive his father for the physical abuse he endured as his mother often looked the other way. He suspects the emotional disapproval caused him to need acceptance from his father even more.

Mark's sad eyes are piercing through his wire-rimmed glasses with magnified lens. His eyebrows, black as coal, stand out in contrast to his long gray hair. I think to myself, "It's as if his body has aged, but his eyebrows didn't, or perhaps they signal to the onlooker that Mark is young at heart." As Mark begins to share his story, his emotions surface immediately, something I have noticed among older male veterans, who seem more willing to violate the stereotypical norm, "Men don't cry." Mark begins by telling the group that he was "not a patriot" in the traditional sense because he tried to leave the Army when he realized he was "fucked up" was up but was told "No, you know too much." As far as Mark was concerned, his commander only had it half right: he "had seen too much," but his mental health credentials kept him in theater and his request was not approved. Instead, his commander punished him and sent him out as a medic, flying Tomahawks daily in and out of fire support. "It was watching these guys maimed and dead," Mark begins but stops abruptly. Tears flow freely and he struggles to continue. "Man, it was really fucked up, really fucked up," he says, looking around the room. "And when I returned, I took the fucking to another level. I did every kind of drug you could think of. You name it, I did it. I was paranoid. I hated the fucking government. It was bullshit, man." He continues as if to answer an anticipated question, "It was from watching these guys, man." I notice Mark is crying heavily now and pressing two fingers to his forehead as if to provide pressure to a wound somewhere in his mind. Gene notices his body language and asks, "Mark what's the image you are holding right now?" Mark moans, eyes closed, as if he is witnessing something horrific in present time. "It was watching these guys, man. It was so fucked up." Gene: "Is that your nightmare?" Mark: "Yeah, one of them." Gene probes further: "What is the image?" Mark puts his hands over his face, leaning forward in his chair, "It was watching them come through the wire [Vietcong soldiers], blown up in the fucking wire. We'd be shooting and they would just keep coming through the wire, limbs missing, still crawling. What the fuck, man?" Mark yells as if asking the soldiers he is seeing in his mind. "I couldn't acknowledge they were human. I couldn't. I couldn't acknowledge their courage." Gene, "So you disrespected them?" Mark, "I had to! They were gooks! I couldn't acknowledge them as human, but they just kept coming even when we were blowing them up. Fuck!"

The room is silent except for Mark's heavy breathing. Gene whispers something to his co-instructor, then turns to Mark: "I've got a hit. We know there are good soldiers on both sides of war, aren't there?" he says rhetorically. "Al Fletcher [Gene's mentor and an early champion of VJH] always used to say, 'It's important to remember there is someone on both ends of the rifle.' It sounds like you thought these soldiers had courage and honor, but you couldn't recognize them as human or you couldn't do your job. Is that right?" Mark nods, adding, "I couldn't! I couldn't see them as human!" Gene nods in agreement, "Yeah, that's war, isn't it?" Veterans around the room are nodding in agreement and Gene continues, offering a role-play scenario, "Mark, what do you think, how would it make you feel if you could get some forgiveness from these brave soldiers?" Mark, "Yeah, I would like that."

Gene asks Mark to choose two people in the room to play the role of the maimed soldiers crawling through the wire, but Mark quickly turns and walks out of the circle, sobbing and shaking his head, saying, "I can't. I can't do this." Gene walks over and stands beside him with one hand on his shoulder. He asks for permission to choose two people on his behalf and Mark agrees. Two staff members are asked to play the role of the men. They are both veterans. Another staff member goes to a large chest at the side of the room and pulls out two items that serve as props for rifles. Both of the men are instructed to position themselves on the floor. Mark is still standing with his back to the men as they begin to inch forward on the floor in a slow crawl. Gene gently nudges Mark to turn around and face the soldiers. Mark sighs deeply, and his head and eyes roll back as he loses his balance. Gene is now supporting him with one hand on his back and the other on his shoulder. A staff member is motioned to come over and help support Mark, whose eyes are shut tight. Gene coaxes him to open his eyes and to face the two men on the floor.

As the men inch forward on the carpet, Terri, the co-instructor, whispers to them to imitate being wounded and maimed. Mark is now on his knees facing the two men. "Do you see the courage they have?" Gene asks. "Yeah," Mark says, turning back to the two staff members crawling toward him. "How could you keep coming? How could you do that? Why? Why? Why?" The role players are now instructed to speak softly to Mark: "I love my country." "I am protecting my family." "You are in my country." Mark is crying heavily and Gene kneels beside him. "Let them know that, let them know what you want to say so they can go on their way. Tell them you know." Mark: "Shit. This is very hard." He looks at one of the role players, asking, "Can I touch you?" He places his hand on the shoulder of the role player on the floor and speaks with his head down. "We were wrong. It was fucking wrong. I am so fucking sorry." Terri directs Mark to look into the eyes of both men. Mark continues, "I'm sorry. Oh, God, and I'm sorry for your families, how we fucked up your country. I'm sorry for the Agent Orange. I'm sorry for your pain. I couldn't have you be human, man. I'm sorry. I'm really so sorry."

The role players now say to Mark, one after the other, "I forgive you." Mark responds, "Thank you for your courage. I can't imagine if it was in my back yard." Gene places his hand on Mark's shoulder. "Can you let them go?" Mark: "This is too hard." Gene: "Mark, this is your chance to let them go." Mark is standing now as he looks down at the men. "Bless you on your journey." Gene asks: "Can they bless you?" As both of the role players begin to back away from Mark on the floor, they look up to Mark, saying, "Bless you on your journey as well." They are helped to their feet by other staff members and escorted quietly out of the room. Mark's body is shaking as if he is experiencing a light seizure or somatic discharge. Gene encourages him to take several deep breaths. "Breathe in love. Breathe in their forgiveness." Mark now turns to Gene, and Gene places his left hand on his own chest and his right hand on Mark's. "Feel your heart beat and fill that empty spot." "Mark, where in your body are you holding their forgiveness?" Terri interjects. "I don't know," Mark responds, appearing calm now. "Where would you like it to be?" Terri asks. "In my heart," he says, placing both hands on his chest.

Next a staff member is instructed to bring a mirror out from the closet. Terri speaks to Mark, "There is someone else that needs forgiveness." Turning Mark toward the mirror, she instructs him to speak to the twenty-something soldier who was confronted with the terror of watching soldiers die. She whispers to Mark, who then places his hand on the mirror. "I love you. I'm sorry for all the shit. Come home. Let's do some fucking work." Gene looks in the mirror alongside Mark and together they repeat several times, "I'm sorry. I forgive you. I love you." "Take it in," Terri adds, "feel that self-forgiveness. You've had a Ph.D in self-hate and now you can become a Doctor of self-love." Mark and the other veterans chuckle. "Dr. Love," someone says jokingly. Mark turns to the group. "I am able to feel my feet and my legs now. I feel connected to the earth." A small box is brought to the center of the circle and Mark draws a card from the box and reads it aloud. "How lovely is my world whose purpose is forgiveness." Gene chuckles, "I promise the deck was not stacked. That's the only card in that box that says that." Laughter erupts and we begin to clap and cheer for Mark, "Welcome home, Mark! Welcome home!"

Shame Release, Self-Forgiveness, and the Journey Home

Two especially significant rituals occur after the emotional process work is completed on a VJH weekend. One is a shame release exercise. Both the staff and veterans are invited to participate in this process, which includes forming a circle. Sheets of paper with large print are placed a few feet apart on the floor inside the circle to assist individuals as they verbally fill in the blanks and complete the sentences on the sheets.

This can be a difficult exercise for veterans whose emotions are still raw from the previous day's work. For example, a young veteran from Afghanistan involved in a firefight that killed innocent civilians chokes on his words several times before he is able to read aloud, "I was ashamed because [fills in the blank] 'I thought I was a terrible person.' And now I know [fills in the blank] 'I was a good soldier. I performed my job to the best of my ability with the information I had.' I release my shame and now [fills in the blank] 'I am proud to be a veteran.' I love myself for who I am." Others might acknowledge they thought they were "unlovable" and now they know they were carrying the shame of someone else (e.g., a father, a rapist, a sergeant, a fallen soldier, a civilian). Sometimes a staff member will share that they were ashamed because they were opposed to war and did not provide support for veterans because of their political views, but now they know they can support the warrior without supporting the politics of war. Acknowledging shame serves as a confession of sorts that reveals we are all a work in progress. Thus, the shame release ritual can understandably take some time as individuals may pause to reflect on shame they have carried, sometimes for decades.

Another important ritual is an exercise in forgiveness. Music plays softly during this extremely solemn ritual that is also designed to provide emotional release and closure on old wounds. Veterans are invited to write letters of forgiveness in order to release a particular emotional issue that has had them stuck. Next, they are given the opportunity to write a second letter, this time one of self-forgiveness. The letter-writing ritual is often a difficult exercise to observe. As I glance around the room during each VJH weekend, the sadness on the faces of soldiers who have been placed in situations that outside military service would be an abomination is sometimes too much to absorb. But the exercise is highly effective and veterans often thank staff for the opportunity afterwards.

Once the ritual is completed, each letter is folded and participants are asked to hold on to them momentarily. Next, a military formation is created among all the veterans, staff, and participants as they line up to unfold the flag in unison. As a civilian, I have only witnessed the folding of the flag at military funerals. When the flag ceremony begins, civilian staff members often stand in silence with their hands over their hearts.

Once the flag is unfolded, each veteran is invited to place his or her letters on the flag, to be retrieved later in the day or to be included in a group of letters taken to the Vietnam Wall (a trek made twice a year by VJH staff). The flag is then folded with the same meticulous attention that was given to the unfolding, pulled taut at each triangular fold and handed from one veteran to another. Next, veterans follow the spoken commands of the veteran who now has the flag at his chest and smoothes any creases. He turns and places the flag on a table, then lights a candle, and the veterans remain at attention through the playing of "Taps."

After I have witnessed several flag ceremonies, the symbolism of this ritual sinks in as I observe time and time again what at first seems paradoxical. The wide array of experienced trauma for so many returning veterans happens to them in the name of the flag, yet they handle it with such respect that I am awestruck. Each has suffered and sacrificed so much. I watch the firm hold of a soldier who had to decide whom to help first when the truck in the convoy ahead of him was hit by an IED that blew out the windows along with his comrades. He now lives with the nightmares and flashbacks of his commander's attempt to push the brains back into the skull of a fallen soldier.

I watch as victims of military sexual assault, such as the soldier whose first sergeant did not believe her when she reported being raped by two of her military "brothers," pull the flag taut and stand proud. Standing next to the soldier is another veteran who returned three years ago and is still waiting for the VA to respond to repeated requests for neurological testing. Another stands proudly with tears streaming down her face, a soldier whose child, now 29 years old, still cannot know who her father is because if she knew she was conceived in such violence, it would tear a rip through her heart. I write in my notes that as a civilian, I am a voyeur to something sacred and I'm in wonderment of these proud soldiers who can, without reservation, place these folded letters of *forgiveness* onto a flag that they still so deeply respect. "Words cannot do this justice," I think to myself, but this much I do know—the sentiment and collective will of these wounded hearts transcend any nation, any bureaucracy, any good old boy system or self-serving bureaucracy. And this ritual of forgiveness seems to provide a conduit for deep emotional healing.

Each VJH weekend ends with rituals and celebration. Affirmations are given to veterans by their mentors. Instructors provide discussions of what to anticipate after the weekend along with wellness suggestions. This is especially important after the emotional intensity of the weekend, and participants are provided with tips to keep their immune systems strong. Plans are made for follow-up reunions with VJH participants and staff, and the day ends with a graduation celebration with friends and family members, often accompanied by a color guard ceremony from local veterans, followed by a reception for the veterans and their guests.

The ultimate work done on each VJH weekend is done by the veterans as they share their stories and emotions with other veterans. Even stronger bonds are created among veterans on the weekends, and the group cohesion is obvious by the time goodbyes are offered.[7] Statements such as, "We are here to provide a space for these veterans with no judgment," are not used lightly among VJH staff members as they create a safe container for veterans to share their experiences with one another.

I now realize that most veterans can only trust other veterans with their hearts, and this is the gift that VJH offers them.

Giving Back

Veterans are invited to come back and staff a future Vets Journey Home weekend and most do so, a testament to the effectiveness of healing that occurs on VJH weekends. I met Breezy in the summer of 2010 in Milwaukee when we staffed a VJH weekend together. I wanted to call him "Easy Breezy" for his light humor and demonstrated calm during our weekend together. I learned during our initial staff meeting that Breezy was a veteran who had volunteered to staff the VJH after having gone through it himself in the spring of 2009. I asked if he could share with me the path that led him to participate in VJH some forty years after he returned from Vietnam and why he came back to volunteer. I watched as Breezy listened attentively to the women and men who arrived for the VJH weekend, many sexual trauma victims and all nervous and unsure of what they would experience. He understood their pain. He had carried his own, a combination of guilt and shame, for decades before he was able to experience self-forgiveness, and he did not want this to be the case for this group of fellow veterans.

A baby-faced 19 year old, Breezy arrived in Vietnam on January 20, 1970. He served in the U.S. Army with the 20th brigade, 93rd Engineers, and was attached to the 9th infantry, 3rd brigade, in Dong Tam, Vietnam. His job included building bridges, base camps, and roads throughout the Mekong Delta. His battalion was working on Highway One in the Mekong Delta region in October 1970. Breezy had just dumped a load of asphalt and was headed back to the factory at My Tho, the capital city of Tien Giang province. "It was a typical day in Vietnam during the dry season. The sun was out and it was very hot. I had the pedal to the metal," Breezy remembers. Slow-moving vehicles made better sniper targets, so driving fast was a necessity. He was driving along with his transistor radio, listening to "rock-n-roll" and soaking up the beauty of the Delta with its green rice paddies and fruit orchards, when everything changed.

There had been little traffic on the road, but it was beginning to pick up as he neared the city. "About 100 yards ahead of me I could see a blue Lambretta on the right shoulder picking up some Vietnamese town folks. It was filled with about fifteen people. As I got closer, about twenty-five yards ahead, the Lambretta pulled off of the shoulder and right into my path. I couldn't believe it. Didn't he see me coming? I slammed on the brakes, but it was too close." The five-ton dump truck hit the car at a speed of maybe 20 mph and the impact caused the car to fly forward. Breezy was horrified at the sight of "people flying out of the open sides." When his truck came to a stop, he could see the wounded and lifeless bodies sprawled across the road and the shoulder. Some were still in the car. He remembers the blood and the moans from bodies in "grotesque" positions on the ground. Then his eyes settled on a small boy in a fetal position in the middle of the road, lifeless on the hot asphalt.

Breezy remembers every detail of the surreal scene as it played out in slow motion. "He was lying on his left side. He was wearing a blue shirt and black silk bottoms. I stepped out of my truck. I could see the heat rays coming off of the asphalt. I could feel the heat and my sweat running off me. As I got closer to him, I could see a pool of blood draining out of his skull. It started to coagulate on the hot asphalt. He looked like he was sleeping. He was so cute." Next he saw the body of an ARVN (Army of the Republic of Vietnam) soldier lying on his back on the right shoulder of the road. He wasn't moving, and as Breezy approached him he saw that "his skull was split open."

The wailing and crying continued and people were assisting the injured or standing around the dead when a squad of heavily armed ARVN soldiers came out of the jungle and surrounded Breezy with their weapons pointed. "The lead ARVN started yelling at me in Vietnamese and pointing his finger at me. He grabbed my shirt and yelled in my face. When he backed away, he also pointed his weapon at me. I felt sure they were going to shoot me. There were no Americans around, only Vietnamese." He was likely saved by the military police jeep that rolled up to the accident, and the ARVN soldiers stood down.

Breezy doesn't know how many were killed in the accident. He just knows that he carried guilt and shame for the accident deep in his soul. He struggled for years with alcohol and drugs before he found help. He didn't know he had PTSD, and the term didn't even exist when he first got home. He just knew he came back, 20 years old, a very different person. Readjustment was difficult because of the traumatic memories. He finally made his way to the veterans' group therapy in 2004. While he received great help from the group and continues to go every two weeks, the deep healing came for Breezy when he attended VJH. He had heard about the program through the ManKind Project and applied online. "The staff were wonderful," he explains. "They supported all us participants with love, respect and honor. I was finally able to let go of my deepest, darkest demon that I had been carrying around for thirty-eight years. It was as if a giant weight, a black cloud, was lifted from me. It was through the process and staff support that this happened. It was over! My heart and soul had released the last remnants of my pain." Breezy still deals with symptoms of PTSD but believes his work at VJH helps him "handle them more easily. I can live with them and love myself. It is from this experience that I have become a staff participant on Vet Journey Home weekends. So I can give back. I am dedicated to this program and all the vets that come through."

Jim, a personal friend whom I've known for over thirty years, suffered greatly from his experiences in Vietnam. As an 18-year-old Army medic, Jim learned early not to get close to his fellow soldiers. As an Army medic, Jim served in the Tay Ninh, Cu Chi, 3rd Corp Theater of operations, 25th Infantry Division. He received a number of medals for his service, but to this day the only one that matters to Jim is his combat medical badge. It doesn't just symbolize all the soldiers he helped keep alive, it also serves as a reminder to Jim of all those he could not help. He arrived in Vietnam an energetic and vibrant teenager who believed the world was his oyster. On day 1 the rapid spiral of lost innocence began. A year later, Jim would come home an old man at the age of 19.

On the flight over to 'Nam, Jim and the young man sitting next to him on the plane kept one another company. It was comforting to have someone to talk with "because the talking took your mind off of what was to happen after we land." He liked the other young soldier well enough and was glad to find they were assigned bunks in the same hootch. "I was on my way to get a shower for the first time in three days. I had bumped into him at the hootch door, and we bullshitted a little more." Jim was in the middle of soaping up when he heard the mortar round. "When I heard a bang, I rinsed as fast as my hands could move and went back to my hootch." The damage was already done, and Jim saw the horror that he would witness time and time again as a medic. "I saw that the head of the guy that I had been talking with was separated from his body. All I could think was, 'I am sorry it is you, but I am glad it isn't me.' I learned right then to not open my heart to anyone and I stayed that way for forty years."

Only recently diagnosed with PTSD, Jim had been attending group therapy sessions at the local VA, but "after the first thirteen weeks it just starts over with the same old stuff," so Jim wasn't seeing much progression as the year dragged on. After some heavy prodding that he would likely describe as nagging on my part, Jim finally agreed to attend a VJH weekend in the spring of 2010. As he freely admits, he considered "bolting from the car" in route to the retreat center more than once. Jim tells me that his experience at VJH "changed his life," and he is now a champion of the program that assisted him in letting go of the survivor's guilt and forty years of tortured memories from war. "I was just a fucking kid. I did the best I could but at 18 years old, I had to play God and decide who to treat and who to let die," Jim once told me.

On a recent VJH weekend, Jim and I attended as staff members together. He tells me, "I have not had a nightmare since April. I can honestly say that I like myself and I've forgiven myself. This is the first time I've been able to say that since Vietnam." Like so many of the veterans who staff VJH, Jim now comes to assist other veterans who are coming home with the same wounded hearts. "I am convinced if the veteran participates in this program, it may not have the same impact as it had on my healing, but it will start the veteran on the healing path. I do not want *any* veteran to spend forty years, like myself, running in circles. I would like for them to go through this program ASAP—the earlier, the better!" While much has changed in forty years, the carnage of war remains constant. Just weeks after our staffing at VJH, we read the following post to the Vets Journey Home discussion list, confirming what Jim has told me repeatedly, "It works!"

> *Happy Day after Veterans Day! I hope everyone was able do to everything that they wanted to do yesterday. The main reason that I am writing today is to give testimonial to the power of this program, in the context of my life. On Tuesday, of this week, I was offered a position to go to Afghanistan as a contractor. If this opportunity had come up just last week, I would have probably taken it, as an escape from my current situation. Since it happened after the weekend and I have honestly been feeling like I am seeing my world around me with new eyes, I wholeheartedly declined the position because it's nice to be home! Thank you to all that make it possible for me to come home and stay home!*

CHAPTER EIGHT

The Power of Ritual and the Importance of Storytelling

Western science, which is based on Cartesian dualism, often separates mind and body to the point of arrogance. False dichotomies do not serve us well. One important understanding that I have gotten from this research is a renewed appreciation for the power of rituals, one that comes from both the military and Vets Journey Home. Because we are dependent on social interaction for a deeper sense of ourselves, we will continue to create rituals in search for solidarity and something that transcends and cultivates emotional communion. And as the experiences of these soldiers reveal, sooner or later passion continues to win out over intellect "no matter how imperfect the symbols."[1]

Emile Durkheim noted that "military morality itself is in certain aspects a survival of primitive morality."[2] This remains true in some aspects, but we also see evidence of a shifting perception in the narratives of soldiers, both in the oral histories and in the ethnographic observations of Vets Journey Home. Some do not question the emotionally charged techniques that reinforce traditional masculinity; some engage in self-censorship or emotion work to either adhere to the moral grammar or avoid reprisal; others challenge the military institution head on.[3] The passive obedience that Durkheim predicted may be gone, but the commitment to serve remains. Soldiers still fight for one another, for the nation, and for their beliefs. Once again, military culture is itself a mixed bag.

Something else I have learned is that when it comes to rituals and emotions, there *are* moments that are beyond words, often leaving sociologists and anthropologists at a loss for explanation. Reflecting on his own examination of rituals, anthropologist Victor Turner concluded that researchers who study rituals must acknowledge that they carry emotional weight and are often "informed with powers both transcendental and immanent."[4] Moreover, "feelings and desires are not a pollution of cognitive pure essence"; rather, they are what make us all human.[5] Thus, just as the emotionally charged rituals of basic training cannot be overstated, the same is true for the emotionally charged rituals provided by programs such as Vets Journey Home. They are equally important for soldiers who now must be welcomed back into community, and we simply don't have enough rituals available. More important, as I stated in chapter 5, these rituals must *necessarily* occur outside the margins of military culture and in spite of well-intended military mental health protocols.

One especially important distinction is the contrast between types of rituals. In military rites of passage, power, dominance, obedience, and aggression combined with suppressed emotions are the ideal. In rituals of reintegration, rank and status are necessarily absent. The Vets Journey Home weekend, in contrast, transcends the highly stratified world of the military. It offers a rite of passage that is reminiscent of earlier purification rituals to assist the transformation from soldier to civilian. It builds on the bonds that already exist among veterans to create a space where they can express difficult or vulnerable emotions that many feel are not welcome in the presence of military mental health personnel, commanding officers, and, in some cases, other soldiers. In other words, it offers a space where the full range of human emotions that both male and female veterans experience can be validated, acknowledged, even celebrated—and then reexamined for ways to live lives of deeper meaning. The emotion process work that I have detailed in chapter 7 does not so much challenge masculinity as it merges the masculine with the feminine, moving emotionally repressed and/or numbed-out soldiers toward emotionally expressive citizens who can experience authentic relationships with self and others.

Durkheim, Turner, and psychologist Carl Jung, for that matter, understood the weight of emotional life. Indeed, much of what Jung has written provides a psychological counterpart to a sociological understanding of emotions. For example, Jung writes, "At all events an affective expectation is present in one form or another even though it may be denied."[6] Each reminds us that the sacred originates in emotional life, resulting in a force, if you will, a metaphysical phenomenon created by the social but *felt* in the individual. Much of sociology has lost sight of this fact of life, but it remains true that emotion, not cognition, is the vehicle through which the force is experienced. Rituals that transcend everyday life are emotionally charged, not dependent on or perhaps diluted by cognition, and the body *is present* in these moments.[7]

Sociologists, social workers, and civilian and military mental health practitioners who deal with emotions will be well served to consider the emerging research on emotions, as there is mounting evidence that thought and experience can significantly change the functioning of the brain. This is true not only for understanding experienced trauma but also is evident in therapeutic techniques.[8] For example, psychophysiological benefits have even been found in the use of therapeutic rituals.

In *The Mindful Brain* (2007), Dan Siegel argues that the brain can experience strong positive effects from emotionally positive rituals. Accordingly, rituals that encourage mindfulness can even promote cell growth in the prefrontal cortex.[9] In other words, positive rituals of emotional release like those described in chapter 7 may speak the language of the amygdala in a way that nurtures raw emotions instead of triggering more stress reaction.[10] Shame and forgiveness rituals are already popular as a clinical tool in marital therapy, but their utility far exceeds their conventional therapeutic use.[11] When they are combined with storytelling, they can have dramatic positive effects.

Storytelling is fundamental to the human psyche. And social support through storytelling of traumatic memories has shown to have positive effects.[12] Combined with ritual, storytelling has great potential for deep emotional catharsis. Moreover, veterans agree that sharing their stories is important but they must also have empathic audiences. Telling a civilian is helpful, but telling other veterans is profound. Hearing the stories of other veterans frees those who have been reluctant to talk about their own wounded hearts. It is not a substitute for therapy, but it can be of great assistance to those navigating their own journey home.

Oral histories are personal narratives, or "stories about the self."[13] They are the self's creative constructions that represent a negotiation between past and present and cannot be understood apart from their context. While recollections of basic training and combat are different in meaningful ways, there is a common thread throughout interviews that both males and females share: all are subjected to the management of their emotions against a masculine backdrop; all are proud of their service, consider themselves better for having served, and hold their bonds with fellow soldiers sacred. Some describe their relationships with other soldiers as stronger than ties to their own family units. Many remain in contact with their "brothers" and "sisters" with whom they served; others have since returned to duty, feeling committed to remain in service until their military family returns.

At the end of each oral history conducted, the question was asked, "Why is it important for veterans to share their stories?" I provide a selection of responses to this question here because I believe the collective wisdom provided by this group of soldiers can teach us all why it is so important for veterans to tell their stories. Both storytelling and ritual bring about transformations that "are not intended to be completed in solitude; they are honored in public and integrated into the culture as its shared history."[14]

I think Americans have a tendency to be very selective. We're a very sound-bite society. We don't hear the details and I think what happens and what happened in World War II, we saw it during the McCarthy era during the 1950s, where we tried to go back and we didn't want to hear all these details. Same thing with Vietnam vets, people want to move on and we have to keep that information alive. There's no telling how much we lost, you know, from what it was like for World War II vets or even Korean when they first came back, because it's part of that "If you don't remember history, you're going be doomed to repeat it." It's important that soldiers share their stories because in time they're going lose it. Even the information I share today isn't the same as what I actually remembered two or three days after an event, so I think it's very important, I think, for us to build this collective wisdom about what war's really like and the consequences and the effects on people. [Army Reserve Captain V. DeCoster]

Because first off, I mean, people need to know what is going on and how everything impacts a soldier. And the more knowledge that's out there, the better decisions that can be made. All the information is just coming from single individual sources now. It's not coming from soldiers themselves. It's not coming from what you'd call "the other side." And we [veterans] are "the other side." So it's best if people hear our viewpoints. [Army Lt. Colonel R. Mayes]

Someone may learn from it. You know that old saying, 'Freedom ain't free'?—to learn from it that what you have, someone you don't know has fought for you to have that. That everything in this world—you don't just wake up and it's there. Somewhere along the line, someone has died for you to protest. Someone has died for you to have this way of life. To share that, I think, it would give them more respect for this country because they sit there and they're able to do just about anything and everything they want. But without us fighting, you wouldn't have that choice. [Army Sergeant R. Hewitt]

Well, I think for one reason is it's important for people to know what veterans have gone through. It might be someone who's been in some hard-core hand-to-hand combat, or it might be someone who stayed in Kuwait and, you know, was the designated shooter on the bus that drove us back and forth. It affects each person differently and their perspective on it is different, you know? In Iraq, everybody's a combatant: females, truck drivers, everybody that wears a uniform is a combatant in Iraq. They don't need to keep it inside. They don't need to keep that heritage, that history [inside], and that's what it is. It's history. They don't need to keep it all to themselves. They need to share that so people know. Maybe people will understand eventually how traumatic it is and that'll keep other wars from being fought. [Army Sergeant G.P. Mayfield]

I'm a history major. I believe in the old adage that if you don't know history, you're doomed to repeat it, so I think it's very important that all vets share their story. [Army First Lieutenant M. Iglesias]

Because I think that there are so many different experiences out there, that otherwise nobody would know. The only thing that people know of war is what the media says and being there twice already, it isn't anything like what I've experienced. [Air Force Tech Sergeant H. Douglas]

Just to talk about different things, you know? And just being able to get on the Internet and just listening to troops, just giving up your experiences because you can learn from other people's experiences. I think I have. So I think it's important that we talk to each other. I don't see why we don't have something for veterans to go to, you know, like I'm not sure of the word I'm looking for, but where veterans can go and share their stories, where there won't be any political people involved, any news people, just where they can talk freely and share and won't be retaliated against for any reason. [Army Sergeant R. Knight]

Because it challenges the narrative of war that the people are being fed, the people of this country are being fed. We often talk about counter-insurgencies in other countries like Iraq or Afghanistan, maybe Vietnam maybe South America. But what is rarely discussed when insurgencies are brought to the table is the duality of this strategy. If you are waging a counterinsurgency on another population, you also have to wage it on your own population in order to win the hearts and minds of the people that are paying for the war. The type of information we're fed is purposely cultivating apathy. The average person in this country is completely apathetic to what is happening over there because of what they are being fed, not because they are naturally apathetic. So the government has to win over the hearts and minds of the population for its actions while it attempts to win the hearts and minds of another population with the taxpayers' dollars. [Army Sgt. J. George]

History repeats itself. [laughs] You know, they can, anything they can learn from our experiences helps them [new soldiers] in their deployments, should they get deployed. [Army Sergeant J. Hurt]

I don't know. I guess so maybe people would understand what it was like to be over there, even though you wouldn't know unless you were over there, but it gives you a glimpse. You know, everybody has this movie image of what it was like, or the news or whatever, and it was totally different over there, so I guess just to get the real explanation for things we did. [Navy Corpsman A. Neal]

Three reasons. First, history is written by man. But usually the person that does the writing wasn't there. Two, it actually gives the veterans a chance to relieve some of the stresses they have as far as some of the memories they put in the background. And three, it's good for the future. It's audio documentation of events that anybody can play at any time, and maybe some politicians get a clue of some of the things these veterans are saying. Maybe they'll actually forget the politics for 5 minutes and do what's right and they can definitely come and talk to me if they want to. [Marine Sergeant D. Carpenter]

I don't know, it just depends on what type of person you are. I mean, some people, if they leave something bottled up, they'll, it'll just eventually drive them mad. [Army Specialist B. Coffield]

It's kind of cliché but for history's sake. What's that saying? "Those that don't learn from history are doomed to repeat their mistakes?" or something like that.... And I think it's important for civilians to understand that freedom isn't free. There's a price to be paid for democracy, so we can learn from our mistakes. [Army Sergeant R. Beers]

So history doesn't repeat itself. If you look at World War I and World War II, World War I set the stage for the Great Depression. And then the Great Depression hit and we had Hitler come around and he filled everybody with wonderful nothings.... So I think it's important that veterans share their stories, if it doesn't tear them up emotionally too much, so that soldiers going forward or just society in general will have some kind of basis to see what happened and why and then move forward without making the same mistakes again. [Army Sergeant B. Lewis]

Well, so it's not forgotten, I guess. So people don't do the same stupid shit again. It's going to happen either way, but at least this way we have something to look back on. So you know really how things went down. [Army Specialist C. Gamblin]

Well, to me the most important thing is, well, there is two. Number one is the media. The media doesn't tell the whole story, in my opinion. The media does tell a lot of the bad things that happen because it's sensational and it gets higher ratings. But they don't tell a lot of the good things that happen. And so the American military is a reflection of society. Not everyone in the military is a perfectly good citizen. So we're just a reflection of society. Not everything is good that happens in the military, and not everything that we've done over there has been good. But the good far outweighs the bad. And the American people don't see that on a daily basis or even a weekly or monthly basis via any outlet of information—be it the Internet all the way up to, to TV.... People who haven't served in the military just don't understand what the military is all about, and that's a concern for me. [Army Major C. Taylor]

I'm not really here to share my story. I am more here to educate. As far as veterans sharing their stories, I think it's a positive thing, because guess what, like I said, you're not there, you don't know what happens, you don't know what occurs, you don't know what 15 seconds feels like, you don't know, you know? Sometimes it's all you have to react is 15 seconds. You can look back like, man, 15 seconds, I saved my own life, or in 15 seconds maybe I didn't. Maybe I'm a number printed on the news. Maybe I'm on a wall, or my name is on there. [Army Specialist C. Hooker]

I think that it's good to have a kind of an archive of people's views. You know, where one would see the war as completely negative, for instance, a veteran can give you a positive view of some of the good things that are going on over there. And maybe if people are smart enough and intuitive enough to want to know both sides to the story, they can see the world and what's going on from a different light and maybe not so negatively. [Navy Reserves Master of Arms E. Heath]

The reason I feel that vets should share their stories is to let people know what they see going on over there and there are some that don't talk, and they let it build up on them and then end up crashing around them, and they have problems. They actually need to get things off their chests. [Army Sergeant T. Bruns]

I guess for all of us to know that we are going through this together, and they are not alone, and that there is somebody who cares about them, that wants to hear what they've gone through, and I mean, and not everyone will feel the same way, but to know that support and that camaraderie, that they're leaving a legacy for generations to come. I mean it's just that's probably the greatest thing, for them to know that they are not alone, you know, that we're going through this together. [Army Sergeant T. Spencer]

I think it's important for vets to share their stories. You know, you get young kids thinking about joining the military, yeah, they're going to be deployed. A very select few aren't. You listen to vets' stories, they're going to see this is what it was like. Plus, it's like a history project, you know, reading a book that has a letter from Columbus—that's good history. It's from Columbus himself. Hearing a veteran, that's history from the veteran. It's not some historian's interpretation. It's from them. That's why I think it's important. [Marine Lance Corporeal M. Francis]

Well, I just think, you know, a lot of the times, a lot of the guys, what helps them from being so stressed out or affected by things they've seen or done, no matter what conflict they're involved in, talking about it usually helps, or hearing someone tell a similar story, something close to what you might have gone through. It helps them realize, "I'm not the only person who had to do that," and I just think it'll probably help a lot of them with the coping. There are a lot of people that will go fifteen years and they will never have an effect from it. But then they can be, you know, 50 years old, and all of a sudden they'll start having problems sleeping or remembering things that happened. I think talking about it really does help. I know any time I meet a guy that I know that went over there, we'll usually sit down and I'll try to draw a couple stories out of him, unless he really just doesn't want to talk about it. They might not realize it, but it kind of helps, in my opinion. [Army Reserves Sgt. R. Young]

Native Americans had a huge emphasis in their society on oral tradition and storytelling. You can think about it like, what happens when a layer of human flesh dies and a new generation of skin grows. To get continuity, humanity needs more storytelling, and in order for us to learn from these mistakes we're making, we are going to have to start talking about it, and the responsibilities fall on the veterans, and individually it's healing. I really think that when veterans talk about their wartime experiences, it can penetrate their souls, and sometimes that has not even been penetrated since it happened. [Senior Airman S. Hindmarsh]

Letters September 11, 2001

What follows is the collection of letters I mentioned in the introduction. These are from students in my general sociology course at the University of Arkansas, written at approximately 11:30 a.m. on 9/11. As I said earlier, I had asked them to write a letter that would go into an imaginary time capsule that would be opened and read by their grandchildren. The vast majority of students in the class of 350 were first-semester college students. I have provided a selection of their letters verbatim, with no editorial commentary. Some called for revenge. Others turned to their faith for solace. Some cringed at the thought of war, and others wrote of being stunned and in shock. I believe this collection captures the wide array of feelings of fear and confusion that so many Americans experienced as they witnessed the attacks, feelings that would provide those in political power with the moral justification for more than a decade of war.

> *Dear Grandchild,*
>
> *Today has been, in my opinion, has been [sic] one of the saddest days in history. Four airplanes were hijacked and two were intentionally crashed into the World Trade Center Towers and one into the Pentagon. I have no explanation for the reason that this is happening and I wish I knew why. Thousands of people have been killed because of people's anger and jealousy. I don't even know what to think. Satan's mind control*

is so powerful and it is not my place to ask God why He allows this to happen. We were in the middle of practice when coach Carrie asked us to stop and pray.

Dear Grandson,

Thirty-four years ago, on the morning of September 11, 2001, a very terrible thing happened. I found out about this travesty as I checked my email, but did not fully understand the severity and magnitude of what happened until I got into my car and heard the news broadcast over the radio. Thousands of Americans were maliciously and deliberately killed in a premeditated and vicious attack on the very fabric of what this country stands for. The World Trade Center in Manhattan, the Pentagon in our nation's capital, and other unconfirmed attacks via crashing planes into structures in Pennsylvania and Camp David, were executed. I was in utter shock, and was immediately overwhelmed by a sense of anger. I wanted to drive my fists into the very hearts of those responsible, those ruthless murderous sons of bitches, who rejoice in the mass murders of those who don't share their viewpoint of the world.

Dear Grandchild,

I will never forget this day. I was asleep, dreaming about being at a wedding in Australia when the phone rang. It was my grandmother. "Hello" "Jill, your mom said to turn on TV, the Pentagon has been attacked by terrorists." I got up and went to watch, thinking I am still dreaming. The first tower was already going down. Then I saw the second one, thinking it was a replay. It is kind of funny. I remember a picture of granddaddy, who is 80, reading a paper while working out at his military base as Pearl Harbor was being attacked. I feel almost like I understand his generation better today. This is generation's day that "will live in infamy". My sister lives outside of Dallas and they were evacuated because they have a World Trade Center. I have always been more emotional than her. I just can't believe this. It is weird because I remember not understanding why so many wanted to hurt the Japanese in 1941, but today, that is how I feel. By the end of the day, thousands of innocent people will be dead for no good reason.

To my grandchildren,

I'll never forget the day of September 11. The year was 2001. I was 18 years old going to college at the University of Arkansas. I had gotten up around 8:30 and I was getting ready for class in my small dorm room when I get a call from my boyfriend Jason. He didn't even say hi, he just said turn on the news now. So I turned my TV on and I was shocked by what I saw. The World Trade Center had been hit by a hijacked plane, I think it was a commercial plane, and the building was exploding quickly. Soon after 9:00 both towers had collapsed to the ground and all you could see was smoke everywhere. The news cameras were flashing back and forth from New York to Washington. In Washington, the Pentagon had been hit by a different hijacked plane and it collapsed as well. They rolled the videotape over and over without saying any words at all. There was another plane crash in Pennsylvania and word of another hijacked plane is still out there. Is this real? Are we going to go to war? Everybody is talking about this, and I keep thinking about Pearl Harbor. I am a little scared—why would someone do this? There is word of at least 20,000 people dead today.

To my grandchild,

Hi, how are you? Today I was already having a bad day. I came to Sociology class and I hear my instructor, "Who has family or someone in military?" She kept asking everyone around the class and people raise their hands up. Someone said "middle east", and "Saudi Arabia" and so forth. I was curious about why she wanted to know and she looked so concerned and scared. Then she finally told us about the World Trade centers and Pentagon was hit by two plane hijackers. It doesn't look accidental, maybe we have a war coming. There were over 50,000 people working in the World Trade Center and reports 20,000 of their employees are dead. No one seems to know what or why the cause but it seems very serious.

As I look around the class, I see students fear for their lives and the family members that could be in the military. Everyone looks so scared and afraid. I am scared too. Well you just know that life is very special and we need to cherish every moment with the loved ones as we can because you never know. You may not see that person tomorrow.

Dear Grandson,

Though you may never have to experience something like this again, I want you to know what happened to this United States on this particular day. I was getting ready for my 11:00 sociology class and I turned on the news to find out about the explosions that took place in the Pentagon and the World Trade Center. Both towers of the World Trade Center collapsed and the Pentagon was on fire. I am so devastated about this. I never thought that something like this could happen to the United States. It is probably the most powerful country at this time, though I don't know how the situation will be when you receive this letter. This taught me the lesson that no one can be really safe even if they think they are.

Dear Grandchild,

Until today I felt safe in this country. We had never been under attack and nobody had ever threatened us in such a way until now. Today there were several attacks and bombings on the World Trade Center and the Pentagon. A plane also crashed near where some of our family lives in Pennsylvania. Now I am scared. I am scared for my mother, and aunts, uncles, and cousins in Pennsylvania are hurt or in danger. I am scared that your grandfather and great uncles will get drafted because now we are at war. And we still don't know who we are at war with. I am scared for the safety of everyone in our country because we don't know where the next attack will come. Things will start changing and probably already have. I don't know how your world will be like or what the outcome of this situation will be. But I hope that you feel the safety that I had felt until this day.

Dear Grandson,

Today the World Trade Center was attacked by terrorists. Hijacked planes were flown into both towers. Another plane was flown into the Pentagon. There were the more hijacked planes, one of them, we believe, crashed somewhere in Pennsylvania and we still don't know where the other one is. When we first heard of this, we were sitting in the cafeteria, eating breakfast. My first thoughts were disbelief and then fear. I couldn't believe that someone would do this to America. When it finally sunk in that this was real, I became very scared. Knowing the size of this tragedy, America won't go without fighting back. That means that I may have to leave with all my friends and go to war somewhere. This is a day that won't be forgotten.

Dear Grandchild,

I hope this letter finds you well. Unfortunately, this was a day filled with terror and destruction. Early this morning, the World Trade Center and the Pentagon were destroyed in an act of cruel terrorism. Three airliners were hijacked and crashed into these buildings. It is not yet known how many lost their lives, or who is responsible. As you know, I am a history major. I study wars from the beginning of time but up until now I have never seen one beginning so close to home. Right now I don't think I have realized or accepted the intensity and magnitude of what is occurring right now as I write. I'm very scared of the near future and what it may hold. My life as an American will forever be changed by this day.

Dear children and grandchildren,

Today has proven to be unlike any other in my lifetime. Between classes today, I stopped by work where my mom and grandma explained the strange happenings going on in New York and our nation's capital. Apparently, we have been attacked by terrorists. Civilian planes of U.S. were hijacked and then crashed into some of our most important buildings. The commercial jets hit both our World Trade Towers in New York. Both of our towers were completely destroyed due to clearly calculated point of impact from both planes! A third plane has hit the Pentagon in our nation's capital, and has caused considerable amount of damage. There is a fourth hijacked plane that is unaccounted for currently, and therefore all other planes have been ordered out of the sky. There are also reports of car bombs going off in Washington D.C., as well as reports of attacks on Camp David. One estimate I heard on the news just prior to this class explained at least 20,000 people have lost their lives this morning. Our only hint is the Iranian attempt in 1993. It is hard to put into words how scared I feel today. Not scared that the US may fall, but just scared of the uncertain. It's amazing how we take our security for granted in this nation because I honestly never thought this would happen. I can just hope and pray for the best.

Dearest Grandchild,

On this day, September 11th, only 34 years ago, America thought that they were at the top of the world. Then it all came crashing down. We were attacked by a terrorist group. They destroyed the world trade center and our nation's capital (the Pentagon). At first, I didn't pay attention to it, because I was having a bad day because I couldn't find a parking space on campus. While searching for a spot to park I heard the news on the radio. They said nothing about terrorist attacks so I began to think they were freak accidents. As the day progressed, I found out that we were headed to war. I truly hate war, it is so stupid. It's the dumbest way to solve a conflict. I wish the world were more peaceful and tolerant.

My dearest grandchild,

Today was a sad day in history. September 11th, 2001, walking through the Union, I discovered a large group of students glued to their TV. "The world trade center is down." Tears flooded my eyes. What the hell is going on! As I braced myself for more bad news my knees began to shake. "The Pentagon's been hit". Our government is falling apart right before our eyes. Thoughts of war raced through my mind. What if we go to war with whoever has done this? There will most likely be a draft. They'll take my most prized possession, Jake. If he were to go off to war, what would I do? What would any of us do? So many people have been murdered today. It is a sad, sad time for everyone in our country. Thousands upon thousands of innocent victims working for our government, unaware of what is to come to them. All the lives that have been affected today, what a waste of human life. In my opinion today the world will change forever—our lives, our thoughts, our prayers. Undeniably everything is in uproar.

Dear Grandson,

The most surreal experience has happened today. Two commercial airliners were hijacked and flown into the World Trade Center. The World Trade Center was two buildings in New York City around 110 stories tall. After the collision, the two towers crashed to the ground around thirty minutes apart. Another airliner that was hijacked crashed into the Pentagon destroying a wing of the building. Your great grand-parents, my mom and dad were supposed to be flying this morning. They were flying from Las Vegas to Los Angeles then to Alabama. All the flights in the United States were grounded, so they didn't get, thank the Lord, to take off. This was the most unbelievable thing I have ever experienced. My girlfriend, Fran, woke me up on the phone and told me to turn on the television. I turned it on to see only one of the towers in flames. I hope you never have to see a sight like this.

Dear Sally,

Today a tragedy occurred. I don't know many words that can describe all the lost lives. But, the World Trade Center, and the Pentagon were hit by two planes. We are still unsure who did this horrible act of terrorism, but we are investigating now. My feelings toward all of this are very fearful and confused. I don't know much about what has happened, except for the number of lost lives and the massive destruction. I have always felt safe in America, and I think for the first time I'm wondering what and where something like this could happen again.

Dear Grandchild,

Today is a Tuesday and it is beautiful outside and I am on my way out the door to class of U of A when I hear the TV playing and talking about planes crashing and I just kept on going, thinking it was just a movie. Today, two different planes hit the World Trade Center and both sides collapsed and killed many people. Another plane crashed in PN and I am very confused. I have heard so much "here say", so I really have no idea what is going on. I have no idea if these people are from other countries or just mean people from the United States. I have never heard of such a huge mess, in all my 19 years I've been here. I'm really scared of a war. I never want to go through what my grandpa has told me about WWII. I think something is going to happen and it's going to be bad but I have no idea what it might be. I feel like these days anything will happen. I hope you get this letter and try to understand what is going on this crazy day in September in 2001. Love always,

P.S. Just as a write this a fourth plane just crashed but no clue where or any details!

Dear Grandkids,

Today I woke up and got ready for class like any other day. I didn't turn on the TV or anything, but I met a friend of mine to walk to class together. He asked me if I had been watch the news and I said, "no why, what is going one?" He proceeded to tell me that terrorists had attacked. The World Trade Center had been crashed into and collapsed. Apparently some terrorists hijacked the planes flying from the east and attacked the WTC and the Pentagon. Of course, I haven't heard anything specifically on the news or seen it for myself, so I don't exactly know what's going on. I'm sure that the seriousness of it hasn't sunk in for me yet. I think the New York Stock Exchange is crashing or going down. Anyway, I hope our country will be okay. It is awful all of the innocent lives that have been lost. I suppose we will see. I don't know why people always want to attack us. Why is the desire to kill so great in our world? It is very scary.

Dear Grandkid,

On Tuesday, a plane hit the Pentagon, causing it to burst into a large fire. Also two planes crashed into the center's towers causing them to collapse. A fighter plane was also shot down by the Iraq military. The United States could be at war any day now, but first we have to find out who is our enemy. This is a sad time because many good young men and women will possibly die fighting for the USA. I just pray that it is all resolved and you and your family are free and not being hassled by the stupid ways of mankind. It is in God's hands now, and all we can do is let Him work His will.

Dear Grandchild,

Hey sweetheart, how are you today? It really is a beautiful day outside except for all the horrible things that are happening in the world. When I came to class today, there was a lot of new news and more tragedy in the world. We should really think about how fortunate we are for all we have because you never know when things like this could happen, and everything could easily be taken away from you. It's just crazy how things happen so fast. I haven't really heard a whole lot about what all is happening, but I do know that it is a very sad time for all of America right now.

Dear John Boy,

Today September 11, 2001, is an unforgettable day. Many are dead and some are fearing for their lives. This morning about 20,000 people were killed. The Pentagon and World Trade Center were bombed and about 10,000 people were in each. I was in psychology when I heard the horrible news. The 5th plane has been hijacked and crashed. This could lead to WWIII. I fear for my life because I don't know what is going to happen.

Dear Bill, Bob, and Betty,

Today began just like every other day. I was running late for class— I can still relate—and I was getting ready to leave my dorm room, *when suddenly I heard the breaking news on TV. I had to watch it for a moment. The news was that two planes had crashed into the World Trade Center in New York City. Both of the planes had been hijacked. The Pentagon was also burning. Many people have died. It is a very horrible thing. I just wish peace cold be a reality. I hope you never have to experience this.*

Dear Jimmy,

Today while I was brushing my teeth, I received the news that something catastrophic had happened. Millions of people will be affected by the events of this morning. The World Trade Center and the Pentagon were attacked plus many other places. The White House was evacuated and planes are continuously being hijacked. Several have been reported missing also. I don't understand how and or why this is happening. I never thought that I would see anything like this is my lifetime. My mom says it is the beginning of WWWIII. I remember studying stuff like this is school and thinking what it was like to be those people who lived then. I am nineteen and I am first handedly witnessing what will become probably the most important thing in our nation's history. I am witnessing what you are studying in school. I hope no-one ever has to go through this. It is like not real.

Dear Kyle,

I was thinking of the world today, all the events that have taken place throughout my life and all the ones that have and will take place in yours. I will never forget . . . 34 years ago, on September 11, 2001, I was getting ready for school, at the time I was a freshman at the University of Arkansas in Fayetteville. I turned on the TV, like I always did in the mornings, but to my surprise, every major channel of reporting was reporting on the same subject. On that day, at 8:00 am, the world was shocked. Two aircrafts, carrying innocent passengers, along with hijackers, had crashed into the World Trade Center in New York, and another into the Pentagon. After a while, another plane was reported to have crashed in Pennsylvania. The world was struck with fear and wonder as we waited to see what else would happen. I hope nothing like this ever comes your way. Love, grandma.

Dear Grandson,

 The terroristic attack this morning really scares me. I knew it was going to happen, but you never really expect it to. It scares me to think that this could be the beginning of something even more terrible. I also feel that we will be involved in a war. My dad is a Little Rock police officer and I called him. He told me that the LRPD is on full alert. That also scares me because if anything was to happen he would be required to defend and go to the scene. I am really in shock, and totally scared of what is to come. I just pray for all of the lives lost.

Dear Grandson,

 On my 19th birthday, I turned on the television and absolutely could not believe what was right before my eyes. I was watching the World Trade Center in New York City crumble to the ground. My first thought was, "no, that's not real. It can't be". But then I heard the news anchor state what I already knew, "Ladies and gentlemen, the two towers of the World Trade Center have collapsed". The next picture on the TV screen was a view of Manhattan Island. All that could be seen was a giant cloud of dust and smoke. All of the buildings were blanketed by it. At that moment my heart went out to the innocent victims in this horrible terrorists attack. I thought about them, their families, their children. It was such a senseless act. I couldn't believe that a few crazy individuals would deliberately want to kill so many people who had no idea they were a part of.

Dear Grandchild,

 This morning I got up just like any other, whined about getting up, and got ready for my class in college. On the way down the elevator, I heard a guy ask, "Did ya hear what's happened?" I hadn't turned on the TV that morning, so I grabbed the bits of information from listening to the other people's conversations. By the time I got to my humanities (ironic) class, I'd heard that one tower of the World Trade Center was down due to a suicide plane crash and that a hijacked plane crashed into the Pentagon. After my two hour class was through, I was still unable to find out for myself what was going on because I had my sociology class. Here is where I wrote this letter. The whole situation is surreal and I suppose I am having a bit of a delayed reaction with fear and what not. During this part of my life I'm going through a difficult break up with a boy I truly love. Finding out about the plane crashes, I wanted to find Jacob and just tell him that our little problems between friends—just found out that a fourth plane has crashed, who is doing this? When the sun goes down, who are we as a nation going to declare war on? Is it Revelations? Terrorism? Or just another big war? What? Live and forgive. Make sure you tell those you love that you really do love them.

Dear Grandkid,

Year is 2035 about the day the Twin Towers went down and the Pentagon was hit. I first found out about the news when I went to my first class. At first I felt (since I hadn't seen or heard anything on the television and the radio) was hard to believe it. The more we talked about it in class the more realistic it seemed. Between my first class and my second class, I went to the Student Union. They set up a big screen television in one of the lobbies and a lot of students and professors, cops, and maintenance crew were watching breaking news all together. In a way, I, as a college student, even though this is my second year away from home, I feel a sense that I am not safe. Since, we didn't know who to blame, who the attacker was, we are in a state of blaming someone but don't know who. And we're in a state of shock and a stand still point.

Dear Logan and Britney,

A tragedy has occurred today. Many people have either died or been severely injured. I'm writing this letter to you two today because I may never get to see you guys. This world just doesn't seem to have peace anymore, and the worst thing about today, we don't have a clue as to who would do such a bastard thing. I will always be in your hearts. I will try to keep you two in touch with me.

Dear Sally,

Four planes were hijacked today. As I was going to class I heard on my radio about this terrible disaster. My first thought was how could someone do this? Innocent people murdered for no reason. As I got on the transit to come to class I heard the full story. Well, the full story for now anyways. We unfortunately don't know who our enemy is on this drowsy day. One plane is still unaccounted for. As I sit and write this letter I wonder how people can be so cruel. How could someone make someone so mad that they could do this to our country?

Dear Grandchild,

This day of September 11, 2001 has been a confusing and upsetting day for the United States. Waking up this morning and turning on the television or radio caused quite a stir on my emotions. Today we have experienced a horrible terrorist attack, leaving many dead and injured. Our country is in complete chaos after our World Trade Center and Pentagon have been bombed. There are also four known hijacked US planes. This is such a shock, because of being eighteen and never experiencing anything like this. We are all confused and know nothing about who is behind this. I have been in prayer all day for those involved and even the terrorists. We have to know that everyday God is our protector and comforter, especially in times like this. I am trusting God today. I will write later. I love you. God bless, grandma.

Dear Grandchild,

I was in the shower when I heard the news ... both towers of the World Trade Center and the Pentagon are under attack. Both towers are gone. Probably 20,000 people are dead. I'm numb, shocked, and scared. I don't know what's going to happen. Corey will probably have to go to war and he and Anne Marie have a baby due. Dad's best friends, Bud and Mac McLarty are in Washington and he can't get a hold of them. Bud's daughter goes to NYU ... is she ok? Who would hate the US enough to do this? Will this be WWIII? All the planes in America are grounded ... the CIA is shut down. I still can't believe two airplanes crashed into the World Trade Center. I've been there. My family could have been there. People were jumping out of windows. I'm scared ... a fourth plane just crashed. What's going to happen?

Dear Sally,

 I turned on the television at about 9:00 this morning. I was eating a bagel as Tom Brokaw voice filled the room. A terrorist attack, they think. Two planes were hijacked and crashed into the World Trade Center. Both towers collapsed and over 20,000 people are assumed to be dead. Another plane crashed in front of the Pentagon. There are two other planes that cannot be located at the moment, they are also assumed to have been hijacked. The United States is in a stand still. In a world of cell phones, pagers, email, etc. communication is limited. It is unknown at this moment who has operated this terrible attack. My mom called crying today. Crying, she just kept saying, "It isn't fair, think of all those people!" For the past couple of weeks I have had a feeling that something bad was going to happen. I didn't know it would be to this magnitude. I hope/pray that these attacks are over, and that everything turns around.

Dear Grandchild,

 The night before today, I went to bed on an emotional high. My favorite pro-football had just dominated their first game of the season. I woke up today in despair. My mother called me at 8:00 o'clock to tell me the tragedy of this morning's events. My first reaction was anger, that she woke me so early, but once I realized the extremity of the situation I got right out of bed and glued my eyes to the media. All I can think is why and who. I'm fearful for what's going to happen to our country next. I'm especially terrified that Bush is in control. My feelings are confused on everything. All I really know is I want somebody's ass. Anybody that attacks America should fucking die. I just want death to occur to the terrorist. I want for all of this not to have happened. Why did innocent people have to die over some fucking terrorists?

Dear Johnny,

It's Tuesday, during my 3rd week of college. I woke up at your grand-father's house and the phone rang. His roommate was on the phone, and the first thing out of his mouth was, "We are going to war!" I thought he was kidding. So, I turned on the news. It showed buildings smok-ing, planes crashing, and people running and crying. It was shocking. We don't even know who attacked us. We can only speculate. It's hard to comprehend. This is America. I always thought that the wars were over and during my lifetime I wouldn't have to deal with the thought that we might have to deal with war. I guess I just don't keep up with the news enough because I definitely didn't expect this. Now, all I can think about is my friend Brandon who I haven't talked to in about a year, maybe less. He's stationed in Fort Bragg, North Carolina. I have his address and email, but I don't know where his phone number is. I need to talk to him to catch up and make sure I hear from him and know if he's going to be shipped off. I'm afraid he'll be hurt. I don't know if I could handle that kind of news. I am afraid for Steve because I don't think he could handle it either. It's terrifying to think that our "stable" world could become so vulnerable and fall apart.

Sally,

Today one of my friends Brittany came in the room and woke me up to tell me the news of the terrorist attacks on the World Trade Center and the Pentagon. Right when she told me, my phone started to ring. It was my mom scared to death because Sam (my brother) had just left the day before to go to Italy, he was flying out of New York, but as of right now he should already be there. So as of that moment all I could think about was something had gone wrong. Sam got on the flight that crashed into the World Trade Center Towers and is gone. But Sam will be fine. I couldn't believe that someone could actually attack the United States. I have always believed that we couldn't be attacked. Well we just are going to have to pray for everyone that is in the United States.

Dear Grandchild,

Today is a somber day for the American population. The World Trade Center, both towers, and the Pentagon have just been attacked by terrorists. Two planes were hijacked and flown into the two towers, both collapsed and killed thousands of people. The Pentagon was also attacked and part of it collapsed. Right now speculations are that four planes were hijacked, three being from the Boston airport and there is still one plane that is unaccounted for. All airports around the country are shutting down and cancelling flights. The Lockhead–Martin in east Camden has secured its doors so no one can leave. Total chaos has shocked our nation and I pray I will be able to tell you how I felt in person one day. I love you!

Dear Grandson,

I remember that one morning in 2001. It was my Freshman year in college at the U of A. After studying late the night before, I was awakened at 10:00 am by the phone ringing. When I answered, my mom was on the other end telling me "Did you hear what happened?" With the situation my family had been in, I expected another fire or sick animal. Then, she told me of hijacked planes and the World Trade Center (or lack thereof). I rolled out of bed and turned on the TV. What I saw was Manhattan encompassed in a cloud of smoke. My boyfriend, Shawn, who came up to visit, said "where is the World Trade Center?" We saw replays of airliners crashing into the towers and them collapsing. They wouldn't show the Pentagon. I had one thought, "Holy Shit".

Dear Grandkid,

Today, I woke up and went to class just as I do everyday. However, when I got home I realized that something tragic had occurred. I got to the Sigma Chi house this morning to see everyone huddled around the TV. Then one of my pledge brothers informed me that terrorist had hijacked four planes, two of which flew directly into the World Trade Center and one hit the Pentagon with the only still flying around. The World Trade Center has been completely demolished. The Pentagon, however, is not completely destroyed but definitely will never be the same. When I received the news it seemed as if my body went numb. It is now 11:00 am, two hours after it happened, and my stomach is still turning. This is definitely a tragedy.

Dear Grandchild,

Today apparently, the World Trade Center and the Pentagon were hit by airplanes causing fires and innocent people to die. I have also heard that we are going to war but I do not know with who yet. What do I have to say about this? Well I feel that whoever is responsible deserves what is coming to them.

Dear Grandchild,

Today the World Trade Center was bombed and collapsed. The Pentagon was also attacked. They said there was fire on the mall in DC. The buildings were attacked by hijacked airliners that crashed into the buildings. I guess I feel mostly confused about who would do something like this and why. I am afraid that the country could be headed for a war with the people who are responsible. The whole idea that we have been attacked by surprise on American soil reminds me of the attack on Pearl Harbor.

Dear Johnny,

On September 11th, 2001, the worst event in U.S. history happened. Terrorists hijacked several planes and crashed into the World Trade Center and the Pentagon. I think that today will be a day that people will still talk about hundreds of years from now. I don't think that the US will ever feel as safe as it did before. Ben–Ladin will most likely be hunted down and killed. I was standing on top of the World Trade Center just a few weeks before the attack. I think in a way I am not the same as before. Security will have to be stepped up everywhere.

Dear Sally,

I want you to remember September 11, 2001. I remember driving to class and hearing on the radio how the superior country had been attacked. Growing up, I have always heard about how the United States was indestructible. How we would never have to deal with acts of war on US grounds. Your grandmother's brother is currently in the military. I'm sitting in sociology scared, and wanting to leave and find him, and say how much I love him, and how long I have been dreading this day that I knew could possibly go to war. I was very emotional driving to school, thoughts of the destiny of the world crossed my mind. It was too close to home. Remember how life can be gone in an instant.

Dear Melissa,

I just found out that some terrorists hijacked some planes and crashed them into the World Trade Center and the Pentagon. I am stunned, shocked and afraid. Not really because I think that this will turn into a war or anything big, but because the man I am dating now is in the Army. If he was sent off I don't know because I haven't heard all of the information, just what people have told me. I can't even imagine how the families of the victims feel right now, they said that somewhere around 20,000 were killed or injured. I first heard the news in my sociology class my freshman year in college at the University of Arkansas. I am so nervous at this point, these first few weeks of school have been so hectic and stressful anyway, and this just makes it worse. If this does turn out to be bad, I want to wish you the best of luck—hopefully it won't be and can be figured or worked out for the best.

Dear Grandchild,

The year is September 11, 2001. Something that I would never think be possible, happened today. I woke up and did my daily things like brush my teeth, take a shower, and get ready for my first class at the U of A. It's about 60 outside, so I threw on some shorts and a sweater. Me and my roommate left the house and went swimming. The whole way there we were complaining how cold it was, and dreaded the thought of jumping into a pool. Once we were done, he drove me to my next class ... There was some of my classmates there, but they looked a little bit down. Then, I asked what was wrong, they replied, "what, you haven't heard?" And I said, "no." Then it all came down. Someone had jacked an airplane and drove it through the World Trade Center, and also the Pentagon. Many were dead and no one knows who survived. I couldn't believe it. I have been taking advantage of my life and complaining about my daily stuff, when innocent people were dying. I think I have learned a very important lesson. And I will always remember this day.

Dear Grandkid,

It blows my mind that you'll be learning about today's events in your history class. They said on the news that this is the largest attack on the US since Pearl Harbor and the most devastating terrorist attack ever. I honestly hope that is still will be the most awful event that has happened when you're reading this, but I don't think that will be the case. My heart cries out to the countless victims. I want to cry when I think about the innocent people who were planning to eat dinner with their family tonight or go see the latest movie. When things like this happen I am bewildered by the unpredictability of life. I was in my car when the news came on the radio. I seriously didn't even believe it when I heard it.

Dear John,

How are you? Hopefully doing well ... Today there was a terrible tragedy. I am nineteen now and in classes at the U of A. Today a plane crashed into the World Trade Center in New York and another plane crashed into the Pentagon. Currently there is another plane unaccounted for. There no state to state flights right now and most of the major airports have been shut down. There is probably a casualty rate up around 20,000. This really breaks my heart to think that there are people in this world who want to take the lives of others. One of the most terrifying facts is that this has to be the work of a group and not just a few. It is actually a very scary thought to think about–it is almost like you don't feel safe. I pray neither you or your family ever goes through any of the heartache that something like this could cause.

Dear Grandchild,

I never really thought a day like this would come in my life-time. There are so many movies and documentaries about this kind of thing, but it never really seems real. Today the Pentagon and the World Trade Centers were crashed into by hijacked planes. You know, America is so sure of themselves. We think we are so power-ful and untouchable. But right when our pride is so big, we get a horrible thing like this. Yes, I'll admit that I am very frightened. I feel incredibly vulnerable right now. I don't want to die yet and I don't want any of my male friends to have to go to war. I'm so sick of things like this. I am realistic enough to know that in my lifetime there will never be world peace. I'm sick of death and anger and fear. This is all so surreal. I hope by the time this is real again, people will realize that this is stupid. I'm very scared.

Dear Grandson,

Today started as any other day. I got up and went to my first class at 8:00. Later a guy came in late and asked us if we had seen the news but of course none of us had because most of us were on our way to class or in class when the tragedy struck. He then went on to tell us that the two towers of the World Trade Center had been attacked. Of course, everyone then went into shock. No one expected this. Class ended early, so I went back and turned on the news only to find that the Pentagon had also been attacked. I hadn't realized it before, but all morning I had a sick feeling in the pit of my stomach. Then worry really began to set in. I knew someone in Washington DC. All I could wonder is how is he and also what would happen to all my friends in the Army and Air Forces. I also feel sorrow for all the families and friends of loved ones who have lost their lives today.

Dear Grandchildren,

Today was a very sad day for millions of people. Being in Arkansas, we didn't feel the effects near as great as those who are in New York and Washington DC. I remember turning on the TV this morning. I never watch the news but I did today. When I first saw the burning buildings I was shocked. I couldn't believe it. My heart went out to the families of those who worked or lived in these areas. I was especially scared because my mom, your great grandmother is gone on a business trip to DC. I still have not talked to her, although I have been calling since 9:30. I hope that they find out who did this and they are punished. I don't want us to go to war though. That would defeat the purpose because thousands more would die. What has this world come to? I wonder if now 50 years or so later, you could answer me this question.

Dear Grandchildren,

Well today was a very sad day once again in American history. The world Trade Center was hit by a hijacked plane. This is second time the World Trade Center has been a target. The Pentagon was hit as well by a plane, and we have absolutely no idea who planned this and why it happened. This is a shock, but not something we all knew about today going into my sociology class. This is a sad representation of our culture and the events that take place every so often. We never really get a good event or something to be proud of. It is always somebody wanting to hurt somebody else. It seems like peace between everybody is far fetched. There is virtually nothing we can do about it. I am sorry you have to hear this and I hope there is some kind of improvement in your time.

Dear Grandchild,

On September 11, 2001 my life seemed like an action movie. This day I remember struggling to wake up and hitting the snooze button twice before rolling out of bed. I stopped by our student union and had some breakfast before heading to class. I was unaware of what was going on in the world because I was identifying rocks in Geology Lab. As I was walking back to my room I heard murmurs about the World

Trade Center and plane crashes, but I was still ignorant to what was happening. When I got to my room my grandfather called to check on me and my worried parents filled me in. I was so shaken that I didn't want to see the news. I tried to deny that this attack was really reaping havoc on our country. I'm so afraid of war. I don't want to lose any of my loved ones, let alone my own life.

Dear Johnny,

   Today is about to change many lives in the US and around the world. The World Trade Center and the Pentagon have been destroyed. Several commercial airliners have been hijacked and terrorists are crashing them and, in doing so, are threatening world peace. Maybe in a few hours, we will begin World War III. I do not feel immediately threatened. I have no family in the military to fear for. I feel very distant from the violence, either because I truly am physically distant or because it hasn't hit me. I am overwhelmed though by feelings of fear and concern for the people who are close to these horrific events. Thousands of people are dead or wounded, and many more lives will be lost. I pray that their families and friends will experience peace. I just heard that a fourth plane crashed.

Dear Abby,

   I am so excited and thankful you are beginning your college career. I know you will excel and grow as a young woman and a scholar in leaps and bounds. I remember the year I started school, and one particular day most vividly stands out. The day was Tuesday, September, 11, 2001. The day started off as any other. Rush, rush, rush to class. In the student union I remember walking in, and seeing sad and disheartened faces, many crying and blue. What once were smiles, had turned to sorrow. The planes had crashed into the World Trade Center and one into the Pentagon. Where there once was peace and a society of happiness, there is now total chaos and dysfunction. What once was, is no longer... We go about our lives in such an ordinary and normal fashion. We live day to day, doing what we need to do, what we think we need to do when we

*don't realize what is really happening. We do not think about the extreme
or the taken for granted when we should be and all at once it is gone.*

Grandchildren—

    *Today, September 11th, two thousand and one, terrorists killed
thousands of innocent people. What will happen to America in the future? Is a war coming upon us? There are many scared people in America
wishing they knew the answer to those questions and only time will tell
us, what kind of person could highjack a commercial airplane and fly it
into the World Trade Center and Pentagon? I say just nuke the bastards!*

Dear Grandchild,

    *Today, the United States and its citizens experienced a terroristic
attack from a possible international group. Many Americans are upset
and surprised by this event, for the World Trade Center (a monument
to U.S. capitalism), Pentagon (a monument to U.S. military power),
and many other attacks may have been carried out. Many thousands of
people, citizens, have died this morning. The tragic point to this is the
American government and people should have been prepared for such
an attack. The United States has, for the last ten years, experienced an
economic, political, and social stability that has not been experienced by
any country (economically at least). There are many countries and groups
that do not like the U.S. so this is an event that was a long time coming.*

Dear Johnny,

    *It is the nature of the Beast kiddo. During that time everyone walked
around the street pretty anonymously. Cameras on the streets were a rare
thing indeed. People had privacy to go about as they want. Hell, you
could even surf the net without every place you went being logged on
a server, being scanned by the government. You could have secrets back
then son. But then that day happened, a terrorist action swept across
the east coast. New York City and DC were in a state of confusion. Both
trade towers came down. I saw that on TV. It was a frightening ordeal.
After that, the writing was on the wall. -I could see it plain as day. The*

people in this country would no longer feel safe. Cameras are going to peep on every street. Linked to the international databases, they will be used to scan faces and pick out political undesirables in the crowd. Phone conversations will all be scanned as well as other forms of communication. Yup, that's the day people gave up liberty for safety, order over freedom.

Dear Grandchild,

Today America was attacked. The very symbol for which we stand was viciously blindsided. The nation watches in shock. The unbelievable is reality. Today several government buildings were attacked in our nation's capital. Both towers at the World Trade Center have collapsed. Washington has declared martial law. Someone has declared war against the United States, most likely a terrorist group. How does one fight an enemy in the dark? My anti-everything ideas and feelings have been overwhelmed with patriotism, anger, and lust for revenge. I almost want to take arms myself, and find whoever was responsible for this. For the 20,000 people that died today. I have a gut feeling that one of these parties are responsible. Bin Laden? The nation of Islam? Hussein?

Dear Grandchild,

Today I was in my second day of honors principles of biology lab. I was nodding off from the teacher's lecture. I noticed she went into the hall and when she came back I heard the news that seemed to turn today into a dream. I didn't know what to think. The first thing that came to my mind was the Oklahoma City coming. I later found out that the other tower was attacked and collapsed also. Not only that, but that the Pentagon in Washington DC was also attacked. The new news made me think of Pearl Harbor. This is like mass chaos. I am so scared that we are going to war, but it is scarier because we don't even know who we are going to war with. I know that this day is going to change history because this act of destruction is so mass and will affect millions of people. I am also scared because I am at the age of adult now and so are all of my friends. This means that if there is a war that most of them will be drafted. I have always hated the idea of war and I have prayed thousands of times about my thanks to God what we have never had to worry or suffer through a war. I know that if I keep my faith in God that He will put His Hand in on this day, and give us light.

Dear Grandson,

The World Trade Center and the Pentagon had been attacked. The only feeling I have about this is helplessness. Watching the news, every news anchor I saw seemed a little out of it. They were just as shocked as I was, but they had to report the bad news, not me. I felt helpless for a couple of reasons. First of all, Osama Bid Laden stated three weeks ago that America was going to receive "an unprecedented attack." How in the hell is someone going to get away with seriously stating something as bold as that? If I was president, I would do anything in my power to stop anyone that said something like that. I will feel even more helpless if it was in fact organized by bin Laden. What are we going to do when there's a surprise attack when we can't even stop one that we knew was going to happen? Actually I had no idea, but I am sure as hell that the Pentagon knew.

Dear Grandchild,

I had always thought the United States was invincible to the world, that no other country was able to hurt or harm our country that badly. Today I woke up earlier than usual and got ready for class. I went to breakfast with my best friend Sally. We walked in the cafeteria and we were told of the events that had occurred only one hour before. At first I was in disbelief, shocked. I thought these events can only happen in movies. My thoughts and feelings are all mixed up. I'm worried for the people I know and also for the ones I don't. I'm scared to know what possibly could occur next. Could anyone hate the U.S. so much that they would want to harm so many people and demolish our prized buildings? Events of this nature freak me out and make me want to cry, scream, shout, and throw things. I really want to go and watch the news all day long, so I can get the facts. This is a day in history that no one in our country will ever possibly forget. It's tragic and horrible. I'm terrified of what might come next. We just heard the fourth plane had crashed. Two in the World Trade Center— two towers fell, one in the Pentagon, and fourth we don't know yet. This is horrible.

Sally,

On the morning of September 11, 2001 I woke up expecting to simply get up, and go my Journalism class as I did on any other ordinary Tuesday at the University of Arkansas in Fayetteville. Sarah received a phone call that there had been terrorist acts in Manhattan, Washington, and Pennsylvania. Two planes were hijacked and flown into the twin towers. Bombs were set off in the Pentagon and World Trade Center. Millions of people died and were injured. I began to think about the small things that I often complain about, like being homesick, or missing my boyfriend, or being tired. I soon realized I have so much to be thankful for. My salvation also came to mind. This could be the end of the world, and I was thankful that if it was, I knew I was a Christian. As I walked to class I began to pray for each and every person who was involved in this terrible event. I prayed that God would protect everyone and maybe that people would come to Jesus through this. As the world is in turmoil, I sit here in a Sociology class writing to my grandchild. That right there is grounds for me to be thankful that God is taking care of me. Grandchild, I hope you never witness anything like this. God bless you.

Dear Grandson,

Today the World Trade Center collapsed into giant piles of glass and shrapnel. That was only the beginning. Throughout the day, more planes crashed, bombs went off, buildings were destroyed, tragedy was spread across the U.S. All I could do that day was watch, wait, and pray. Your great uncle Seth was in the Marines, stationed in North Carolina. I worried all day about him because he would be the first group to be shipped off if we went to war. I cried that day for Seth, for those that had died, for their families, for the future of our country and for you. Yes I cried for you. I am scared because I am not sure what this world will be like when you come around. I hope that you will never have to witness or experience anything like what happened September 11, 2001. I just want to say that I love you very much. Cherish life. You never know how much you have left.

Dear Grandchild:

Today is September 11, 2001. This is a extremely devastating time for U.S. citizens. You will probably read about today in your history books, but let me give you some first hand information. Early this morning, while most people were tucked away safely in their beds, two airplanes flew through the sky with explosives, and danger and their mind. The Pentagon, World Trade Center, and local airplanes were hit. We are all very scared, worried, and confused. Thousands of people were killed and injured. This doesn't seem possible, but it became very real as I turned on the TV and saw the smoke filled screens. As you learn today in your history books, know that this could happen to you also, so treasure everyday and the freedom you have.

Dear Grandchild,

Today is September 11, 2001, which is six days after my 18th birthday. This morning the World Trade Center was hit by two planes and has collapsed. Also the Pentagon was hit by a plane. Our country is in a state of panic. One of my best friends is in Active Duty in the United States Army and is packed and ready to leave if he is commanded to do so. He is in the 82nd airborne division in Fort Bragg, North Carolina. I talked to him on the phone last night and it is so, so scary to think that might have been the last time I will ever speak to him. I don't know what to think . . . we are going to war and we don't even know who with. I also have friends in the Reserves that are also waiting for more news. I'm very scared and very sad for all the people and their families who died in all the crashes. Hopefully God will be with America.

Dear Blank,

Watching a large airplane crash into a 110 story building is an event that cannot be described. Both world trade center towers are gone. The Pentagon is in chaos, another plane crashed in Pennsylvania and more planes are still missing. I don't know who is responsible. I don't know what is going to happen. War is coming but for how long I don't know. All I know is that more innocent people died today than I ever thought humanly possible. Men, women, children— all innocent are gone and I am sitting in Sociology writing this letter. The world continues to move around me and I am still contained in my bubble. How balanced is that?

Dear Grandchild,

Today is September 11, 2001 and our Nation has experienced a disaster. Terrorists, "unknown at the time," have bombed and crashed planes into the World Trade Center along with the surrounding areas. It is believed that over 20,000 innocent people have died and many others are injured. This has caused a nationwide shortage of blood and medical officials are encouraging people to donate. The terrorists are believed to be Arabs. "I hate those people!"

Grandchildren—

Today something very tragic and historical happened. The second bombing of the World Trade Center took place. Taking a general perspective of these two events along with all of the terrorists attacks, the public has gotten a fearful image of everyday life. No one knows what could happen in the next year or even the next day. These terrorists are able to do the most horrific and random acts. I am writing you this letter today in hopes that the world is much different now. You should treasure the peacefulness and kindness of your life and never take it for granted.

Dear Grandchild,

Today the World Trade Center and the Pentagon were caught on fire by a total of three planes flying into them after they were hijacked.

I was so scared. I remember thinking this couldn't be happening. It was like I was watching a movie. I thought why was this happening to us? I remember thinking that the U.S. was going to be taken hostage or something (as if that could really happen). I realized how lucky I have been in my life so far to not have to experience something so drastic as the Great Depression or WWII. But then I became so afraid that this was my time to experience something so horrible and painful. I am so afraid of what's going to happen next. Will these terrorists, if they are indeed terrorists, try more? Will the president by killed? Will we go to war which will cause many of my friends to be drafted? I'm terrified. I've always thought that the U.S. was untouchable, that we were so powerful that no one could hurt us. But, this was crazy! We were hurt!

Dear Grandchild,

I don't know what is going on. I've only heard that four commercial airliners have been hijacked and maybe a few buildings bombed? I really don't know. I only know these rumors and hints of rumors scare me because I am truly afraid of where we are going. Where is this world headed? We speak of the goodness of our nature, but I've only seen the worst parts, the hatred that has marked our men, and the wars, tyranny and oppression that has marked our nations. I only hope that you exist in a place that is safe and that if such a place does not exist, by 2035, I hope you do not exist. This world is only too awful for you. Hope is not enough, because what are we hoping in? Humanity? Corporations? Men? Some say God is dead.

Methodological Appendix

Oral Histories

Data collection for the Oral History project began in June 2007. I received permission from the University of Arkansas Institutional Review Board for the project in April 2007 after obtaining partnership with the Library of Congress's (LOC) American Folklife Center online archive repository, "Experiencing War Series." Next, I applied for and received a small grant from the University of Arkansas Women's Giving Circle for $7,500 in June 2007. I later received a small grant supplement from the University of Arkansas Jones Community Foundation. As I neared the end of this work, I fell short of the needed funds to complete my research for Vets Journey Home. I am especially grateful to colleagues Brent Smith and Ania Zajicek, who provided unsolicited financial support to this project as it neared completion.

Between June, 2007, and May, 2010, fifty-six oral histories were conducted by a research team, including myself and two sociology graduate students working under my supervision (Melodie Griffis and Crosby Hipes). Forty-six interviewees are males (four African American and two Latino) between the ages of 22 and 42. Ten interviewees are female (two African American and two Latina) between the ages of 23 and 39. Contacts with participants were made via snowball sampling, researcher participation and solicitation at "welcome home" events sponsored by local veterans' groups, and public service announcements on both local public access television and a local public radio station. Most of the interviews were conducted in neutral locations and work settings, although several were conducted in the homes of the interviewees. Verbal consent was provided at the start of each interview.[1]

Each participant received a personal copy of either a DVD or CD, depending on their preference. Some opted for audio only.[2] Eight more interviews have been donated and are pending posting online. Those veterans who are Arkansas residents were also given the option to have their oral histories placed in the Barbara and David Pryor Center for Oral and Visual History at the University of Arkansas, Mullins Library–Special Collections. Thus, confidentiality is not provided to participants who consented to submit their interviews to the online archives. Ten oral history participants opted not to have their interviews donated to the Library of Congress. Six of those opted for confidentiality. Finally, four participants withdrew from the study and their DVDs were returned to them along with the required forms from the Library of Congress.

Verbatim audio and/or video of the oral histories are available for those archived with LOC and most have written transcriptions available as well. Oral histories were conducted in Arkansas, Missouri, Texas, Wisconsin, and Maryland. In November 2009, I wrote to each of the veterans to announce that I would be writing up the research of oral histories and that I would be choosing a select group for the book, as I could not include all of the oral histories. I regret that I was unable to tell each story because they vary in important ways but each one is important to tell. One soldier who experienced severe combat trauma and has since been reactivated, wrote back to me and asked that he be excluded from the book. I hope the stories told by other veterans in this book honor his experience.

Oral history interviews loosely followed the suggested topics provided by the Library of Congress's Oral History Kit, also available online (http://www.loc.gov/vets/kit.html). This is an excellent resource for family members and researchers who are interested in conducting oral histories of veterans. Interview times varied greatly, ranging from

45 minutes to 3 hours, and were recorded with digital audio and video equipment for online repositories.

Topics covered in the oral history interviews included a variety of issues, from motivation to join, basic training experiences, job descriptions and experiences during service, transition to civilian life, and contribution of the war experience to current attitudes about the military. Questions were added to the interview guide that included readjustment to civilian life, stress conditions, coping strategies, difficult emotions experienced both while serving and on arriving home, and perceptions of Iraqi and Afghanistani people and culture. A conversation-style approach to interviews was adopted in order to allow veterans to guide the researcher. This approach assisted our research team greatly because it provided the opportunity to learn how returning veterans understand themselves in relation to military culture and how they make sense of their unique experiences upon returning home. A breakdown of the various branches of service and rankings represented are provided as follows.

Army 16	Army Reserves 5	Marines 2	Navy 2	Air Force 4	National Guard 23
4 specialists	1 captain	1 first	2 petty	2 tech	1 captain
7 sergeants	4 specialists	sergeant	officers	sergeants	16
1 first		1 lance cpl.		3 senior	specialists
sergeant		(reservist)		airmen	4 sergeants
1 first					1 sergeant
lieutenant					first class
1 captain					1 captain
1 major					
1 lieutenant					
colonel					

Mental Health Professionals

In addition, eight in-depth interviews with mental health workers associated with the Veterans Health Administration (VHA) were conducted between January 2008 and February 2009. This group was included in order to examine the organizational narratives that inform their encounters with returning veterans. Two mental health workers interviewed served in Iraq, including one mental health official [113th Medical Company] who conducted "critical event debriefings" and trauma counseling. Others are mental health professionals employed by the Veterans Health Administration who treat veterans with a wide variety of conditions. These individuals are strong advocates of veterans, but they are also constrained by protocol. Several voiced frustration in treating the deep wounds of soldiers and fully understood the stigma associated with treatments that ranged from sleeping disorders, anger management and depression to PTSD and TBI. Mental health workers opted for confidentiality and generic job titles are provided for those individuals. Their interviews were also recorded and transcribed verbatim but are not included in the archived Veterans Oral History Project.

Two thesis projects were generated from this data as well. Graduate students Crosby Hipes and Melodie Griffis wrote their sociology M.A. theses on topics related to this work. Crosby's thesis, "The Framing of PTSD: A Comparison of Mental Health Workers and Soldiers," examines the ways in which mental health professionals negotiate between the needs of veterans the bureaucratic constraints of the VA. Melodie's thesis, "Voices of Combat: Gender and Emotion Work in the Military," examines the gendered aspect of military edgework. Both theses are available through interlibrary loan from Mullins Library, University of Arkansas. Also available for review is Joshua Rohrich's thesis, mentioned in chapter 5 of this book, "Post-Traumatic Disorder in the Military: The Deviantization of Emotions." Crosby Hipes now attends the University of Maryland and continues to study veterans' issues for his graduate work.

Vets Journey Home

Permission to attend and observe Vets Journey Home was obtained in January 2010. After learning about the program through a mutual friend, I contacted Patricia Clason and Gene McMahon for permission to include the program in my research. They welcomed my presence and provided permission on the condition that I would honor the confidentiality of all participants, including staff and veterans.[3] Because of the sensitive nature of military service, self-disclosure, and emotional process work, confidentiality for all those involved is especially important. Thus, names of participants are eliminated and pseudonyms are provided. Branch of service is used only to contextualize the experiences of veterans and gender and race are provided only where they cannot be eliminated. Staff members were given the option of a pseudonym. Some have opted to use their actual names. These include Breezy, Christan Kramer, Patricia Clason, and Gene McMahon. Sam Luna—the Texas Coordinator for VJH, is referred to as "John" in the Houston setting and has given permission to be identified.

I asked for feedback from Christan Kramer, Patricia Clason, and Gene McMahon for all content related to VJH. This was agreed on at the start of the research project in order to protect the identities of VJH participants. They have all read and provided useful comments and insight on the content of chapters 6 and 7 and have provided permission as per our consent agreement. I am especially grateful for their feedback and, more important, for their willingness to allow me access to VJH.

In addition to a trauma-training seminar, I attended five VJH programs over the course of one year as a participant-observer, accumulating approximately 200 hours of observation. I admit that I was nervous at the start of the research because my role of sociologist and ethnographic researcher was made known at the start of each retreat, hampering the "fly on the wall" approach many ethnographers prefer. Fortunately, I was allowed to take verbatim notes during the weekends, and this greatly assisted my ability to capture the trajectory of each weekend, especially the emotional process work. After each weekend, I expanded my ethnographic fieldnotes with descriptive narrative of each program.

I was initially concerned that my presence as a researcher might somehow inhibit the process, but my concerns were put to rest the first weekend and this remained consistent throughout the year. I was amazed by the willingness of veterans to allow me to observe their work. Over the course of one year, only two veterans chose not to provide permission. Veterans spoke freely about their war experiences and from their hearts, and I quickly learned my presence was not going to hinder their participation in any way.

As I stated in the introduction to this book, I entered this research in 2007 with a heavy heart for young returning veterans and could not help but become emotionally invested as time went on. Hearing from young men and women who carry memories of war on their shoulders, proud of their service but wounded in various ways, I too began to mourn their loss of innocence and their youth at a time when so many are searching to find their own moral compass. Most were still teenagers when they enlisted. Thus, I confess that I entered the last phase of this project with a personal desire—to find a program that works for veterans.

When I arrived at my first observation, what struck me immediately was the willingness of VJH staff members to welcome me to the organization. As most ethnographers can attest, gaining entry is often so very difficult in the beginning of a research endeavor. However, this was not the case with the VJH staff members, who receive no money for their services. In fact, staff volunteers pay a fee in order to help cover the costs for veterans in attendance.

I remember my first encounter with the VJH program in January 2010. It was snowing in Arkansas and the weather forecast predicted 13 inches by day's end, so I changed my flight to arrive earlier in the day only to realize I was showing up at rush hour. "Not a good first impression," I thought to myself, but "Rose" and "Paul," my hosts for the evening, greeted me warmly at the airport and we visited en route to a local cafeteria, where they treated me to dinner.

Paul, who reminds me of the folklore character "Paul Bunyan," served in Vietnam in the late 1960s but was only recently diagnosed with PTSD. I learn that Paul suffers from a variety of physical ailments. His stoop reveals his body's wear and tear. During our first evening together, Paul and his wife share their frustration over waiting so many years for a diagnosis. Rose is understandably frustrated over the years of torment they experienced without a diagnosis. Paul struggles as he answers my barrage of questions about his war experiences. Rose interjects, "It will take too much out of him—he was in an ambush with a unit of 60 and 58 were killed." As we visit through the evening, I learn that Paul and Rose will participate in the couples retreat that I have come to observe. Rose, self-described as "the short one" (and she is, compared to Paul) has been advocating for wives of PTSD and has formed a group that meets in her home. The group draws from "military ministries" to use a faith-based approach to working with women veterans and military wives. As Rose explains, "Wives suffer from war, too."

At first glance they appear to be the traditional couple, married so many years they seem to know what the other is about to say, and there is a sweet charm to their interactions. I like them both immediately. As the evening progresses, the traumatic memories that accompanied Paul home from war reveal themselves. Our conversations vacillate between the program, family, grandchildren, and I notice that Paul often wanders off in thought or tears up, and Rose steps in to complete his thoughts. "He reminds me of my father," I think to myself, surprised to find I am now holding back tears.

Paul explains, "I can be under this chair," he says, pointing toward the carpet. "I can be level or I can be way up on the roof, but the drugs they give you don't help. I'll try to stay in the back of the house tonight," he adds. At first I am confused but Paul continues, "I am often up between 1:30 and 5 if not up right at 2 a.m.—that's when we were ambushed. I get up and I hear sounds, guns going off, but the dogs aren't barking and I ask Rose, 'Did you hear that?' She says, 'Hear what?'" Lately I've been hearing rockets. They have a unique sound." Then he's gone again. Silent, he motions upward with his index finger, "Were it not for God, I would not be here." As we turn in for the evening, Rose says warmly, "Sleep well, dear, because we are in for a long weekend. Tomorrow is an encounter and nothing like a retreat. You'll see what we mean." She seems tired and weary at points throughout the evening, but I learn as time goes on that when Paul is awake, she too is "on point." I would come to learn that Rose's experiences were not uncommon. Spouses and partners of those diagnosed with PTSD and TBI often serve much like comrades of war–they must remain on alert to protect themselves and their families.

"T. J." picks me up the next morning and is my escort to the VJH location. Our day will start early. On our way to the retreat center, T. J. shares that he, too, was in Vietnam. His first words about his service are, "I was 19 and I saw things that I should not have seen." I'm immediately reminded of a conversation I had with a young veteran who served in Iraq just weeks before, a testament to the lost innocence of soldiers.

T. J. was a radio man in Vietnam and went on 24-hour missions on the rivers. He recalls the hypervigilance that accompanied waiting for the gunships and remembers he and his fellow soldiers "had better be there to be picked up or we were left." The missions were classified, and he found that more often than not they were "off the grid." He recalls the one and only time he commented, "Sir, we are off the grid," to which his commander responded, "Then turn the radio off." When he protested, he was met with, "Turn off the fucking radio!" T. J. understands only too well the moral anguish of war, and as a young soldier he learned early on the important lesson, "You don't make friends, because they die."

As we near the retreat center, T. J. explains that he was "used up" in Vietnam, labeled "damaged goods" by the time his commander sent him home a few months short of two tours. As we make our way into the building, I thank T. J. for sharing his own story with me. He responds, "We need a voice for this program. I'm glad you're here."

Each weekend I attended, volunteers would offer to transport me to and from the airport. They opened their homes to me, and when I had to leave abruptly for a family emergency at the end of a weekend in May I received follow up e-mails of encouragement from fellow staff members. In short, the VJH community is more like an extended family of veterans and civilians who share one mission, to heal other veterans. Thus, to all those who staff and participate in VJH, who welcomed me into your homes, your hearts, and your community, I offer my sincere gratitude.

Notes

Introduction

1. David Altheide, *Terrorism and the Politics of Fear* (New York: Altamira Press, 2006), 5. See also Barry Glasner, *The Culture of Fear: Why Americans Are Afraid of the Wrong Things* (New York: Basic Books, 1999).

2. *Washington Post*, September 12, 2001, A29.

3. "Soldiers Face Obstacles to Mental Health Services," *All Things Considered*, National Public Radio, December 4, 2006.

4. I am especially thankful for the small grant I received in 2008 from the University of Arkansas, Women's Giving Circle. With their assistance and the use of audiovisual equipment from the special collections department of the Mullins Library, University of Arkansas, I was able to hire several graduate students to assist in the project.

5. See Leslie Gelb with Jeanne–Paloma Zelmati, "Mission Unaccomplished," *Democracy Journal*, Summer 2009, for their critique of media coverage in Iraq.

6. Edward Tick, *War and the Soul: Healing Our Nation's Veterans from PTSD*, (Wheaton, IL: Quest Books, 2005), 169.

7. Ilona Meagher, *Moving a Nation to Care* (Brooklyn, NY: Ig Publishing, 2007), xxii.

8. U.S. Substance Abuse and Mental Health Services Administration (SAMHSA), Office of Applied Studies National Survey on Drug Use and Health, "Major Depressive Episode and Treatment for Depression among Veterans Aged 21 to 39," November 6, 2008, accessed October 4, 2010, http://oas.samhas.gov/2k8/veteransDepressed/veteransDepressed.htm.

9. Larry Scott, "Army Says Soldier Suicides May Set Record." September, 5, 2008, accessed October 4, 2010, http://www.vawatchdog.org/08/nf08/nfsep08/nf090508-3.htm.

10. Craig Schneider, "Rising Tide of Veterans Need Services," *Atlanta Journal Constitution*, November, 10, 2010, accessed November 11, 2010, http://www.ajc.com/news/rising-tide-of-veterans-736523.html.

11. Tick, *War and the Soul*, 19.

12. The term was coined by Peter Salovey and John Mayer in "Emotional Intelligence." *Imagination, Cognition, and Personality* 9 (1990):185–211.

13. Jacob L. Moreno, *Psychodrama*, vol. 1 (New York: Beacon Press, 1946).

14. The term *mythopoetic* was coined by Shepard Bliss (1995) to describe the use of mythology in redefining masculinity for men in contemporary culture. It's been popularized by others such as Robert Bly (1990) and Sam Keen (1991) and used by a variety of organizations, such as the ManKind Project, to assist men in challenging standards of hypermasculinity and incorporating feminine energy as part of their personal growth. These programs are informed by the Jungian psychology framework that dictates a need to incorporate both our feminine and masculine counterparts for a healthy psyche.

15. Donations can be made to Veterans Journey Home through its parent organization, the Starfish Foundation @ www.starfishfound.org. All donations are tax deductible.

Chapter One

1. EMediaMillworks, Inc., "Our Unity is a Kinship of Grief," *Washington Post*, September 15, 2001, A13; David von Drehle, "Congress Approves Use of Military Force; Bush Addresses N.Y. Relief Workers, Says U.S. Must 'Rid the World of Evil," *Washington Post*, September 16, 2001, A3.

2. Timothy Williams, "Insurgent Group in Iraq Declared Tame, Roars," *New York Times*, September 27, 2010, accessed October 4, 2010, http://www.nytimes.com/2010/09/28/world/middleeast/28qaeda.html. See also Jane Arraf, "Wave of Iraq Suicide Bombings Target Police," *Christian Science Monitor*, August 25, 2010, accessed October 13, 2010, http://www.csmonitor.com/World/Middle-East/2010/0825/Wave-of-Iraq-suicide-bombings-target-police.

3. Ernesto Londono, "U.S. Struggles to Counter Taliban Propaganda," *Washington Post*, October 1, 2010, accessed October 6, 2010, http://www.washingtonpost.com/wp-dyn/content/article/2010/10/01/AR2010100106644.html?hpid=topnews.

4. U.S. Congressional Budget Office, "The All-Volunteer Military: Issues and Performances" (Washington, D.C.: U.S. Government Printing Office, 2007), accessed October 10, 2010, http://www.cbo.gov/doc.cfm?index=8318&type=0&sequence=1.

5. Center for Military Policy Research, *Invisible Wounds of War: Psychological and Cognitive Injuries, Their Consequences, and Services to Assist Recovery* (Santa Monica, CA: RAND Corporation, 2008), accessed June 5, 2010, http://www.rand.org/pubs/monographs/MG720.

6. Josh Dougherty, "Iraq Death Toll Soars Post War," accessed October 1, 2010, http://news.bbc.co.uk/2/hi/middle_east/3962969.stm. The U.S. military does not keep statistics on civilian casualties.

7. Center for Military Policy Research, *Invisible Wounds of War.*

8. U.S. Department of Defense, Task Force on Mental Health, *An Achievable Vision: Report of the Department of Defense Task Force on Mental Health* (Falls Church, VA: Defense Health Board, 2007), accessed September 5, 2010, http://www.ha.osd.mil/dhb/mhtf/MHTF-Report-Final.pdf.

9. Ibid., 11–12.

10. It is worth noting that most Vietnam active force troops were enlistees, although admittedly many enlisted in order to control where they were placed and avoid being drafted.

11. National Priorities Project, "Military Recruitment 2008: Significant Gap in Army's Quality and Quantity Goals," January 21, 2009, accessed October 3, 2010, http://www.nationalpriorities.org/military recruiting2008.

12. Ibid., 2.

13. U.S. Congressional Budget Office, "All-Volunteer Military."

14. Ibid.

15. See David R. Segal, Thomas J. Burns, William W. Falk, Michael P. Silver, and Bam D. Sharda, "The All-Volunteer Force in the 1970s," *Social Science Quarterly* 79, 2(1998): 390–411.

16. Meredith Kleykamp, "College, Jobs, or the Military? Enlistment During a Time of War," *Social Science Quarterly* 87, 2 (2006): 272–90.

17. Cynthia Gimbel and Alan Booth, "Who Fought in Vietnam?" *Social Force* 74, 4(1996): 1137–57.

18. See also Alair McLean and Nicholas Parsons, "Unequal Risk: Combat Occupations in the Volunteer Military," *Sociological Perspectives* 53, 3(2010): 347–52.

19. U.S. Congressional Budget Office, "All-Volunteer Military."

20. Robert Connell, *Masculinities* (Berkeley, CA: University of California Press, 1995).

21. Michael Schwalbe, *Unlocking the Iron Cage: The Men's Movement, Gender Politics, and American Culture* (Oxford and New York: Oxford University Press, 1996).

22. For exceptions, see Helen Benedict, *The Lonely Soldier: The Private War of Women Serving in Iraq* (Boston: Beacon Press, 2009).

23. David Morgan, "Theater of War: Combat, Military, and Masculinities," in Harry Brod and Michael Kaufman [Eds.] *Theorizing Masculinites* (Thousand Oaks, CA: Sage, 1994), 165–82; Andrew Huebner, *The Warrior Image* (Chapel Hill, NC: University of North Carolina Press, 2008); Edward Tick, *War and the Soul: Healing Our Nation's Veterans from PTSD* (Wheaton, IL: Quest Books, 2009).

24. Hanns Pols, "The Repression of War Trauma in American Psychiatry after World War II," in R. Cooper, M. Harrison, and S. Strudy, eds., *Medicine and Modern Warfare* (Atlanta, GA: Rodopi, 1999), 261.

25. P. J. Bracken, "Post-Modernity and Post-Traumatic Stress Disorder," *Social Science and Medicine* 53 (2001): 733–43.

26. Huebner, *Warrior Image*, 287.

27. William Styron, "The Enduring Metaphors of Auschwitz and Hiroshima," *Newsweek*, January 11, 1993, accessed October 6, 2010, http://www.newsweek.com/1993/01/10/the-enduring-metaphors-of-auschwitz-and-hiroshima.

28. Huebner, *Warrior Image*, 129.

29. Evan Wright, *Generation Kill: Devil Dogs, Iceman, Captain America, and the New Face of American War* (New York, Berkeley Caliber, 2004).

30. U.S. Department of Defense, "Comprehensive Review of the Issues Related to 'Don't Ask Don't Tell,'" appendix B, 165, November 20, 2010, accessed January 11, 2011, http://www.defense.gov/home/features/2010/0610_gatesdadt/DADTReport_FINAL_20101130(secure-hires).pdf.

31. Stephen Webster, "Army 'Revisiting' Ban on Female Soldiers in Combat Units, Gen. Casey Announces," *The Raw Story*, January 17, 2001, accessed February 17, 2011, http://www.rawstory.com/rs/2011/01/army-revisiting-ban-female-soldiers-combat-units/.

32. See U.S. Department of Defense, "Comprehensive Review," appendix B, 204.

Chapter Two

1. Emile Durkheim, *The Elementary Forms of Religious Life* (New York: The Free Press 1962 [c. 1912]), 222.

2. Ibid., 35.

3. Ibid., 37.

4. Ibid., 221–22.

5. Ibid., 224.

6. Emile Durkheim, *Suicide* (New York: The Free Press, 1951 [1897]), 238.

7. *The Ground Truth: After the Killing Ends* (Los Angeles: Plum Productions, 2006), DVD, directed by Patricia Foulkrod.

8. Ibid.

9. Jeff Hearn, "Emotive Subjects: Organizational Men, Organization Masculinities and the (De)construction of Emotions," in Stephen Fineman, ed., *Emotions in Organizations* (Thousand Oaks, CA: Sage, 1993), 143.

10. Sion Liora and Eyal Ben-Ari, "Imagined Masculinity: Body, Sexuality, and Family Among Israeli Military Reserves," *Symbolic Interaction,* 32,1 (2009): 21–43.

11. See, for example, M. W. Ashford and Y. Huet-Vaughn, "The Impact of War on Women," in B. S. Levy and V. W. Sidel, eds., *War and Public Health,* updated ed. (Washington, DC: American Public Health Association, 2000). See also L. Millier, "Not Just Weapon of the Weak: Gender Harassment as a Form of Protest for Army Men," *Social Psychology Quarterly,* 60, 1(1997): 320–51.

12. *NBC News,* January 3, 2011.

13. Peter Lyman, "The Fraternal Bond as a Joking Relationship: A Case Study in the Role of Sexist Jokes in Male Group Bonding," in M. S. Kimmel, ed., *Changing Men: New Directions in Research on Men and Masculinity* (Newbury Park, CA: Sage, 1987), 148–62.

14. Liroa and Ben-Ari, "Imagined Masculinity," 35.

15. Erving Goffman, quoted in Arlie Hochschild, "Emotion Work, Feeling Rules, and Social Structure," *American Journal of Sociology* 85 (1979): 556.

16. The 2008 documentary film, *Lioness,* by codirectors and producers Meg McLagan and Daria Sommers, portrays a group of women placed in a combat situation and their ability to demonstrate warrior qualities equal to men. On the other hand, women continue to be victims of the militarized masculinity. In *The Lonely Soldier,* Benedict (2009) describes the sexual violence and institutional backlash many women have experienced in the wars in Iraq and Afghanistan, reminding us that there remains a link between sexual aggression and war (Brownmiller 1976; Morgan 1994; Theweleit 1987). This is an issue I address in a paper in progress on women in the military.

17. Thomas Scheff discusses this process in *Goffman Unbound* (Boulder, CO: Paradigm, 2006).

18. Elizabeth Lemerise and Kenneth Dodge, "The Development of Anger and Hostile Interactions," in Michael Lewis and Jeanette Haviland, eds., *Handbook on Emotions* (New York: Gilford, 1993), 537–46.

19. K. A. Dodge, "The Structure and Function of Reactive and Proactive Aggression," in D. Pepler and K. Rubin, eds., *The Development and Treatment of Childhood Aggression* (Hillsdale, NJ: Erlbaum, 1991), 201–18.

20. Scheff, *Goffman Unbound*, 162.

21. Ibid., 161.

22. For further discussion of masculinity in military training, see R. Wayne Eisenhart, "You Can't Hack It, Little Girl: A Discussion of the Covert Psychological Agenda of Modern Combat Training," *Journal of Social Issues* 31,4 (1975), 13–23.

23. Laura Miller, "Not Just Weapons of the Weak: Gender Harassment as a Form of Protest for Army Men," *Social Psychology Quarterly* 60,1 (1997), 32–51.

24. Jeff Hearn, "Emotive Subjects: Organizational Men, Organization Masculinities and the (De)construction of Emotions," in Fineman, *Emotions in Organizations*, 153.

25. J. Allen and D. Haccoun, "Sex Differences in Emotionality: A Multidimensional Approach," *Human Relations* 28,8(1976): 711–22.

26. Tours are typically shorter (120 days) for Air Force personnel.

27. Victor Turner, *The Ritual Process: Structure and Anti-Structure* (Chicago: Aldine, 1969), 94.

28. Ibid., 2.

29. Erving Goffman, *Asylums* (New York: Anchor Books, 1961).

30. John Hewitt, *Dilemmas of the American Self* (Philadelphia: Temple University Press, 1989).

31. Ibid., 170.

32. Ibid., 192.

33. Ibid., 213.

Chapter Three

1. Dave Grossman, *On Killing* (Boston: Little, Brown and Company, 1995), 312–16.

2. World Bank Report, part 1, *Cry Havoc: Why Civil War Matters*, accessed September 24, 2010, http://www-wds.worldbank.org/external/default/WDSContentServer/IW3P/IB/2003/06/30/000094946_0306190405396/additional/310436360_200500070100004.pdf.

3. Helen Haste, *The Sexual Metaphor* (New York: Harvester/Wheatsheaf, 1993), 90.

4. In their investigation of PTSD among those in peacekeeping missions in Somalia, Litz and colleagues found that the frustrations involved with peacekeeping, such as restrictive rules of engagement, were the best positive predictor of PTSD development. Brett T. Litz, Susan M. Orsillo, Matthew Friedman, Peter Ehlich, and Alfonso Batres, "Posttraumatic Stress Disorder Associated with Peacekeeping Duty in Somalia for U.S. Military Personnel," *The American Journal of Psychiatry*, 154, 2 (1997): 178–84.

5. Jeremy Scahill, *Blackwater: The Rise of the World's Most Powerful Mercenary Army* (London: Serpent's Tail, 2007). Scahill reveals that Blackwater mercenaries earn in one day what most GIs earn in a week ($600–$800).

6. Stephen Lyng, "Edgework: The Social Psychology of Risk Taking," *American Journal of Sociology* 95(1990): 851–86.

7. Ibid., 872.

8. Lyng's original (1990) research focused on skydivers.

9. Jeff Ferrell, Dragan Milovanovic, and Stephen Lyng, "Edgework, Media Practices, and the Elongation of Meaning," *Theoretical Criminology* 5,2 (2001):177–202.

10. Richard Mitchell, *Mountain Experience: The Psychology and Sociology of Adventure* (Chicago: University of Chicago Press, 1983).

11. Stephen Lyng, ed., *Edgework: The Sociology of Risk Taking* (New York: Routledge Press, 2005).

12. Lori Holyfield, "Manufactured Adventure: The Buying and Selling of Emotions," *Journal of Contemporary Ethnography* 28,1 (1999):1–27. See also Lori Holyfield, Lilian Jonas, and Anna Zajicek, "Adventure Without Risk Is Like Disneyland," in Lyng, *Edgework*, 173–86.

13. Jonathan Simon, "Edgework and Insurance in Risk Societies: Some Notes on Victorian Lawyers and Mountaineers," in Lyng, *Edgework*, 203–26.

14. Charles Smith, "Financial Edgework: Trading in Market Currents," in Lyng, *Edgework*, 187–202.

15. Ulrich Beck, *Risk Society* (London: Sage, 1992).

16. Jennifer Lois, "Gender and Emotion Management in the Stages of Edgework," in Lyng, *Edgework*, 117–52.

17. Lyng, "Edgework," 857.

18. Stephen Lyng, Introduction, in Lyng, *Edgework*, 7.

19. Ibid., 10.

20. U.S. Department of Defense, "Report on the Comprehensive Review of the Issues Associated with a Repeal of 'Don't Ask, Don't Tell,'" Final Report, November 2010 accessed January 11, 2011, http://www.defense.gov/home/

features/2010/0610_gatesdadt/DADTReport_FINAL_20101130(secure-hires).pdf.

21. Dragan Milovanovic, "Edgework: A Subjective and Structural Model of Negotiating Boundaries," in Lyng, *Edgework*, 51–59.

22. Ibid., 58.

23. Jack Katz, *The Seductions of Crime: Moral and Sensual Attractions in Doing Evil* (New York: Basic Books, 1988), 284.

24. Katz, *Seductions of Crime,* quoted in Milovanovic, "Edgework," 17–50.

25. Private contractors now constitute approximately 20 percent of today's U.S. military presence. In 1991, one in 60 US military personnel deployed on active service was a private contractor. By 2006, the 100,000 mercenaries operating in Iraq had brought the ratio to almost 1:1. Scahill, *Blackwater,* 161.

26. *Killbox* is the name given to a situation in which soldiers are caught in enemy territory without support. Under these conditions, soldiers are authorized to use deadly force.

27. Stephen Lyng, Introduction, in Lyng, *Edgework,* 5.

28. The M-2 is a 50-caliber mounted weapon that shoots up to 200 rounds per minute.

29. Martha Raddatz, *The Long Road Home: A Story of War and Family* (New York: Penguin, 2007).

30. The Liseks' situation is similar to that of many military families who are now being asked to pay back overpayment. Some of these overpayment balances are being turned over to credit agencies for collection. The frustration surrounding this practice is reported in a U.S. Government Accountability Office report, "Challenges Encountered by Injured Service Members in Their Early Recovery Process," accessed September 5, 2010, http://www.gao.gov/new.items/d07606t.pdf.

31. Edward Tick, *War and the Soul: Healing Our Nation's Veterans from Post-Traumatic Stress Disorder* (Wheaton, IL: Quest Books, 2005), 171.

Chapter Four

1. The film *Lioness,* by directors Meg McLagan and Daria Summers (Los Angeles: Room 11 Productions, 2008), documents the combat experiences of female support soldiers.

2. Stephanie Gutmann, *A Kinder, Gentler Military: How Political Correctness Affects Our Ability to Win Wars* (San Francisco: Encounter Books, 2001).

3. Associated Press, "Fort Sill Changes Basic Training after 30 Years," March 16, 2010, accessed August 8, 2010, http://www.kfor.com/news/local/kfor-news-basic-trainging-changes-story,0,6501237.story?track=rss.

4. See blog comments, "Fort Sill Changes Basic Training after 30 Years," March 16, 2010, accessed August 8, 2010, http://www.topix.net/forum/source/kfor/T9JF9IN4SK2OQFP8J.

5. See, for example, Lisa A. Boyce and Ann M. Heard, "The Relationship Between Gender Role Stereotypes and Requisite Military Leadership Characteristics," *Sex Roles* 49,7/8(2003): 347–365. See also Jamie L. Callahan, "Women in a 'Combat, Masculine-Warrior' Culture: The Performance of Emotion Work," *The Journal of Behavioral and Applied Management* 1,1 (2000):104; John W. Howard III and Laura C. Prividera, "Rescuing the Patriarchy or Saving 'Jessica Lynch': The Rhetorical Construction of the American Woman Soldier," *Women and Language* 27,2 (2004): 89; and Clyde Wilcox, "Race, Gender, and Support for Women in the Military," *Social Science Quarterly* 73, 2 (1992): 310–23.

6. Nathaniel Frank, "What Does the Empirical Research Say about Impact of Openly Gay Service on the Military?" March 2, 2010, accessed October 1, 2010, http://www.palmcenter.org/publications/dadt/what_does_empirical_research_say_about_impact_openly_gay_service_military.

7. Laura L. Miller, "Not Just Weapons of the Weak: Gender Harassment as a Form of Protest for Army Men," *Social Psychology Quarterly* 60,1(1997): 1–32.

8. Operation Anaconda occurred in March 2002 in the Shahi-kot Valley Afghanistan. It was the first major battle for coalition forces after the Tora Bora special ops battle in 2001. Sergeant Douglas was stationed with a unit of Army Rangers involved in the rescue mission of U.S. troops ambushed by Taliban and al-Qaeda forces.

9. Wilcox, "Race, Gender, and Support."

10. R. W. Connell, *Masculinities* (Berkeley, CA: University of California Press, 1996), 77.

11. Demekratis Z. Demetriou, "Connell's Concept of Hegemonic Masculinity: A Critique," *Theory and Society* 22 (2001): 643–75.

12. See J. A. Holstein and J. F. Gubrium, *The Self We Live By: Narrative Identity in a Postmodern World* (New York: Oxford University Press, 2000) for their discussion of the symbolic resources associated with identity construction. See also P. Higate, "Traditional Gendered Identities: National Service and the All Volunteer Force," *Comparative Social Research* 20 (2002); 229–35.

13. See Anne Sadler, Brenda Booth, and Diane Cook, "Factors Associated with Women's Risk of Rape in the Military Environment," *American Journal of Industrial Medicine* 43 (2003): 262–72. See also Rachel Natelson, "A Case for Federal Oversight of Military Sexual Harrassment," *Journal of Poverty, Law, and Policy* 43, 5/6 (2009): 277–81.

14. See Nancy Gibbs, "Sexual Assaults on Female Soldiers: Don't Ask, Don't Tell," *Time*, August 18, 2008, accessed October 6, 2010, http://www.time.com/time/magazine/articles/0,9171,1968110,00.html.

15. Jane Harman, quoted in Nancy Gibbs "Sexual Assaults on Female Soldiers: Don't Ask, Don't Tell," *Time*, August 18, 2008, 17.

16. Rachel Lipari, Paul Cook, Lindsay Rock, and Kenneth Matos, "Gender Relations Survey of Active Duty Members," Defense Manpower Data Center, DMDC Report No. 2007-022, accessed January 11, 2011, http://www.sapr.mil.

17. U.S. Department of Defense, Sexual Assault Prevention and Response, *Annual Report on Sexual Assault*, accessed October 6, 2010, http://www.sapr.mil/media/pdf/reports/fy09_annual_report.pdf.

18. Rachel Natelson, "Separate, Unequal, and Unrecognized," *The Huffington Post*, August 4, 2010, accessed October 8, 2010, http://www.huffingtonpost.com/rachel-natelson/separate-unequal-and-unre_b_670302.html, reproduced at http://www.veteranstoday.com/2010/08/05/military-sexual-trauma-not-addressed-fully/. See also Gibbs, "Sexual Assaults on Female Soldiers."

19. Helen Benedict, *The Lonely Soldier: The Private War of Women Serving in Iraq* (Boston: Beacon Press, 2009). See also Madeline Morris, "By Force of Arms" Rape, War, and Military Culture," *Duke Law Journal* 45,4 (1996): 716–20.

20. Borrowed from Michael Schwalbe's *Unlocking the Iron Cage* (New York: Oxford, 1996).

Chapter Five

1. Michael Schwalbe, *Unlocking the Iron Cage: The Men's Movement, Gender Politics, and American Culture* (New York: University of Oxford Press, 1996).

2. By some estimates, the limbic system works approximately 80,000 times faster than the conscious cerebral cortex. Robert K. Cooper and Ayman Sawaf, *Executive EQ* (New York: Grosset/Putnam, 1997), 88–89.

3. Babette Rothschild, *The Body Remembers: The Psychophysiology of Trauma and Trauma Treatment* (New York: W.W. Norton, 2000), 21.

4. Ibid., 47. See also G. G. Gallup and J. D. Maser, "Tonic Immobility: Evolutionary Underpinnings of Human Catalepsy and Catatonia," in M. E. P. Seligman and J. D. Maser, eds., *Psychopathology: Experimental Models* (San Francisco: W. H. Freeman, 1997), 334–57.

5. See James Wilson, *Adrenal Fatigue: The 21st Century Stress Syndrome* (Petaluma, CA: Smart Publishing, 2002).

6. George Herbert Mead, *The Philosophy of the Act* (Chicago: University of Chicago Press, 1938), 20.

7. In *Emotional Survival for Law Enforcement* (Tucson, AZ: E-S Press, 2002), K. Gilmartin states that it takes approximately eight months to recover from an eleven-month tour, and that is without the presence of PTSD.

8. For in-depth discussion of the physiological changes to the brain of trauma victims, see also David Nutt, "Evidence Based Guidelines for the Pharmacological Treatment of Anxiety Disorders," *Journal of Clinical Psychology* 61,5 (2000): 24–29; and Roger Pitman, "Post-Traumatic Stress Disorder: Hormones and Memory," *Biological Psychiatry* 26 (1989): 221–23.

9. See also J. L. Hanley and N. Devine, *Tired of Being Tired* (New York: Berkeley, 2001).

10. Edward Tick, *War and the Soul: Healing Our Nation's Veterans from PTSD* (Wheaton IL: Quest Books, 2005).

11. See D. M. Elliot, "Traumatic Events: Prevalence and Delayed Recall in the General Populations," *Journal of Consulting and Clinical Psychology* 65,8(1997): 811–20.

12. Ibid., 11–12.

13. U.S. Department of Defense Task Force on Mental Health, *An Achievable Vision: Report of the Department of Defense Task Force on Mental Health* (Falls Church, VA: Defense Health Board, accessed January 5, 2009, http://www. ha.osd.mil/dhb/mhtf/MHTF-Report-Final.pdf.

14. Center for Military Policy Research, *Invisible Wounds of War: Summary and Recommendations for Addressing Psychological and Cognitive Injuries* (Santa Monica CA: Center for Military Policy Research, 2007), accessed June 5, 2010, http://www.ha.osd.mil/dhb/mhtf/MHTF-Report-Final.pdf.

15. "Thousands of Returning Soldiers Face a New Enemy," *All Things Considered*, National Public Radio, September 2, 2010, accessed September 5, 2010, http://www.npr.org/templates/story/story.php?storyId=129651881&surl=htt p%3A//www.northcountrypublicradio.org/news/npratc.html&f=module-2.

16. Greg Zoroya, "Simple Blood Test May Identify Mild TBI," *USA* Today, October 15, 2010, accessed October 16, 2010, http://www.armytimes.com/news/2010/10/gannett-blood-tests-find-mild-tbi-101510.

17. Mandy Stahre, Robert Brewer, Vincent Foneseca, and Timoth Naimi, "Binge Drinking among U.S. Active-Duty Military Personnel," *American Journal of Preventive Medicine*, 36,3 (2009): 208–17.

18. "Thousands of Returning Soldiers Face a New Enemy," *All Things Considered*, National Public Radio, September 2, 2010, accessed September 5, 2010, http://www.npr.org/templates/story/story.php?storyId=129651881&surl=http%3A//www.northcountrypublicradio.org/news/npratc.html&f=module-2.

19. Judith Lorber, *Gender and the Construction of Illness* (Thousand Oaks, CA: Sage, 1997), 1.

20. For a full description of the trajectory of PTSD diagnosis, see Allan Young's *The Harmony of Illusions: Inventing Post-Traumatic Stress Disorder* (Princeton, NJ: Princeton University Press, 1995).

21. Wilbur J. Scott, "PTSD and Agent Orange: Implications for a Sociology of Veteran's Issues," *Armed Forces and Society* 18,4 (1992): 592–612.

22. See Lewis Yealland, *Hysterical Disorders of Warfare* (London: McMillan, 1918).

23. See Scott, "PTSD and Agent Orange," 596.

24. American Psychiatric Association, *Diagnostic and Statistical Manual of Mental Disorders I* (Washington, DC: American Psychiatric Association, 1952), 40.

25. See Erving Goffman, *Stigma* (Englewood Cliffs, NJ: Prentice-Hall, 1963).

26. Agent Orange was a combination of defoliants and herbicides used against the Vietnamese in what some called herbical warfare. U.S. troops were also exposed to the poisons.

27. For a discussion of the four dimensions of stereotypical masculinity, see Deborah David and Robert Brannon, "The Forty-Nine Percent Majority: The Male Sex Role, in Deborah David and Robert Brannon, eds., *Sex Roles* (Reading, MA: Addison and Wesley, 1976).

28. American Psychiatric Association, *Diagnostic and Statistical Manual for Mental Disorders III-R* (Washington, DC: American Psychiatric Association, 1988), 247.

29. American Psychiatric Association, *Diagnostic and Statistical Manual of Mental Disorders IV-TR* (Washington, DC: American Psychiatric Association, 2000), 464.

30. Ibid., 467.

31. "Overview of Traumatic Event Management," chap. 6 in U.S. Army, *Combat and Operational Stress Control,* Field Manual 4-02.51 (Washington D.C.: Headquarters, Department of the Army, 2006), 48–53.

32. Greg Jaffe, "Therapists Take On Soldiers Trauma in Iraq," *Wall Street Journal,* November 28, 2005, accessed August 1, 2008, http://www.postgazette.com/pg/05332/613785.stm.

33. U.S. Army Medical Research and Material Command, Walter Reed Army Institute of Research, "10 Tough Facts About Combat," accessed October 4, 2008, http://www.armyg1.army.mil/dcs/docs/10%20Leaders%20Tough%20Facts%20About%20Combat%20Brochure%2011%20SEP%2006.pdf.

34. See Stephen Soldz, "To Heal or Patch: Military Mental Health Workers in Iraq," *Counterpunch,* November 30, 2005, accessed September 2, 2009, http://www.counterpunch.org/soldz11302005.html.

35. Stephen Robinson, quoted in "A Soldier's Heart," *PBS Frontline,* Broadcast March 1, 2005. Interview transcript accessed October 4, 2009 at http://www.pbs.org/wgbh/pages/frontline/shows/heart/interviews/robinson.html.

36. Lynda Warren, "Male Intolerance of Depression: A Review with Implications for Psychotherapy," *Clinical Psychology Review* 3,2 (2002): 147–56.

37. See Elaine Showalter, *The Female Malady* (New York: Pantheon, 1985).

38. Robert Connell, *Masculinities* (Berkeley, CA: University of California Press, 1995), 611.

39. Mark Thompson, "America's Medicated Army," *Time,* June 5, 2008, accessed October 4, 2010, http://www.time.com/time/nation/article/0,8599,1811858,00.html.

40. There is also concern that Mefloquine, a common antimalaria drug, has caused neurological and psychological contraindications for those taking a variety of prescription drugs. See Nevin Remington, Paul Pietrusiak, and Jennifer Caci, "Prevalence of Contraindications to Mefloquine Use among USA Military Personnel Deployed to Afghanistan," *Malaria Journal* 7, February 11, 2008, accessed October 2, 2010, http://www.ncbi.nlm.nih.gov/pmc/articles/PMC2259366/.

41. Shaun McCanna, "It's Easy for Soldiers to Score Heroin in Afghanistan," *Salon,* August 7, 2008, accessed January 15, 2011, http://www.salon.com/news/feature/2007/08/07/afghan_heroin.

42. Scott Gaulin, "Facing Consequences," *Temple Daily Telegram,* December 20, 2009, A1.

43. Eric's letter and profiles of other military who have refused to return for multiple deployments can be found at http://www.couragetoresist.org/x/content/view/837/1/(accessed September 1, 2010).

44. See Kelly Kennedy, "Mental Health Issues Rising Among Vets," *The Army Times*, July 22, 2009, accessed November 1, 2009, http://www.armytimes.com/news/2009/07military_mental health_072209w/.

45. CNN U.S. online, "Case Dropped against U.S. Soldier Initially Accused of Cowardice," July 15, 2004, accessed September 3, 2010, http://articles.cnn.com/2004-07-15/us/army.dropped.charges_1_cowardice-charge-pogany-panic-attacks?_s=PM:US.

46. See Stephen L. Robinson, *Hidden Toll of the War in Iraq: Mental Health and the Military* (Washington, DC: Center for American Progress, National Gulf War Resource Center, 2004).

47. Austin Comancho, "Project DE-STRESS Helps Treat Traumatic Stress," American Forces Press Service, August 3, 2004, accessed January 3, 2010, http://www.defense.gov/news/newsarticle.aspx?id=25599.

48. Charles Hoge et al., "Combat Duty in Iraq and Afghanistan: Mental Health Problems and Barriers to Care," *The New England Journal of Medicine* 351,1(2004, July 1): 13–22.

49. Arlene Kaplan Daniels, "The Social Construction of Military Diagnoses," in Jerome G. Manis and Bernard N. Meltzer, eds., *Symbolic Interaction: A Reader in Social Psychology*, 3rd ed. (Boston, MA: Allyn & Bacon, 1978), 381.

50. Richard O'Connor, "Collateral Damage: How Can the Army Best Serve a Soldier with PTSD?" *The Land Warfare Papers* 71 (2009), 4.

51. Kennedy, "Mental Health Issues."

52. See also Rick Maze, "Expert Cites Gaps in PTSD Research," *The Navy Times*, October 9, 2006, accessed October 1, 2010, http://www.armytimes.com/news/2009/07military_mental health_072209w.

53. U.S. Department of Defense Task Force on Mental Health, *An Achievable Vision: Report of the Department of Defense Task Force on Mental Health* (Falls Church, VA: Defense Health Board, 2007).

54. Ibid.

55. See Joshua Rohrich, "Post-Traumatic Disorder in the Military: The Deviantization of Emotions," M.A. thesis, Department of Sociology and Criminal Justice, University of Arkansas, 2007.

56. David A. Snow and Robert D. Benford, "Ideology, Frame Resonance, and Participant Mobilization,"*International Social Movement Research* 1(1988): 197–217.

57. See, for example: Bremner et al. (1996); Fontana, Rosenheck, and Horvath (1997); Murdoch et al. (2006); Prigerson, Maciejewski, and Rosenheck (2002); West, Mercer, and Altheimer (1993); and Yehuda et al. (2005).

58. See, for example: Emery et al. (1991); Gerlock (2004); Hermann and Goran (1994); Kishon-Barash, Midlarsky, and Johnson (1999); Ruef, Litz, and Schlenger (2000); Schnurr, Friedman, and Rosenburg (1993); and Watson et al. (1998).

59. Wilbur J. Scott, "PTSD and Agent Orange: Implications for a Sociology of Veteran's Issues," *Armed Forces and Society* 18,4 (1992): 592–612.

60. Institute of Medicine and National Research Center, *PTSD and Military Compensation,* (Washington D.C. National Academic Press, 2007), 14, accessed August 10, 2010, http://www.pdhealth.mil/downloads/PTSD_Compensation_and_Military_Service2.pdf.

61. Christopher Lee, "Official Urged Fewer Diagnoses of PTSD," *Washington Post,* May 16, 2008, accessed September 4, 2010, http://www.washingtonpost.com/wp-dyn/content/article/2008/05/15/AR2008051503533.

62. "Fighting the Army," *Now,* Public Broadcasting Service, broadcast June 13 2008, transcript accessed August 1, 2009, http://www.pbs.org/now/shows/424/transcript.html; Rick Maze, "Filner says PTSD Misdiagnosis Cheats Vets," *The Army Times,* June 28, 2007, accessed August 1, 2009, http://www.armytimes.com/news/2007/06/military_misdiagnosedvets_070628w/; Daniel Zwerdling. "Army Dismissals for Misconduct Rise," *All Things Considered,* National Public Radio, broadcast November 15, 2007, accessed August 1, 2009. http://www.npr.org/templates/story/story.php?storyId=16330374.

63. Kelly Kennedy. "PTSD victim booted for misconduct." *The Army Times.* January 7, 2009, accessed August 1 2009, http://www.armytimes.com/news/2009/01/military_ptsd_discharge_010709w/.

64. Donileen Loseke, "The Study of Identity as Cultural, Institutional, Organizational, and Personal Narratives: Theoretical and Empirical Integrations," *The Sociological Quarterly* 48 (2007): 661–88.

65. Jaber Gubrium and James Holstein, *Institutional Selves: Troubled Identities in a Postmodern World* (Oxford and New York: Oxford University Press, 2001).

66. Roy Clymer, "The Puzzle of PTSD: Does the PTSD Diagnosis Do More Harm than Good?" *Psychotherapy Networker Magazine,* November 2, 2010, accessed November 14, 2010, http://sychotherapynetworker.org/magazine/currentissue.

67. Thomas Degloma, "Expanding Trauma through Space and Time: Mapping the Rhetorical Strategies of Trauma Carrier Groups," *Social Psychology Quarterly* 72,2 (2009): 105–22.

68. See Eric J. Leed, *No Man's Land: Combat and Identity in World War I* (London: Cambridge University Press, 1979).

69. See Michael Orbans, *Souled Out: A Memoir of War and Inner Peace* (Candler, NC: Silver Rings Press, 2007).

70. Edward Tick, *War and the Soul: Healing Our Nation's Veterans from PTSD* (Wheaton IL: Quest Books, 2007), 106.

71. Ibid., 261.

72. Ibid., 262.

73. Peggy Thoits, "Self-Labeling Processes in Mental Illness: The Role of Emotional Deviance," *American Journal of Sociology* 91 (1985): 221–49.

74. Arlie Hochschild, *The Managed Heart* (Berkeley: University of California Press, 1983).

75. A number of sociologists (e.g. Thomas Scheff, Randall Collins, Jonathan Turner, and Theodore Kemper) have written on the role of social emotions in response to interactions with power and deference.

76. Norman Denzin, *On Understanding Emotion* (San Francisco, CA: Jossey Bass, 1984), 126.

77. Ibid., 125.

78. Ibid.

79. Tick, *War and the Soul,* 107.

80. John Hewitt, *Dilemmas of the American Self* (Philadelphia: Temple University Press, 1989), 153.

81. Ibid.

82. Erving Goffman, *Presentation of the Self in Everyday Life* (New York: Anchor Books, 1959).

83. Harold Garfinkel, "Conditions for Successful Degradation Ceremonies," *American Journal of Sociology* 61 (1956): 420–44.

84. Thomas Scheff, "Shame and Conformity: The Deference-Emotion System," *American Sociological Review* 53,3 (1988): 397.

85. Susan Shott, "Emotion and Social Life: A Symbolic Interactionist Analysis," *American Journal of Sociology* 84 (1979): 1317–32.

86. Jonathan Turner and Jan Stets, *The Sociology of Emotions* (Cambridge and New York: Cambridge University Press, 2005), 108.

87. Martin Wong and David Cook, "Shame and Its Contribution to PTSD," *Journal of Traumatic Stress* 5,4 (1992): 557–62.

88. Claude M. Chemtob, Gordon B. Bauer, Gary Neller, Roger Hamada, Charles Glisson, and Victor Stevens, "Post-traumatic Stress Disorder among Special Forces Vietnam Veterans," *Military Medicine* 155,1 (1990): 16–20.

89. Michelle Rosaldo, "Toward an Anthropology of Self and Feeling," in R. Shweder and R. LeVine, eds., *Culture Theory* (Cambridge, MA: Cambridge University Press, 1984), 137–57.

90. Herbert Thomas, *The Shame Response to Rejection* (New York: Albanel, 2005), 27.

91. Babette Rothschild, *The Body Remembers: The Psychophysiology of Trauma and Trauma Treatment* (New York: W. W. Norton, 2000), 11–12.

92. David McMillan, *Emotion Rituals: A Resource for Therapists and Clients* (New York: Routledge, 2006), 48.

93. Peter Levine with Ann Frederick, *Waking the Tiger: Healing Trauma* (Berkeley, CA: North Atlantic Books, 1997).

Chapter Six

1. Clason is also the founder and certified instructor for Taking It Lightly and owner of Patricia Clason, LLC, Accountability Coaching Associates.

2. Rich Tosi, a former marine and leader in the ManKind Project, was invited to assist Christan, helping him through his emotional process work around a war experience and was especially helpful, Christan remembers.

3. See Gene McMahon's biography link, accessed December 2, 2009, http://vetsjourneyhome.org.

4. Two influential books during this period were Chris Harding's *Wingspan: Inside the Men's Movement* (New York: St. Martin's Press, 1992) and its feminine counterpart by Clarissa Pinkola Estes, *Women Who Run with Wolves: Myths and Stories of the Wild Woman Archetype* (New York: Ballantine, 1992). Other influential works included Alan Chinen's *Beyond the Hero* (New York: Putnam. 1993), and Connie Zweig and Jeremiah Abrams, eds., *Meeting the Shadow* (New York: Putnam, 1991). Other feminist responses to Jung included Naomi Goldenberg's earlier book, *Changing of the Gods: Feminism and the End of Traditional Religions* (Boston: Beacon Press, 1979). Perhaps the most influential book cited among staff who volunteer is a book popular among attendees of the ManKind Project, Robert Moore and David Gillette's *King, Warrior, Magician and Lover* (New York: Harper-Collins, 1980). Others refer to the Shadow Work Seminars offered by Cliff Barry and incorporated into the "guts" or "carpet work" done at ManKind initiations, a widely popular but cost-prohibitive program.

5. As a sociologist, I cannot endorse and am more critical of gender-exclusive programs, but I am quick to admit that individuals can and do experience

personal growth in these programs. I feel it important to disclose this because while many if not most of my fellow advocates for veterans would disagree, some vehemently, it is important to distinguish the gender-neutral pedagogy that informs Vets Journey Home from the "mythopoetic" masculinity that drives confrontational "guts work" and "carpet work" done in men's groups with what sociologist Michael Schwalbe describes as "strategic anti-intellectualism."

6. Michael Schwalbe, *Unlocking the Cage: The Men's Movement, Gender Politics, and American Culture* (Oxford and New York: Oxford University Press, 1996).

7. Ibid., 229.

8. For further critique of the gender politics behind the mythopoetic framework, see Cynthia Eller's *Living in the Lap of the Goddess* (New York: Crossroad, 1993); Kay L. Hagan, ed., *Women Respond to the Men's Movement* (San Francisco: Harper Collins, 1992), and Gordon Murray, "Homophobia in Robert Bly's Iron John," *Masculinities* 1 (1993): 52–54.

9. Schwalbe, *Unlocking the Iron Cage*, 149.

10. See Jacob L. Moreno, *Psychodrama*, vol. 1 (New York: Beacon Press, 1946).

Chapter Seven

1. "I'm in" is a term that is used throughout the weekends as an indication that one's focus and intention are on the veterans.

2. Each aspect of the weekend is timed to the minute, which I find challenging as an ethnographer. There are few opportunities to retreat for writing. For example, Friday's program reads: 9:30–9:45 *Staff arrives*, 10–12:30 *Opening staff meeting and site prep*, 12:30–1:15 *lunch break*, 1:15–4:30 *complete site prep*, 4:30 *light staff dinner*, 5:15–5:45 *free time*, then it's another meeting for staff prior to participants arrival and greeting period.

3. It is also sometimes referred to as "Al's Chair." Al Fletcher was a Vietnam veteran who passed away recently but was an early champion of the program and, as I have come to learn, was loved by many.

4. Positive emotion management entails guiding participants by soliciting expression of felt emotional states and then providing affirmations, meanwhile discouraging emotional responses that are considered emotionally dysfunctional.

5. While EQ speaks best to primary emotional states, such as fear, anger, sadness, and joy, I am also reminded of the role of secondary or socially constructed

emotions. For example, Cooley (1902) provides a metaphor of the "looking glass self" to illustrate how social interaction informs our privately held views of our selves. We imagine how others perceive us and then respond to the imagined or real judgments of others. For Cooley, our responses are driven by socially constructed emotions of either pride or shame. These are emotions that arise out of deference either given or withheld through social interaction. Our sense of who we are, then, results from a combination of reflected appraisals (real or imagined) and our own self-views. The values or filters that Carl teases out, such as "Boys don't cry," are the messages that we receive and internalize from social norms. For Cooley, there are two basic responses to these messages, either shame or pride.

6. A large body of work speaks to these concepts in emotional intelligence. See, for example, Robert Cooper and Ayman Sawaf, *Executive EQ* (New York: Putnam, 1997); Daniel Goleman, *Emotional Intelligence* (New York: Bantam Books, 1995).

7. For a discussion on the positive effects of social sharing of emotions, see Bernard Rimc, "The Social Sharing of Emotions as an Interface between Individual and Collective Processes in the Construction of Emotional Climates," *Journal of Social Issues*, 63,2 (2007): 307–22.

Chapter Eight

1. Emile Durkheim, *The Elementary Forms of Religious Life* (New York: The Free Press [1912] 1965), 206.

2. Ibid., 238.

3. For example, Spencer Hindmarsh, a veteran who served two tours in Afghanistan, has joined veteran Jacob George and other Iraq and Afghanistan veterans against the war (IAVAW) on a cross-country bicycle ride. Their organization, "A Ride 'til the End," involves public speaking to communities and college campuses about their experiences in the wars in Iraq and Afghanistan. "Essentially there is a culture of war in this nation," Spencer tells me, "especially when you consider that we're corporatizing war. And we've got wars on videogames, permeating our entire society." He continues, "For me, it [the ride] transcends bipartisan politics, all that rhetoric, all the fickle debate and we put truth on the line." Spencer's father, a Vietnam veteran, suffered for years from PTSD and Spencer knows firsthand the collateral damage of war trauma, both as a veteran and as a child of a veteran. "The truth is impervious," Spencer explains, "and we [veteran activists] are in a unique position to present the truth."

4. Victor Turner, *From Ritual to Theatre: The Human Seriousness of Play* (New York: Performing Arts Journal Publications, 1982).

5. Ibid., 86.

6. Carl Jung, *Memories, Dreams and Reflections* (New York: Vintage Books, [1961] 1989), 25.

7. A small number of sociologists have always concerned themselves with emotions and/or responses to emotions (Durkheim 1897; Weber 1946; or Mead 1938). For example, sociologists Theodore Kemper (1978) and Thomas Scheff (1985) have attempted to keep *psychosocial* and *psychophysiological* debate alive within sociology. Kemper named it the "positivist/antipositivist" debate, while Scheff describes it as the "instinctivist/culturalist" debate. Scheff describes "course" emotions (e.g., grief, fear, anger, shame, joy) that we experience and monitor through our own thoughts and behaviors as well as the standpoint of others. Kemper distinguishes between "primary" and "secondary" emotions. Like "course" emotions, "primary" emotions include fear, anger, depression, and happiness. "Primary" emotions result from situations that bring about physiological arousal. "Secondary" emotions that consist of feelings such as shame, pride, love, and nostalgia are experienced in the context of the "primary" emotions, then are grafted onto them as we attempt to make sense of them in a social context.

8. See J. Forgas, *Feeling and Thinking* (Cambridge: Cambridge University Press, 2000); D. Fosha, *The Transforming Power of Affect: A Model of Accelerated Change* (New York: Basic Books, 2000); L. Greenberg and J. Pascual-Leone, "A Dialectical Constructivist View of the Creation of Personal Meaning," *Journal of Constructivist Psychology* 14(2001): 165–86; J. E. LeDoux, *The Emotional Brain: The Mysterious Underpinnings of Emotional Life* (New York: Simon and Schuster, 1996); Ronald Ruden, *When the Past Is Always Present: Emotional Traumatization, Causes and Cures* (New York and London: Routledge, 2010).

9. Daniel Siegal, *The Mindful Brain: Reflection and Attunement in the Cultivation of Well-Being* (New York: W.W. Norton, 2007).

10. See for example, Robert Scaer's *The Trauma Spectrum: Hidden Wounds and Human Resiliency* (New York: W.W. Norton, 2005). See also Peter Levine's *Waking the Tiger: Healing Trauma* (Berkeley, CA: North Atlantic Books, 1997).

11. See for example, R. P. Fitzgibbons, "The Cognitive and Emotive Use of Forgiveness in the Treatment of Anger," *Psychotherapy* 23 (1986): 629–633. See also S. Freedman, "Creating an Expanded View: How Therapists Can Help Their Clients Forgive," *Journal of Family Psychotherapy* 11,1 (2000): 87–92.

12. See, for example, Z. Solomon, M. Mikulincer, and E. Avitzur, "Coping, Locus of Control, Social Support and Combat-Related Stress Disorder:

A Prospective Study," *Journal of Personality and Social Psychology* 55,2 (1988): 279–85. See also D. R. Baerger and D. P. McAdams, "Life Story Coherence and Its Relation to Psychological Well-Being," *Narrative Inquiry* 9,1 (1999): 69–96. Finally, see K. J. Burnell, N. Hunt, and P. G. Coleman, "Using Narrative Analysis to Investigate the Role of Social Support in the Reconciliation of Traumatic War Memories,"*Health Psychology Update* 15,3 (2006): 37–39.

13. D. E. Polkinghorne, "Narrative and Self-Concept," *Journal of Narrative and Life History* 1,2 (1991): 135–53.

14. Tick, *War and the Soul*, 217.

Methodological Appendix Notes

1. Informed Consent Script for Oral Histories: "Before we begin I would like to thank you for participating in this interview and for your willingness to be part of the Veterans Oral History Project. I also want to confirm that you can receive a copy of the interview in CD format for your own use if you choose, and I also want to be sure that you realize that your information is being used for research purposes by Dr. Holyfield and if you agree, will be made available along with copies of the audio tape today to the Library of Congress Veterans Oral History Project: "Experiencing War" Series and also will be housed with the Special Collections Department, David and Barbara Pryor Center for Oral and Visual History in the Mullins Library at the University of Arkansas. While there are no physical risks involved in this research, this interview will cover possible topics that cause emotional discomfort such as recalling traumatic events. I want to confirm that you understand, and you've looked at the forms of consent to participate, and that you also realize that you can stop at any time during the interview. You can choose not to participate and there'll be no penalty for choosing to do so. And finally, if you have questions or concerns regarding the study you can contact Dr. Lori Holyfield at 479-575-3807 and I'll also leave a card with you today for that. If you have any concerns that are not addressed and if you have any other questions regarding your rights as a research subject, you can contact the University of Arkansas Institutional Review Board at 479-575-3845."

2. Thirty-four oral histories are currently available online (http://lcweb2. loc.gov/diglib/vhp/html/search/search.html) via "donor/interviewer" search term using the author's name.

3. Release for Publication Form: "With my signature below, I give my permission to Lori Holyfield to write about this retreat with the understanding

that my identity or my story will not be disclosed in any way, including gender, time frames, branch of service, residence, or detail of any personal experience that I share, that would make it possible for anyone to identify me or my story. I give this permission with the understanding that the instructors and coordinators of this weekend and the director of Vets Journey Home have the opportunity to approve this story before it goes into publication to assure anonymity and confidentiality are maintained. I understand that the instructors, coordinators, and/or director may bring the writing to me for approval if there is any question at all about confidentiality and anonymity in the way in which the article is written."

Bibliography

Abrams, Jeremiah and Connie Zweig. 1991. *Meeting the Shadow: The Hidden Power of the Dark Side of Human Nature.* New York: Putnam.

Allen, J. and D. Haccoun. 1976. "Sex Differences in Emotionality: A Multidimensional Approach." *Human Relations.* 28(8), 711–22.

Altheide, David. 2006. *Terrorism and the Politics of Fear.* New York: Altamira Press.

American Psychiatric Association. 1952. *Diagnostic and Statistical Manual of Mental Disorders.* I. Washington, DC: American Psychiatric Association.

_____. 1988. *Diagnostic and Statistical Manual of Mental Disorders.* III-R. Washington, DC: American Psychiatric Association.

_____. 2000. *Diagnostic and Statistical Manual of Mental Disorders.* IV-TR. Washington, DC: American Psychiatric Association.

Arraf, Janef. "Wave of Iraq Suicide Bombings Target Police." *Christian Science Monitor.* August 25, 2010. Retrieved October 13, 2010. http://www.csmonitor.com/World/Middle-East/2010/0825/Wave-of-Iraq-suicide-bombings-target-police.

Baerger, D. R. and D. P. McAdams. 1999. "Life Story Coherence and Its Relation to Psychological Well-Being. *Narrative Inquiry.* 9 (1), 69–96.

Beck, Ulrich. 1992. *Risk Society.* London: Sage.

Benedict, Hellen. 2009. *The Lonely Soldier: The Private War of Women Serving in Iraq.* Boston: Beacon Press.

Bly, Robert. 1990. *Iron John: A Book about Men.* Reading, MA: Addison-Wesley.

Boyce, Lisa A. and Ann M. Heard. 2003. "The Relationship between Gender Role Stereotypes and Requisite Military Leadership Characteristics." *Sex Roles.* 49 (7/8), 347–65.

Bracken, P. J. 2001. "Post-Modernity and Post-Traumatic Stress Disorder." *Social Science and Medicine.* 53, 733–43.

Bremner, J. Douglas., Southwick, Steven M., Darnell, Adam, and Dennis S. Charney. 1996. "Chronic PTSD in Vietnam Combat Veterans: Course of Illness and Substance Abuse." *The American Journal of Psychiatry.* 153(3), 369–75.

Burnell, K. J. Hunt, N. and Coleman, P. G. 2006. "Using Narrative Analysis to Investigate the Role of Social Support in the Reconciliation of Traumatic War Memories." *Health Psychology Update.* 15(3), 37–39.

Callahan, Jamie L. 2000. "Women in a 'Combat, Masculine-Warrior' Culture: The Performance of Emotion Work." *The Journal of Behavioral and Applied Management.* 1(1), 104–126.

Center for Military Policy Research. 2007. *Invisible Wounds of War: Psychological and Cognitive Injuries, Their Consequences, and Services to Assist Recovery.* Santa Monica, CA: Rand Corporation. Retrieved June 5, 2010. http://www.rand.org/pubs/monographs/MG720.

_____. 2008. *Invisible Wounds of War: Summary and Recommendations for Addressing Psychological and Cognitive Injuries.* Santa Monica, CA. Rand Corporation. Retrieved September 10, 2008. http://www.ha.osd.mil/dhb/mhtf/MHTF-Report-Final.pdf.

Chemtob, Claude M., Bauer, Gordon B., Neller, Gary, Hamada, Roger, Glisson, Charles and Victor Stevens. 1990. "Post-Traumatic Stress Disorder among Special Forces Vietnam Veterans." *Military Medicine.* 155(1), 16–20.

Chinen, Alan. 1993. *Beyond the Hero.* New York: Tarcher Putman.

Comancho, Austin. 2004, August. "Project DE-STRESS Helps Treat Traumatic Stress." American Forces Press Service. Retrieved January 3, 2010. http://www.defense.gov/news/newsarticle.aspx?id=25599.

Connell, Robert. 1995. *Masculinities.* Berkeley, CA: University of California Press.

Cooley, Charles. 1902. *Human Nature and the Social Order.* New York: Charles Scribner's Sons.

Cooper, Robert and Ayman Sawaf. 1997. *Executive EQ.* New York: Putnam.

Clymer, Roy. 2010, November 2. "The Puzzle of PTSD: Does the PTSD Diagnosis Do More Harm than Good?" *Psychotherapy Networker Magazine.* Retrieved November 14, 2010. http://sychotherapynetworker.org/magazine/currentissue.

Daniels, Arlene Kaplan. 1978. "The Social Construction of Military Diagnoses." Pp. 380–92 in *Symbolic Interaction: A Reader in Social Psychology.* 3rd ed. Jerome G. Manis and Bernard N. Meltzer (Eds.). Boston: Allyn & Bacon.

David, Deborah, and Robert Brannon. 1976. David, Deborah, and Robert Brannon. 1976. "The Forty-Nine Percent Majority: The Male Sex Role." In *Sex Roles.* Deborah David and Robert Brannon (Eds.). New York: Random House.

Degloma, Thomas. 2009. "Expanding Trauma through Space and Time: Mapping the Rhetorical Strategies of Trauma Carrier Groups." *Social Psychology Quarterly.* 72 (2), 105–22.

Demetriou, Demekratis Z. 2001. "Connell's Concept of Hegemonic Masculinity: A Critique." *Theory and Society.* (22), 643–75.

Denzin, Norman. 1984. *On Understanding Emotion.* San Francisco, CA: Jossey Bass.

Dodge, K. A. 1991. "The Structure and Function of Reactive and Proactive Aggression." Pp. 201–18 in *The Development and Treatment of Childhood Aggression.* D. Pepler and K. Rubin (Eds). Hillsdale, NJ: Erlbaum.

Dougherty, Josh. 2010. "Iraq Death Toll Soars Post War." BBC news online report. Retrieved October 1, 2010. http://news.bbc.co.uk/2/hi/middle_east/3962969.stm.

Durkheim, Emile. 1951 [c. 1897]. *Suicide.* New York: The Free Press.

_____. 1961 [c. 1912]. *The Elementary Forms of Religious Life.* New York: The Free Press.

Eisenhart, R. Wayne. 1975. "You Can't Hack It, Little Girl: A Discussion of the Covert Psychological Agenda of Modern Combat Training." *Journal of Social Issues.* 31(4): 13–23.

Eller, Cynthia. 1993. *Living in the Lap of the Goddess.* New York: Crossroad.

Elliot, D. M. 1997. "Traumatic Events: Prevalence and Delayed Recall in the General Populations." *Journal of Consulting and Clinical Psychology.* 65(8), 811–20.

Emery, V. Olga., Emery, Paul E., Shama, Delek K. and Nancy A. Quiana. 1991. "Predisposing Variables in PTSD Patients." *Journal of Traumatic Stress.* 4(3), 325–43.

Ferrell, Jeff, Milovanovic, Dragan and Stephen Lyng. 2001. "Edgework, Media Practices, and the Elongation of Meaning." *Theoretical Criminology.* 5(2), 177–202.

Fitzgibbons, R. P. 1986. "The Cognitive and Emotive Use of Forgiveness in the Treatment of Anger." *Psychotherapy.* 23, 629–633.

Fontana, Alan, Rosenheck, Robert and Thomas Horvath. 1997. "Social Support and Psychopathology in the War Zone." *Journal of Nervous and Mental Disease.* 185(11), 675–681.

Franks, David. 1985. "Introduction to the Special Issue on the Sociology of Emotions." *Symbolic Interaction.* 8(2), 161–170.

_____. 1989. "Power and Role-Taking: A Social Behaviorist's Synthesis of Kemper's Power and Status Model." In *The Sociology of Emotions: Original Essays and Research Papers.* David D. Franks and E. Doyle McCarthy (Eds.) Greenwich CT: JAI Press.

Freedman, S. 2000. "Creating an Expanded View: How Therapists Can Help Their Clients Forgive." *Journal of Family Psychotherapy.* 11 (1), 87–92.

Gallup, G. G. and J. D. Maser. 1997. "Tonic Immobility: Evolutionary Underpinnings of Human Catalepsy and Catatonia." Pp. 334–57 in *Psychopathology: Experimental Models.* M. E. P. Seligman and J. D. Maser (Eds.). San Francisco: W. H. Freeman.

Garfinkel, Harold. 1956. "Conditions for Successful Degradation Ceremonies." *American Journal of Sociology.* 61, 420–44.

Gelb, Leslie with Jeanne-Paloma Zelmati. 2009, Summer. "Mission Unaccomplished." *Democracy Journal.*

Gerlock, April A. 2004. "Domestic Violence and Post-Traumatic Stress Disorder Severity for Participants of a Domestic Violence Rehabilitation Program." *Military Medicine.* 169(6), 470–474.

Gibb, Nancy. "Sexual Assaults on Female Soldiers: Don't Ask, Don't Tell." *Time.* August 18, 2008. Retrieved October 6, 2010. http://www.time.com/time/magazine/articles/0,9171,1968110,00.html.

Gilmartin, Kevin. 2002. *Emotional Survival for Law Enforcement.* Tucson AZ: E-S Press.

Gimbel, Cynthia and Alan Booth. 1996. "Who Fought in Vietnam?" *Social Forces.* 74(4), 1137–157.

Goffman, Erving. 1959. *Presentation of the Self in Everyday Life.* New York: Anchor Books.

_____. 1961. *Asylums.* New York: Anchor Books.

_____. 1963. *Stigma.* Englewood Cliffs, NJ: Prentice-Hall.

Goleman, Daniel. 1995. *Emotional Intelligence.* New York: Bantam Books.

Goldenberg, Naomi. 1979. *Changing of the Gods: Feminism and the End of Traditional Religions.* Boston: Beacon Press.

Grossman, David. 1995. *On Killing.* Boston: Little Brown. *The Ground Truth.* 2006. DVD. Los Angeles, CA. Plum Productions. Directed by Patricia Foulkrod.

Gubrium, Jaber and James Holstein. 2001. *Institutional Selves: Troubled Identities in a Postmodern World.* Oxford and New York: Oxford University Press.

Gutman, Stephanie. 2001. *A Kinder, Gentler Military: How Political Correctness Affects Our Ability to Win Wars.* San Francisco: Encounter Books.

Hagan, Kay L. 1992. *Women Respond to the Men's Movement.* San Francisco: HarperCollins.

Hanley, J. L. and N. Devine. 2001. *Tired of Being Tired.* New York: Berkeley.

Harding, Chris. 1992. *Wingspan: Inside the Men's Movement.* New York: St. Martin's.

Haste, Helen. 1993. *The Sexual Metaphor.* New York: Harvester/Wheatsheaf.

Hearn, Jeff. 1993. "Emotive Subjects: Organizational Men, Organization Masculinities and the (De)construction of Emotions. Pp. 142–66 in *Emotions in Organizations.* Stephen Fineman (Ed.). Thousand Oaks, CA: Sage.

Hermann, Nathan and Goran Eryavec. 1994. "Posttraumatic Stress Disorder in Institutionalized World War II Veterans." *American Journal of Geriatric Psychology* 2(4), 324–31.

Hewitt, John. 1989. *Dilemmas of the American Self.* Philadelphia, PA: Temple University Press.

Higate, P. 2002. "Traditional Gendered Identities: National Service and the All Volunteer Force." *Comparative Social Research.* 20, 229–35.

Hochschild, Arlie. 1979. "Emotion Work, Feeling Rules, and Social Structure." *American Journal of Sociology.* 85, 551–75.

_____. 1983. *The Managed Heart.* Berkeley: University of California Press.

Hoge, Charles, Castro, Carl, Messer, Stephen, McGurk, Dennis, Cotting, Dave and Robert Kauffman. 2004. "Combat Duty in Iraq and Afghanistan: Mental Health Problems and Barriers to Care." *The New England Journal of Medicine.* 351 (1), 13–22.

Holstein J. A. and J. F. Gubrium. *The Self We Live By: Narrative Identity in a Postmodern World.* Oxford and New York: Oxford University Press.

Holyfield, Lori. "Manufactured Adventure: The Buying and Selling of Emotions." *Journal of Contemporary Ethnography.* 28 (1), 1–27.

_____. Jonas, Lillian and Anna Zajicek. "Adventure without Risk Is like Disneyland." Pp. 173–186 in *Edgework: The Sociology of Risk Taking.* Stephen Lyng (Ed.). New York: Routledge.

Howard III, John W. and Laura C. Prividera. 2004. "Rescuing the Patriarchy or Saving 'Jessica Lynch': The Rhetorical Construction of the American Woman Soldier." *Women and Language.* 27(2), 89.

Huebner, Andrew. 2008. *The Warrior Image.* Chapel Hill, NC: University of North Carolina Press.

Institute of Medicine and National Research Center. "PTSD and Military Compensation." Washington D.C. National Academic Press. Retrieved August 10, 2010. http://www.pdhealth.mil/downloads/PTSD_Compensation_and_Military_Service2.pdf.

Jaffe, Greg. 2005. "Therapists Take on Soldiers' Trauma in Iraq." *Wall Street Journal.* Retrieved August 1, 2008. http://www.postgazette.com/pg/05332/613785.stm.

Jung, Carl. 1961. *Memories Dreams and Reflections.* New York: Vintage Books.

Katz, Jack. 1988. *The Seductions of Crime: Moral and Sensual Attractions in Doing Evil.* New York: Basic Books.

Kemper, Theodore. 1978. *A Social Interactional Theory of Emotions*. New York: John Wiley and Sons.

Kennedy, Kelly. 2009. "Mental Health Issues Rising among Vets." *The Army Times*. Retrieved November 1, 2010. http://www.armytimes.com/news/2009/07military_mentalhealth_072209w/.

_____. "PTSD Victim Booted for Misconduct." *The Army Times*. January 7, 2009. Retrieved August 1, 2009. http://www.armytimes.com/news/2009/01/military_ptsd_discharge_010709w/.

Kishon-Barash, Ronit, Midlarsky, Elizabeth and David R. Johnson. 1999. "Altruism and the Vietnam Veteran: The Relationship of Helping to Symptomatology." *Journal of Traumatic Stress*. 12(4), 655–62.

Kleykamp, Meredith. 2006. "College, Jobs, or the Military? Enlistment During a Time of War." *Social Science Quarterly*. 87(2), 272–90.

Lee, Christopher. 2008, May 16. "Official Urged Fewer Diagnoses of PTSD." *Washington Post*. Retrieved September 4, 2010. http://www.washingtonpost.com/wp-dyn/content/article/2008/05/15/AR2008051503533.

Leed, Eric J. 1979. *No Man's Land: Combat and Identity in World War I*. Cambridge and London: Cambridge University Press.

Lemerise, Elizabeth and Kenneth Dodge. 1993. "The Development of Anger and Hostile Interactions." Pp.537–546 in *Handbook on Emotions*. Michael Lewis and Jeanette Haviland (Eds). New York: Gilford.

Levine, Peter. 1997. *Waking the Tiger: Healing Trauma*. Berkeley CA: North Atlantic Books.

Lipari, Rachel, Cook, Paul, Rock, Lindsay and Kenneth Matos. 2008. "Gender Relations Survey of Active Duty Members." Defense Manpower Data Center, DMDC Report No. 2007-022. Retrieved January 11, 2011. http://www.sapr.mil.

Litz, Brett T., Orsillo, Susan M., Friedman, Matthew, Ehlich, Peter and Alfonso Batres. 1997. "Posttraumatic Stress Disorder Associated With Peacekeeping Duty in Somalia for U.S. Military Personnel." *The American Journal of Psychiatry*. 154(2), 178–184.

Lois, Jennifer. 2005. "Gender and Emotion Management in the Stages of Edgework." Pp. 117–52 in *Edgework: The Sociology of Risk-Taking*. Stephen Lyng (Ed). New York: Routledge.

Londono, Ernesto. 2010, October 1. "U.S. Struggles to Counter Taliban Propaganda." *Washington Post*. Retrieved October 6, 2010. http://www.washingtonpost.com/wp-dyn/content/article/2010/10/01/AR2010100106644.html?hpid=topnews.

Lorber, Judith. 1997. *Gender and the Construction of Illness*. Thousand Oaks, CA: Sage.

Loseke, Donileen. 2007. "The Study of Identity as Cultural, Institutional, Organizational, and Personal Narratives: Theoretical and Empirical Integrations." *The Sociological Quarterly*. 48, 661–88.

Lyman, Peter. 1987. "The Fraternal Bond as a Joking Relationship: A Case Study in the Role of Sexist Jokes in Male Group Bonding." Pp. 148–62 in *Changing Men: New Directions in Research on Men and Masculinity*. M. S. Kimmel (Ed.). Newbury Park, CA: Sage.

Lyng, Stephen. 1990. "Edgework: The Social Psychology of Risk Taking." *American Journal of Sociology*. 95, 851–86.

_____. 2005. *Edgework: The Sociology of Risk Taking.* Stephen Lyng (Ed.) New York: Routledge.

MacLean, Alair and Nicholas Parsons. 2010. "Unequal Risk: Combat Occupations in the Volunteer Military." *Sociological Perspectives.* 53(3), 347–52.

Maze, Rick. 2006, October 9. "Expert Cites Gaps in PTSD Research." *The Navy Times.* Retrieved October 1, 2010. http://www.armytimes.com/news/2009/07military_mentalhealth_072209w.

McCanna, Shaun. 2007. "It's Easy for Soldiers to Score Heroin in Afghanistan." Retrieved January 15, 2011. http://www.salon.com/news/feature/2007/08/07/afghan_heroin.

McMillan, David. 2006. *Emotion Rituals: A Resource for Therapists and Clients.* New York: Routledge.

Mead, George Herbert. 1938. *The Philosophy of the Act.* Chicago, IL: University of Chicago Press.

Meagher, Ilona. 2007. *Moving a Nation to Care.* Brooklyn: Ig Publishing.

Mestrovic, Stjepan. 1997. *Postemotional Society.* Thousand Oaks, CA: Sage.

Miller, Laura L. 1997. "Not Just Weapons of the Weak: Gender Harassment as a Form of Protest for Army Men." *Social Psychology Quarterly.* 60 (1), 1–32.

Milovanovic, Dragan. 2005. "Edgework: A Subjective and Structural Model of Negotiating Boundaries." Pp. 51–59 in *Edgework: The Sociology of Risk Taking.* Stephen Lyng (Ed.). New York: Routledge.

Mitchell, Richard. 1983. *Mountain Experience: The Psychology and Sociology of Adventure.* Chicago: University of Chicago Press.

Moore, Robert and David Gillette. 1980. *King, Warrior, Magician and Lover.* New York: HarperCollins.

Moreno, Jacob L. 1946. *Psychodrama.* 2 vols. New York: Beacon Press.

Morgan, David. 1994. "Theater of War: Combat, Military, and Masculinities." Pp. 165–82 in *Theorizing Masculinities.* Harry Brod and Michael Kaufman (Eds.). Thousand Oaks, CA: Sage.

Morris, Madeline. 1996. "By Force of Arms: Rape, War, and Military Culture." *Duke Law Journal.* 45(4), 716–20.

Murdoch, Maureen., Polusny, Melissa A., Hodges, James and Diane Cowper. 2006. "The Association between In-Service Sexual Harassment and Post-Traumatic Stress Disorder among Department of Veterans Affairs Disability Applicants." *Military Medicine.* 171(2), 166–73.

Murray, Gordon. 1993. "Homophobia in Robert Bly's Iron John."*Masculinities.* 1, 52–54.

Natelson, Rachel. 2009. "A Case for Federal Oversight of Military Sexual Harassment." *Journal of Poverty, Law, and Policy.* 43(5/6), 277–281.

_____. 2010, August 4. "Separate, Unequal, and Unrecognized." *The Huffington Post.* Retrieved October 8, 2010. http://www.huffingtonpost.com/rachel-natelson/separate-unequal-and-unre_b_670302.htmlhttp://www.veteranstoday.com/2010/08/05/military-sexual-trauma-not-addressed-fully/.

National Priorities Project. 2009, January 21. "Military Recruitment 2008: Significant Gap in Army's Quality and Quantity Goals." Retrieved October 3, 2010. http://www.nationalpriorities.org/military recruiting2008.

Nutt, David. 2000. "Evidence Based Guidelines for the Pharmacological Treatment of Anxiety Disorders." *Journal of Clinical Psychology.* 61(5), 24–29.

O'Connor, Richard. 2009. "Collateral Damage: How Can the Army Best Serve a Soldier with PTSD?" *The Land Warfare Papers.* 71(4). Retrieved September 2, 2010. http://www3.ausa.org/marketing/LWP71weboptimized03_07.pdf.

Orbans, Michael. 2007. *Souled Out: A Memoir of War and Inner Peace.* Candler, NC: Silver Rings Press.

Pinkola-Estes, Clarissa. 1992. *Women Who Run with Wolves: Myths and Stories of the Wild Woman Archetype.* New York: Ballantine.

Pitman, Roger. 1989. "Post-Traumatic Stress Disorder: Hormones and Memory." *Biological Psychiatry.* (26), 221–23.

Polkinghorne, D. E. 1991. "Narrative and Self-Concept." *Journal of Narrative and Life History.* 1(2), 135–53.

Pols, Hanns. 1999. "The Repression of War Trauma in American Psychiatry after World War II." Pp. 251–76 in *Medicine and Modern Warfare.* R. Cooper, M. Harrison and S. Strudy (Eds.). Atlanta, GA: Rodopi.

Prigerson, Holly G., Maciejewski, Robert A. and Robert A. Rosenheck. 2002. "Population Attributable Fractions of Psychiatric Disorders and Behavioral Outcomes Associated with Combat Exposure among U.S. Men." *American Journal of Public Health.* 92(1), 59–63.

Remington, Nevin, Pietrusiak, Paul and Jennifer Caci. 2008, February 11. "Prevalence of Contraindications to Mefloquine Use among USA Military Personnel Deployed to Afghanistan." *Malaria Journal.* Retrieved October 2, 2010. http://www.ncbi. nlm.nih.gov/pmc/articles/PMC2259366/.

Rime, Bernard. 2007. "The Social Sharing of Emotions as an Interface between Individual and Collective Processes in the Construction of Emotional Climates." *Journal of Social Issues.* 63 (2), 307–322.

Robinson, Stephen L. 2004. "Hidden Toll of the War in Iraq: Mental Health and the Military." Washington, DC: *Center for American Progress.*

Rosaldo, Michelle. 1984. "Toward an Anthropology of Self and Feeling." Pp. 137–57 in *Culture Theory.* R. Shweder & R. LeVine (Eds.). Cambridge, MA: Cambridge University Press.

Rothschild, Babette. 2000. *The Body Remembers: The Psychophysiology of Trauma and Trauma Treatment.* New York: W.W. Norton.

Ruden, Ronald. 2010. *When the Past Is Always Present: Emotional Traumatization, Causes and Cures.* Psychological Stress Series. New York and London: Routledge.

Ruef, Anne Marie, Litz, Brett T. and William E. Schlenger. 2000. "Hispanic Ethnicity and Risk for Combat-Related Posttraumatic Stress Disorder." *Cultural Diversity & Ethnic Minority Psychology.* 6(3), 235–51.

Sadler, Anne, Booth, Brenda and Diane Cook. 2003. "Factors Associated with Women's Risk of Rape in the Military Environment." *American Journal of Industrial Medicine.* 43, 262–72.

Salovey, Peter and John Mayer. 1990. "Emotional Intelligence." *Imagination, Cognition, and Personality.* (9), 185–211.

Scaer, Robert. 2005. *The Trauma Spectrum: Hidden Wounds and Human Resiliency.* New York: W.W. Norton.

Scahill, Jeremy. 2007. *Blackwater: The Rise of the World's Most Powerful Mercenary Army.* London: Serpent's Tail.

Scheff, Thomas J. 1985. "Universal Expressive Needs: A Critique and a Theory." *Symbolic Interaction.* 8(2), 241–62.

_____. 1988. "Shame and Conformity: The Deference-Emotion System." *American Sociological Review.* 53(3), 395–406.

_____. 2006. *Goffman Unbound! A New Paradigm for Social Science.* Boulder, CO: Paradigm.

Schnurr, Paula P., Friedman, Matthew J. and Stanley D. Rosenburg. 1993. "Preliminary MMPI Scores as Predictors of Combat-Related PTSD Symptoms." *American Journal of Psychiatry.* 150(3), 479–83.

Schwalbe, Michael. 1996. *Unlocking the Iron Cage: The Men's Movement, Gender Politics, and American Culture.* Oxford and New York: Oxford University Press.

Scott, Wilbur J. 1992. "PTSD and Agent Orange: Implications for a Sociology of Veteran's Issues." *Armed Forces and Society.* 18(4), 592–612.

_____. 2004 *Vietnam Veterans Since The War.* Norman, OK: University of Oklahoma Press.

Segal, David R., Burns, Thomas J., Falk, William W., Silver, Michael P. and Bam D. Sharda. 1998. "The All-Volunteer Force in the 1970s." *Social Science Quarterly.* 79(2), 390–411.

Shott, Susan. 1979. "Emotion and Social Life: A Symbolic Interactionist Analysis." *American Journal of Sociology.* (84), 1317–1332.

Siegal, Daniel. 2007. *The Mindful Brain: Reflection and Attunement in the Cultivation of Well-being.* New York: W.W. Norton.

Simon, Jonathan. 2005. "Edgework and Insurance in Risk Societies: Some Notes on Victorian Lawyers and Mountaineers." Pp. 203–26 in *Edgework: The Sociology of Risk Taking.* Stephen Lyng (Ed.). New York: Routledge.

Sion, Liora and Eyal Ben-Ari. 2009. "Imagined Masculinity: Body, Sexuality, and Family among Israeli Military Reserves." *Symbolic Interaction.* 32(1), 21–43.

Showalter, Elaine. 1985. *The Female Malady.* New York: Pantheon.

Smith, Charles. 2005. "Financial Edgework: Trading in Market Currents." Pp. 187–202 in *Edgework: The Sociology of Risk Taking.* Stephen Lyng (Ed.). New York: Routledge.

Snow, David A. and Robert D. Benford. 1988. "Ideology, Frame Resonance, and Participant Mobilization." *International Social Movement Research.* 1, 197–217.

Soldz, Stephen. 2005, November 30. "To Heal or Patch: Military Mental Health Workers in Iraq." *Counterpunch.* Retrieved September 2, 2009. http://www.counterpunch.org/soldz11302005.html.

Solomon, Z., Mikulincer, M. and E. Avitzur. 1988. "Coping, Locus of Control, Social Support and Combat-Related Stress Disorder: A Prospective Study." *Journal of Personality and Social Psychology.* 55 (2), 279–85.

Styron, William 1993, January 11. "The Enduring Metaphors of Auschwitz and Hiroshima." *Newsweek.* Retrieved October 6, 2010. http://www.newsweek.com/1993/01/10/the-enduring-metaphors-of auschwitz-and-hiroshima.

Thoits, Peggy. 1985. "Self-Labeling Processes in Mental Illness: The Role of Emotional Deviance." *American Journal of Sociology.* 91, 221–49.

Thomas, Herbert. 2005. *The Shame Response to Rejection.* New York: Albanel.

Thompson, Mark. 2008, June 5. "America's Medicated Army." *Time.* Retrieved October 4, 2010. http://www.time.com/time/nation/article/0,8599,1811858,00.html.

Tick, Edward. 2005. *War and the Soul: Healing Our Nation's Veterans from PTSD.* Wheaton IL: Quest Books.

Turner, Johnathan and Jan Stets 2005. *The Sociology of Emotions.* Cambridge and New York: Cambridge.

Turner, Victor. 1969. *The Ritual Process: Structure and Anti-Structure.* Chicago, IL: Aldine.

_____. 1982. *From Ritual to Theatre: The Human Seriousness of Play.* New York: Performing Arts Journal Publications.

U.S. Army. *Combat and Operational Stress Control.* 2006. Field Manual 4-02.51. Washington D.C.: Headquarters, Department of the Army.

U.S. Army Medical Research and Material Command. Walter Reed Army Institute of Research. "10 Tough Facts about Combat." Retrieved October 4, 2008. http://www.armyg1.army.mil/dcs/docs/10%20Leaders%20Tough%20Facts%20About%20Combat%20Brochure%2011%20SEP%2006.pdf.

U.S. Congressional Budget Office. 2007, July. "The All-Volunteer Military: Issues and Performance." Retrieved October 10, 2010. http://www.cbo.gov/doc.cfm?index=8318&type=0&sequence=1.

U.S. Department of Defense. Task Force on Mental Health. 2007. *An Achievable Vision: Report of the Department of Defense Task Force on Mental Health.* Falls Church, VA: Defense Health Board. Retrieved January 5, 2009. http://www.ha.osd.mil/dhb/mhtf/MHTF-Report-Final.pdf.

U. S. Department of Defense. 2009. Sexual Assault Prevention and Response. *Annual Report on Sexual Assault.* Retrieved October 6, 2010. http://www.sapr.mil/media/pdf/reports/fy09_annual_report.pdf.

_____. 2010, November. "Report on the Comprehensive Review of the Issues Associated with a Repeal of 'Don't Ask, Don't Tell.'" Final Report. Retrieved January 11, 2011. http://www.defense.gov/home/features/2010/0610_gatesdadt/DADTReport_FINAL_20101130(secure-hires).pdf.

U.S. General Accounting Office. "Challenges Encountered by Injured Service Members in their Early Recovery Process." Retrieved September 5, 2010. http://www.gao.gov/new.items/d07606t.pdf.

U.S. Substance Abuse and Mental Health Services Administration (SAMHSA). Office of Applied Studies National Survey on Drug Use and Health. 2008, November 6. "Major Depressive Episode and Treatment for Depression among Veterans Aged 21 to 39." Retrieved October 4, 2010. http://www.oas.samhsa.gov/2k8/veteransDepressed/veteransDepressed.pdf.

von Drehle, David. 2001, September 16. "Congress Approves Use of Military Force; Bush Addresses N.Y. Relief Workers, Says U.S. Must 'Rid the World of Evil.'" *Washington Post.* A3.

Watson, Charles G., Davenport, Ernest, Anderson, Patricia E.D., Mendez, Claudia and Lee P. Gearhart. 1998. "The Relationships between Premilitary School Record Data and Risk for Posttraumatic Stress Disorder among Vietnam War Veterans." *Journal of Nervous and Mental Disease.* 186(6), 338–44.

Weber, Max. 1947. *The Theory of Social and Economic Organization*. New York: Oxford University Press.

Webster, Stephen. 2001, January 17. "Army 'Revisiting' Ban on Female Soldiers in Combat Units, Gen. Casey Announces." *The Raw Story*. Retrieved February 17, 2011. http://www.rawstory.com/rs/2011/01/army-revisiting-ban-female-soldiers-combat-units/.

West, Lola., Mercer, Susan O. and Edith Altheimer. 1993. "Operation Desert Storm: The Response of a Social Work Outreach Team." *Social Work in Health Care*. 19(2), 81–98.

Wilcox, Clyde. 1992. "Race, Gender, and Support for Women in the Military." *Social Science Quarterly*. 73(2), 737–749.

Williams, Timothy. 2010, September 27. "Insurgent Group in Iraq Declared Tame, Roars." *New York Times*. Retrieved October 4, 2010. http://www.nytimes.com/2010/09/28/world/middleeast/28qaeda.html.

Wilson, James. (2002) *Adrenal Fatigue: The 21st Century Stress Syndrome*. Petaluma CA: Smart Publishing.

Wong, Martin and David Cook. 1992. "Shame and Its Contribution to PTSD." *Journal of Traumatic Stress*. 5 (4), 557–62.

World Bank. 2006. *Cry Havoc: Why Civil War Matters*. Retrieved September 24, 2010. http://www-wds.worldbank.org/external/default/WDSContentServer/IW3P/IB/2003/06/30/000094946_0306190405396/additional/310436360_200500070100004.pdf.

Yealland, Lewis. 1918. *Hysterical Disorders of Warfare*. London: McMillan.

Yehuda, Rachel, Golier, Julia A., Tischler, Lisa., Stavisky, Karina and Philip D. Harvey. 2005. "Learning and Memory in Aging Combat Veterans with PTSD." *Journal of Clinical and Experimental Neuropsychology*. 27(4), 504–15.

Young, Alan. 1995. *The Harmony of Illusions: Inventing Post-Traumatic Stress Disorder*. Princeton, NJ: Princeton University Press.

Zoroya, Greg. 2010, October 15. "Simple Blood Test May Identify Mild TBI." *USA Today*. Retrieved October 16, 2010. http://www.armytimes.com/news/2010/10/gannett-blood-tests-find-mild-tbi-101510.

Index

versus cognition, 156, 182, 232
Enlisted forces. *See* Armed forces

Fear, 2, 25, 32, 36, 40, 44, 47, 48,
    64, 115–116, 130, 153, 194
Ferrell, Jeff, 237
Fitzgibons, R., 250
Fontana, et al., 245
Forgiveness, 136, 160, 174–175
    as ritual, 172–179, 186
Franks, David, 245
Freedman S., 250

Gallup, G., and J. Maser, 241
Garfinkel, Harold, 246
Gelb, L., and J. Paloma Zelmati,
    231
Gerlock, April, 245
Gibb, Nancy, 250
Gilmartin, Kevin, 241
Gimbel, Cynthia, and A. Booth,
    235
Goffman, Erving, 32, 133, 235, 236
    and embarrassment, 133
    and stigma, 242
    and total institution, 43
Goldenberg, Naomia, 247
Goleman, Daniel, 107, 249
Grief, 130, 144, 146
Grossman, Dave, 23, 24, 236
Gubrium, J., and J. Holstein, 239,
    245
Guilt, 32, 110, 112, 117, 122, 131,
    134, 136, 162, 179, 182
    Survivor's, 134
Gutmann, Stephanie, 238

Hanley, J., and N. Devine, 241
Harding, Chris, 247
Herman, N., and G. Eryavec, 245
Hewitt, John, 43, 236, 246

Higate, P., 239
Hijacked brain. *See* Amygdala
Hippocampus, 107–108, 110
Hochschild, Arlie, 35, 36, 131, 235,
    246
Hoge, Charles, et al., 244
Holstein, J., and J. Gubrium, 239,
    245
Holyfield, Lori, 237
Howard, John, and Laura Prividera,
    239
Huebner, Andrew, 17–18
Hussein, Saddam, 12
Hyper-Alert/Vigilance, 52–54, 57,
    60, 63, 64, 69, 74
    in Post Traumatic Stress Disorder,
    110, 116, 120, 125, 134
Hypothalamus, 107–108

Injuries, 14
    See also Signature Injuries
Institute of Medicine and National
    Research Center, 245

Jaffe, Greg, 243
Jasinski, Eric, 120–124
Jung, Carl, 186

Katz, Jack, 238
Kay, Hagan, 248
Kemper, Theodore, 246, 250
Kennedy, Kelly, 244
Killbox, 65, 66, 68
    definition of, 238
Killing
    avoidance of, 45
    and military jargon, 49
    psychology of, 23, 24, 28
    and sociopath, 45, 137
Kishon-Barash, et al., 245
Kleycamp, Meridith, 245